"Concise and helpful...an excellent guide to creating your own best style."

—Linda Allard, Director of Design for Ellen Tracy

HOW TO BE THE BEST-DRESSED PLUS-SIZE WOMAN

Over a third of American women wear size 14 and up, and designers are quickly tapping into his booming market. Plus-size boutiques are featured at the best retail chains, from Macy's to Bloomingdale's, Nordstrom to Saks. As manufacturers provide a new range of options, every woman has the opportunity to look and feel great. Now, a leading consultant in the plus-size market—whose clients include top designers and retailers—provides step-by-step guidance to planning, buying, and caring for a wardrobe that is both fashionable and flattering. You will discover:

- How to use patterns and lines to focus on your best qualities—and downplay others
- Which skirts, pants, and dresses complement your body type
- What kind of swimwear you can live with—even love
- How to do your own makeover, including hairstyle, makeup, and accessories
- Mistake-proof shopping strategies
- And more

"Suzan Nanfeldt's gentle voice and practical advice on creating beauty and positive self-image can help every plus-size woman transform her fashion fears into stylish sense. A no-nonsense, no-shame, empowering resource for women who want to look great in the bodies they already have!"

—Cheri K. Erdman Ed.D, author of
Nothing to Lose: A Guide to Sane Living in a Larger Body

"This book is destined to become an excellent resource for all plus-size women."

—Diane Parente, CEO of Image Development and Management, Inc., and
co-author of *Mastering Your Professional Image*

PLUS
STYLE

The Plus-Size
Guide to
Looking Great

SUZAN
NANFELDT

ILLUSTRATED BY
SHAWN BANNER

A PLUME BOOK

PLUME
Published by the Penguin Group
Penguin Books USA Inc., 375 Hudson Street,
New York, New York 10014, U.S.A.
Penguin Books Ltd, 27 Wrights Lane,
London W8 5TZ, England
Penguin Books Australia Ltd, Ringwood,
Victoria, Australia
Penguin Books Canada Ltd, 10 Alcorn Avenue,
Toronto, Ontario, Canada M4V 3B2
Penguin Books (N.Z.) Ltd, 182–190 Wairau Road,
Auckland 10, New Zealand

Penguin Books Ltd, Registered Offices:
Harmondsworth, Middlesex, England

First published by Plume, an imprint of Dutton Signet,
a division of Penguin Books USA Inc.

First Printing, September, 1996
10 9 8 7 6 5 4 3 2 1

Cover photographs by Michael Keel. Top row: Katy Hansz in Carole Little II and The Gap; second row (left to right): Catherine Schuller in Carole Little II; Maryellen Kernaghan in Carole Little II; bottom row: Tanya Jeremy in Harper Greer; Jeanette Baez in Tamotsu.

Ⓟ REGISTERED TRADEMARK—MARCA REGISTRADA

LIBRARY OF CONGRESS CATALOGING-IN-PUBLICATION DATA:
Nanfeldt, Suzan.
    Plus style: the plus-size guide to looking great / Suzan Nanfeldt ;
Illustrated by Shawn Banner.
        p.   cm.
    Includes index.
    ISBN 0-452-27596-2
    1. Fashion. 2. Clothing and dress. 3. Overweight women—Costume.
4. Beauty, Personal. I. Title.
TT507.N26 1996   96-14935
646'.34–dc20   CIP

Printed in the United States of America
Set in Avant Garde
Designed by Michaelis/Carpelis Design

BOOKS ARE AVAILABLE AT QUANTITY DISCOUNTS WHEN USED TO PROMOTE PRODUCTS OR SERVICES. FOR INFORMATION PLEASE WRITE TO PREMIUM MARKETING DIVISION, PENGUIN BOOKS USA INC., 375 HUDSON STREET, NEW YORK, NEW YORK 10014.

Contents

Acknowledgments

This book is the result of much love, understanding, dedication, commitment, and support of some magnificent individuals, proving indisputably that people want to care, want to be involved, want to give, if you only ask. And I asked a lot.

I will be forever grateful to my parents and siblings for their love and constant support. Special thanks goes to my mother for teaching me the basics and demonstrating the power of creativity, elegance, and style at any size, any age.

Harold Levine has been a great friend in every way, and was the impetus for *Plus Style* by encouraging me to *make lemonade*. As a most stylish writer, strategist, conversationalist, virtuoso, thinker, gourmet, humorist, philanthropist, houseguest, and perfect road trip pal, he has been a friendly ear, warm shoulder, constant inspiration, and a pragmatic cheerleader. Thanks, H.

Catherine Schuller arrived just when I needed her most. Not only is she the most beautiful plus model and a talented actress, comedienne, speaker, writer, and violinist, she can get more things done in an hour than any human alive. Her good spirit never lags—no matter what lunacy the world throws at us. She is my #1 fan, and I'm hers. Love you, Cath.

Betsy Leichliter dragged me into the twentieth century just in time for the twenty-first. If it weren't for her beneficence—technical, spiritual, operational, physical, and intellectual—I'd be nowhere. She saved me from countless crises, both real and imagined, and never lost her cool or her concern. You're the best, Bets.

Lisa Cunningham taught me nearly everything I know about image analysis. She's a beautiful, selfless individual whose genius and gumption are unparalleled. What a pioneer! Thanks, Lisa.

Thanks to Carolyn Gustafson for her brilliant input, sage advice, great humor, warmth, and unquestioning belief in me. Princess Squeegee and her HHBL are in a class by themselves.

Special thanks goes to some wonderfully gifted people for their contributions: Ann Zacasian for "getting it" immediately, and for her love, support, insight, motivation, and tremendous efforts on my behalf; Dr. Setrag Zacarian, not only for his medical brilliance, but his inspiration; to Jan Larkey for her contributions and willingness to listen; to the great Angie Michael for her teachings and ministrations; to Miss Jean Patton for her mind, her humor, and her style; to Sharon Craig for her love and support; to Julian Petrocelli, John Antony, and Kim Lépine for their contribution and creativity; to Dolly M. Wilson for eyewear advice; to Irene Carpelis of Michaelis/Carpelis for her inspired book design; and to the incomparable, magical Shawn Banner for putting up with much while turning out brilliance.

Many thanks to Dana Buchman and Karen Harmon, the great design duo for their time, thoughts, support, and faith in the beauty of plus-size women; Robin Scheer Ettinger, and Karen Greenberg at Liz Claiborne for their support, Joya Paterson of S&S Industries for her advice; Dr. Cheri Erdman and Carol Johnson, for giving plus-size women tools to build their self-esteem; my friends at Tomatsu, Carol Little, Ellen Tracy, Marina Rinaldi, Mondi, and George Simonton for their help; Alice Ansfield at *Radiance* magazine for her ground-breaking work and interest in my projects; *BBW* magazine for showing that size and style are not mutually exclusive; my friends at Nordstrom all over the country who have supported our events, and who define personal service every day; all the people and organizations who have shown support for plus-size women, and developed products and services to meet their needs and desires.

I owe more than I can repay to some wonderful, brilliant women—image consultants, writers, speakers, and entrepreneurs who have inspired and supported me with their time, thoughts, and creativity: the brilliant, loving, and gifted Mary Rudder; Diane Parente, Mina Bancroft, Alyce Parsons, Judith Rasband, Gwen Mazer, Renai Ellison, Dominique Isbecque, Donna Fujii, Devora Lissack, Lauren Solomon, Veda Cassells-Jones, Debra Kuhns, Doris Grant, Linda Arroz, Jo Beacham, Linda Fidelman, and the late Beth Kuhn-Purk.

And lastly, my heartfelt thanks to B. Mellinger & Company, who lit my lamp so that I could find my way; Oprah Winfrey, who daily inspires, motivates, and makes me proud to be a woman; the great DV, who is still teaching me about style and glamour; and lastly, but never, ever, least, to the late Cary Schroeder, a most stylish fella, with whom life was always an adventure, and without whom this world is just not the same.

introduction:
Our Clothes and Ourselves

You Are Unique, but You Are Not Alone

At least 35 million women in the United States—one in three—wear a size 14 or over. Although you certainly couldn't tell by reading a magazine or looking at television, there are as many size 18s as there are size 8s. Perhaps most surprising is that plus-size women have the same demographics as the rest of the population—the same ages, incomes, lifestyles. Larger people have such a negative image in our culture, and yet study after study reveals that many Americans fall outside standard height/weight tables.

And whatever the current statistics, we are all heading in the same direction; the group of women aged thirty-five to sixty-four who wear plus sizes will grow 16.5 percent in this decade as the whole of our population ages (and expands). The truth is, the real American woman looks nothing like what you may think. *The average woman is 5'4" tall, weighs 144 pounds, is a size 12 on the top and a 14 on the bottom.* Though this woman repre-

> *"A beautiful thing is never perfect."*
>
> EGYPTIAN PROVERB

sents the average, she's nearly plus-size by fashion industry standards!

These days we're fortunate to have a much broader interpretation of beauty, which incorporates a little more of the natural variations on the female form. Undoubtedly many of us still suffer to meet unrealistic standards of perkiness, thinness, and other valued qualities, but now at least variation in eye, hair, and skin colors has become "acceptable." Whether you are seventeen or seventy, you can learn a few skills that will make the most of what you have and help you feel better about yourself, knowing that you're taking control for *you*, not to meet someone else's ideal.

This book is for you—the average American woman who is over size 14. If you have never thought of yourself as a fashion everywoman, or as belonging to a large group of women who look, live, and feel the same as you, here's where you start to change your outlook, your self-image, and the image you project. You'll find out that while unique in mind and body, you are definitely not alone, and that you can look great and feel not only okay, but *terrific* about yourself—without losing a pound. By changing your perspective about yourself and what defines beauty or style, you can reclaim your stake in the female style mainstream.

How We Feel About These Larger-Than-Life Bodies

And now, a word from my soapbox ... Do you feel embarrassed or guilty buying clothes? Do you always think, "I really don't have the right things to wear, but I shouldn't buy anything until I lose weight"? Do you think you will automatically look better a few pounds lighter? Do you think it's impossible for you to look attractive until you are no longer a size 18? 16? 14?

Well, you're not alone. Despite their numbers, our culture takes an exceptionally dim view of women who fall outside "normal" size/weight ranges. You know what I mean—sometimes it feels as if we're the last group in America it's okay to disrespect! But together we can turn around this naive way of thinking by shifting our own perspective, and changing the way we look at ourselves.

Perhaps this narrow thinking (pardon the pun) is influenced by our Puritan background, which idealizes self-denial and makes us feel guilty for self-indulgence and acceptance of a less-than-perfect self. The popular biased thinking goes like this: *If you're overweight you must be giving in to temptation all the time, and you should feel guilty about being so weak. You aren't entitled to feel okay or buy anything new until you toe the line, restrain yourself, and lose weight. You sinful bad thing! How dare you expect anything better for yourself!*

Our media images reinforce this negative thinking. Magazines, TV, and movies portray unreasonable physical expectations that even healthy, active, normal teenage girls have a hard time living with. The sizism message says if you're large (large being a relative term, of course—some girls see anything over size 6 as too large) you are guilty of breaking some sort of cultural taboo, that you shouldn't be taking up so much space, that you must be out of control. Larger women are made to feel they have no right to look good or feel good about themselves, as if a woman's only value is in her degree of attractiveness. Sometimes even very thin but tall girls are made to feel ungainly and unattractive because they fall outside the bounds of the popular ideal of beauty. (Ironically, many fashion models, who average 5'10" or more, feel awful about themselves because of their height, even while representing the ultimate image of glamour and beauty.) Every single young girl gets the message loud and clear: You must be thin to be acceptable.

Yes, we tell ourselves, *I look horrible, I am horrible.* We don't stop to question the thought process or the reality of our bodies. Why does large have to mean horrible? Can't you look and feel wonderful, project confidence and goodwill, and be a happy, stylish, well-dressed large person? Of course you can, and it's easier than you think. It's also fun to poke holes in negative thinking and negate a few myths.

For starters, we already know that not all women are small. We also know— and science is finally starting to confirm—that large body size doesn't necessarily mean a person is unhealthy, unfit, or unacceptable. Many women eat normally, exercise regularly, and are still large. That's just their normal state of being, and it has nothing to do with out-of-control eating or any other damaging behavior. Some large-size models are athletes in world-class condition, but are naturally a little larger than the average woman.

Unfortunately, today we all seem to be focused on control. Control over time, money, lifestyle, behavior, everything. In the 1980s we strove to amass the right possessions. Now we grapple with control, and she who has the most (perceived) control wins. Of course, control is really an illusion. That's what makes getting it and keeping it so very difficult. But if you wrestle with drugs, alcohol, workaholism, abusive behavior, or some other nasty, the world doesn't see the burden you carry. If you wrestle with body weight—either inherited or created—the world sees the evidence of your struggle in every ounce. In many people's unconscious minds, you become the personification of a person out of control, a person that represents their worst fears. And sometimes people hate what they fear.

So it's not hard to see why some plus-size women believe that it's impossible to look good as they are, without losing weight. At best, they think they can only look acceptable, inoffensive. And it usually follows that looking acceptable means looking as thin as possible, or covering up one's true size by camouflage.

While it may seem obvious to an outsider that a large woman is not ever going to look waif-model thin, the plus woman fights to keep that possibility alive in her own mind, and in the perceptions of the world around her. Since the media and our entire culture place such a high value on attractiveness for women at the expense of all other virtues, nearly every woman wants (whether on a conscious level or not) to be attractive. But the media also tells her that female attractiveness is directly linked to thinness. Ergo, she is not, and cannot be, attractive or truly valuable until she is thin. Right?

Face It

When I was a teenager poring over *Cosmopolitan* or some other magazine, I would gaze into my mirror, trying unsuccessfully to see how my face might compare to the pictures of the perfect models on the page. According to the fashion and beauty doyenne, you had to wear your hair a certain way, figure out how to shade, camouflage, and otherwise persuade your face to conform to the classic oval with mile-high cheekbones.

At sixteen I *knew* I had an "ugly" body but I tried hard to do as much as possible to rise to the challenge. I grew my mousy blond hair very long to meet rigid teenage social standards, and spent hours forcing out the natural wave so that when I parted it down the middle it fell as straight as a stick. Do you remember the gossamer tresses of Jan on the "Brady Bunch"? Her lovely oval face supported the style well. On my oblong face, well …

Next, I headed for the bleach bottle when Mom wasn't looking, to achieve that Christie Brinkley/Cheryl Tiegs golden-blonde goddess look. Then, with the help of a lot of blue eye shadow and a "healthy" tan, I thought I might fit in well enough to escape rejection. How many of us suffered the pain and blisters of turning unwilling white skin reddish brown for a few days? How many of us will pay a second time for adhering to unrealistic or even unsafe beauty practices like this?

Now when I walk through malls and see teenage girls suited up to follow the lead of strict social codes of dress, hair, makeup, body posture, and attitude, I'm always struck by how *every single girl* could look much more attractive—yet fashionable—if she dressed with her own body in mind instead of some mythic ideal. Of course, when you're a teenager conformity is acceptance, and acceptance is everything. Fortunately we grow up and learn about ourselves separate and apart from the rest of the world.

Thinking back to myself at seventeen, I see a clear-skinned, strong majorette who marched every day and was in very good physical condition, with twenty-five pounds of "extra" weight! Unfortunately I didn't feel very good about myself. I hated my body and was ashamed of its size, which kept me from wearing the miniskirts, sleeveless blouses, skintight jeans, and bikinis I thought every self-respecting girl should wear. And my darned face wanted to be an oblong shape with a high forehead, small upturned nose, and less-than-prominent cheekbones. It simply refused to be what I thought it should be, with the requisite angles that insured beauty. Nonetheless I tried to wear the type of clothes, makeup, and hairstyles of my idols. Surely that would make me more attractive, right?

Naturally, my ideal of beauty at the time was pretty limited to what I saw on TV and in magazines, and had less to do with reality than with what a handful of fashion stylists thought was the look of the moment. Times change, and the looks of the supermodels of the 1990s share very little with the hot models of the 1970s. But real beauty is eternal, and any woman can learn to look more attractive with a little knowledge in place of blind hopes.

Mirror, Mirror, on the Wall . . .

When a woman looks in the mirror, her self-esteem looks back at her. Unfortunately, in our society there is little correlation between high self-esteem and large body size. In fact, studies confirm that even thin, attractive women don't like their bodies—or themselves. Clearly, thinness is only part of the self-esteem issue, but you can't discount its part in making us love or hate ourselves. I think the major issue with our mirrors is this: *Women don't have a real gauge of what shapes, lines, colors, textures, and patterns flatter their bod-ies—and why.* Most of us lack the training and skills to achieve what we want for ourselves. So looking good is driven by whether our bodies are small, and whether we're wearing the latest, most expensive fashions.

Good news! On the path to looking good (and the high self-esteem that comes from liking and respecting ourselves) there is an alternative course to looking thin—it's dressing right for you. It's about understanding proportion and balance, and about choosing color and texture that will flatter your body, your style personality, and your lifestyle. Dressing well and looking good have more to do with easily learned skills than the size of your bank account and how much time you have to devote to shopping. Getting dressed can be simple and fun, not an exercise in feeling bad about yourself.

We can learn to bridge the gap between size and attractiveness by changing the focus from body size to body shape and the overall coordina-tion and style of the clothing we choose to wear. In other words, you can know what makes you look attractive, and why. You can learn the secrets of how to look *put together,* and know that the image you portray is flattering to your body and personal coloring, appropriate, and stylish. You can learn to look in the mirror and like what you see.

Your Clothes Are Talking— Do You Know What They're Saying?

Have you ever noticed a woman who isn't particularly beautiful either in face or figure, but still somehow appears very attractive, confident, and stylish? She's working with her assets and minimizing her shortcomings. You can, too. Don't ever believe thin equals beautiful. There are many thin women in the world who don't know how to dress to flatter themselves! Beauty is style, it's confidence, and, above all else, it's a positive attitude.

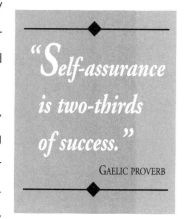

"*Self-assurance is two-thirds of success.*"

GAELIC PROVERB

Recognizing and learning to use proportion, scale, color, and perspective is the key to polishing appearance, keeping a wardrobe updated, following trends, and feeling great about yourself—regardless of your size, age, beauty, or financial situation. If knowledge = power = confidence = beauty, by following a few simple steps you'll be *Einstein gorgeous*!

Did you know that the average American woman spends 80 percent of

9

her time in 20 percent of her clothing? Plus-size women like yourself also tend to wear more of what they have (that fits), but they don't like their clothes as much as most women do. Why? My research shows that plus women have much lower expectations for their clothing. They don't think they can look really good at their present size, whatever that happens to be. So they settle for whatever they can find instead of *insisting* on good fit, quality fabric and construction, and garments that suit their coloring, shape, fashion personality, and lifestyle. These compromises add up, though, and the world notices and judges you on them.

I've always puzzled over the woman who runs around, sometimes for years, in the same old ill-fitting, out-of-date clothes, thinking that when she's *thin*, she will shop for a new wardrobe and look great. Until then, she expects you to reserve judgment on the *real her*. Well, yes I do understand that wearing clothes is sometimes easier when there is less of you, but why wait to go on living? What if you never change size? Who said you must? The reality is that people encounter you every day, make judgments about who and what you are now. Why give them any extra negative ammunition by looking your worst? If you get thinner, fine—buy clothes that make you happy then. Meanwhile, you're missing out on the terrific feeling that comes with looking your best and appearing confident in the presentation you make to the world.

You wouldn't neglect buying furniture and a few comforts for your home just because it wasn't the house of your dreams, would you? Even if it's an itty-bitty studio apartment, it's home. A few towels, some pots and pans, maybe even a sofa is indispensable until you move into that 5,000-square-foot dream house on ten acres with the tennis courts and pool.... If you're going to live in a house, you have to furnish it. Ditto on the wardrobe.

Seven Seconds to Image Impact...

Why should you pay special attention to what you wear? Because appearance and clothing are some of the most important criteria we have by which to judge others. It may surprise you to know that when people meet you they form lasting impressions that take a long time to change. Studies have shown that over 55 percent of the very first impression you make is based on your appearance and actions, 38 percent is based on your tone of voice, and only 7 percent is based on the actual words you say! Like it or not, people develop ideas about us based more on what they see and feel than on what you say. We are just naturally visual creatures.

Furthermore, in the first seven seconds of seeing you (before you even open your mouth) the other person is consciously and unconsciously making ten or more value judgments about you based only on your appearance. These include:

Value Judgments

Economic Level	Educational Level
Trustworthiness	Social Position
Level of Sophistication	Level of Success
Economic Heritage	Social Heritage
Educational Heritage	Moral Character

Whew! So you see, even if you keep your mouth closed, your appearance speaks volumes about you. What is yours saying? People are going to form an impression anyway, so wouldn't you like to have some say in the matter? This is what image management is all about—being in control of the message other people get from your appearance and nonverbal communications. Knowing that so many people in the world subject plus-size women to a discriminatory standard, we need to pay even closer attention to the overall image we convey, even if it's just to guarantee that the world is seeing our whole selves, and not just our bodies.

The Well-Dressed Woman

Well dressed has less to do with fashion trends than fabulous fit; less to do with your body size than your shape, colors, and proportions; less to do with the amount of money you spend than what you choose; and less to do with dressing up than dressing right. As many professional image consultants point out, a well-dressed woman wears clothes that are right for her body, fit her perfectly, coordinate in color, fabric, and pattern, are current, and are appropriate for the occasion. (There aren't any inappropriate clothes, really, only inappropriate occasions to wear certain clothes.)

Oh sure, you think, easy for you to say, but you haven't gone shopping with me. You don't know how hard it is to find things that fit, that I can afford. Ah, but I have! I constantly tour the market for research, shop with clients, and select and present clothes in seminars, workshops, and retail fashion shows. I know perfect clothes may not jump off the racks the moment you walk into your nearest clothing store, but with a little knowledge, time, and persistence, you can have whatever you want.

There have never been more beautiful clothes offered to plus women than right now. The recession of the early '90s forced manufacturers to look for new markets for their product, and for the first time in over seventy-five years they found us! New labels crop up monthly, stores are expanding their plus-size departments all over the country, and the number of catalogs devoted to large women is growing in leaps and bounds.

The key, of course, is selecting those things that are perfect for your body, your style, your life, and your budget. Here's how....

Your Body Type: The Key to Dressing

Go Figure

Ever notice that two women with the same dress size can have very different shapes? That's the natural variation of female bodies. Besides the variations in clothing size, women differ in shape due to bone structure and placement of their body mass. These differences are most obvious in overall height, but they also affect the length, width, and diameter of arms, legs, torsos, and every other body part.

> *"Vive la différence."*
>
> FRENCH PROVERB

Naturally there's no such thing as right or wrong bodies, just variations on the theme of female. If you find that clothes in the stores don't fit you right, it's not your body's fault; it doesn't mean you have a bad body, it means you have a body different from the one the designer was thinking of when developing those clothes.

Most clothing is cut to fit an average, evenly proportioned model's body, not necessarily your body. This system is designed to fit as many women as possible by using the most average measurements. The designer develops a consistent idea about the look her clothes convey, and she uses the same model to achieve perfect fit against that ideal. If that fit model has a very different body than yours, the clothes won't flatter you—even if you're a "perfect size."

Two things are happening here. First, no two designers use the same bust, waist, and hip measurement in their sizing scales; and second, a whole lot more goes into fit than bust, waist, and hip measurements!

We're all individuals with interesting and beautiful variations. Because every woman is unique, in the next few chapters we will explore the individual aspects of each body, and make specific dressing recommendations for you—no matter what your size, age, lifestyle, or budget. To begin to determine the right fashion silhouettes for you, we start with a careful examination of your body. We will outline four body types that incorporate all the configurations of plus-size bodies, and help you recognize the best clothing silhouettes for you based on your body type. These four types are derived from classical design elements and have been used by dressmakers and image consultants forever. They were most notably presented for the plus-size woman by Mary Duffy in her seminal book *The HOAX Fashion Formula.*

> **The Elements of Design**
>
> ◆ **Proportion:** Length and ratio of body sections
>
> ◆ **Dimension:** Body height and width
>
> ◆ **Shape:** Body silhouette

The Body as Canvas

The first step in the process of learning to make the most of your physical best is an honest, nonjudgmental examination of your body. I realize that some of you may have never looked in the mirror without finding flaws, but try to think about what your body *is* versus what it's *not*. Focus on the proportions you see. Try not to judge yourself as you relate to anyone else or to some fantasy image. Look for the lines, shapes, and proportions of your body as if it were a work of art on canvas, not as compared to any other body, or the body you used to have. (You might imagine yourself describing your body in great detail to an alien creature unfamiliar with our judgments about beauty and size. What proportions, dimensions, and shapes would you see and report on if you weren't being negatively judged?) *The key to Plus-Style dressing is in manipulating and balancing your proportions—not in making your body look smaller.*

To start, you should stand comfortably in front of a full-length mirror, preferably in a leotard or close-fitting top and hose and your best-fitting, nonminimizer bra. Using a tape measure, record the following measurements. Ask a friend to help. Don't ask anyone who might be at all judgmental or react negatively to your size.

What do you see? Are your hips rounded or more square? Is your waist very noticeably smaller than your bust or hips? Do your shoulders appear very rounded or somewhat square? Are your thighs or your hips the broadest part of your body? Are your legs relatively slender compared to your torso? Do you appear bigger above the waist or below it? We're looking at the big picture first, then the details.

The Nitty-Gritty Details of Proportion, Size, and Shape

Proportion

In theory, in the art of the ancient Greeks and in the minds of all designers, a "perfect" figure is evenly proportioned top to bottom, seven and a half or eight heads tall translating to four equal measurements: top of the head to the underarm, underarm to the break of the leg, leg break to the knee, and knee to the floor.

Of course, most people don't measure the theoretical ideal, but it's really helpful to know your own proportions. Many women don't know what to wear because they don't recognize their proportions, dimensions, or shape. (This isn't just a problem for plus-size women by the way, smaller women are just as confused!) For instance, one woman finds regular plus sizes way too long but may not fit plus-size petite styles. Careful measurements would reveal that her torso was about average, but her legs and arms were very short. Petite bodies aren't petite all over, and long bodies can be average or even short in some places. Another lovely woman was totally average in upper torso, lower legs, and elbow to wrist measurements, but very short in upper arms and thighs, as well as rise, or waist to crotch. Now that she knows her differences versus the average, or what most designers are constructing clothes for, she can shop for the correct styles and shapes more knowledgeably and do less altering. You can, too.

Your Body's Proportions

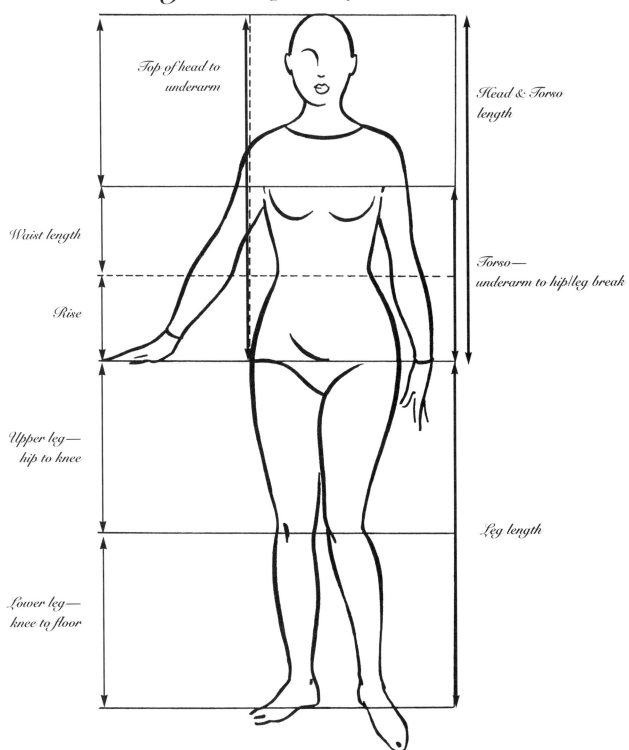

Top of head to underarm

Head & Torso length

Waist length

Torso— underarm to hip/leg break

Rise

Upper leg— hip to knee

Leg length

Lower leg— knee to floor

How to Measure

At this stage you are measuring your bone structure, so don't be concerned with your relative size or shape. Keep in mind that your body undoubtedly differs from the "classic" proportions somewhere—in head length, upper torso, rise, leg length, etc. Your measurements will be your general guide in analyzing how your genes configured the overall blueprint of your body. *Knowledge is power in dressing!*

It's very, very important that you take the time to take the plunge and measure yourself. You can't begin to meet a challenge, solve a problem, or gain self-esteem by hiding your head in the sand. Besides, the actual numbers that you measure are less important than the proportions they reveal. (If it makes you more confident, measure yourself in centimeters, which have less meaning for most of us and can be found on the back of most tape measures.) You can do this—it's easy, it's revealing, it's empowering!

Get a friend to assist you with a flat-edge ruler and a tape measure. (For the original stick/string method of figure analysis, see Jan Larkey's Flatter Your Figure™ System.) You may find it easier to stand against a wall and lightly mark these lengths in pencil, or to mark them on a full-length mirror in black marker (this will come off with glass cleaner), then measure.

Height_____ inches	
Torso vs. Legs	
Top half _____ inches	
Bottom half _____ inches	

Are you longer in the torso or the legs? Measure the top half of your body (head to hipbone/leg break) versus the bottom half (hip/leg break to bottom of feet) and see if you are longer, shorter, or even in torso or legs. (If you need help in finding that hipbone, stand up straight while holding onto a chair or other stable object for support, and raise your leg slightly. Where your leg "breaks" is your hipbone). If these two measurements are equal, you are evenly proportioned.

Waist Length

Some torsos are evenly proportioned, some are long on the bottom, and some are longer on the top. The "average" waist is halfway between the underarm and the leg break/hip joint. To determine if you are short-, long-, or even-waisted, evaluate these three measurements:

- Underarm to your hipbone/leg break. For this, keep your arm at your side and measure just from the underarm crease to your hipbone. (The underarm is usually halfway between the top of the head and the crotch/hip joint. If not, your arm may be placed higher or lower than average, which would affect the best suit jacket cuts for your body.) _____ inches

- Measure the distance from your underarm to your waist. (Trouble finding your waist? Lean sideways and see where you bend! You might want to tie a string around your waist to keep the mark point clearly defined.) _____ inches

I am	
Short-waisted	_____
Long-waisted	_____
Evenly proportioned	_____

Longer on top? You're long-waisted; shorter? short-waisted.

- Measure from your waist to your hipbone/leg break. _____ inches

Rise

The average rise is the same as the waist length. If you are short-waisted, you're probably long in the rise, too. Conversely, if you are long-waisted, you may be short in the rise. Or are you even?

Shoulder Width

An equal circumference at the shoulders and the hips is considered average. Stand facing the mirror, and clasp your arms behind you. A straight edge placed

| My rise is: |
| Short _____ |
| Long _____ |
| Evenly proportioned _____ |

from the outer shoulder corner to the edge of your hip will reveal which is wider. Is the line perpendicular—straight up and down, showing your shoulders and hips equally wide? Or is the line significantly angled out, showing your hips

Average

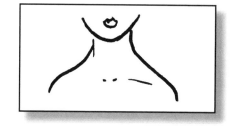

Sloping

Narrow

Broad

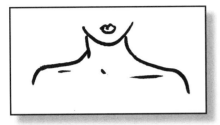

Square

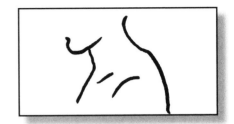

"Dowager's Hump"

Are my shoulders:

Narrow _____

Broad _____

Average _____

Sloping _____

Square _____

Do I have:

"Dowager's hump" _____

to be wider than your shoulders, or your shoulders wider than your hips?

Look also at the angle of your shoulders from your neck to the outer shoulder corner (you can have your helper hold the yardstick or broom handle across your shoulders from behind to compare your natural shoulder line with the straight edge).

Look at your back where your neck joins your shoulders. Is your shoulder line smooth and flat, or is it more rounded, also known as "dowager's hump"?

Hip/Leg Break to Knee, Knee to the Floor

The knee is usually about halfway between leg break/hip joint and feet. If not, are your legs shorter in the thigh or lower leg?

Upper leg:

Hip/leg break to knee_____ inches

Lower leg:

Knee to the floor _____ inches

In all of the measuring, the important issues are these: Your torso length—long or short—has everything to do with the jackets and tops you choose and how you balance skirt lengths with tops. It's also critical to gauge whether you are short- or long-waisted, which will influence how you balance the proportions of tops and bottoms, as well as your choice of dress style. The upper and lower leg length proportions determine how you wear your skirts. Lastly, rise is critical to choosing the right trouser design for your body.

Body Dimension

In addition to your overall proportions, it's crucial to know your exact measurements when identifying your body type and foundation/clothing sizes. Once your dimensions are on paper, it's also a little easier to understand how your proportions affect your clothing selections, and how to achieve proper fit.

Bustline

Measure straight across the back and around the fullest part of the bustline. _____ inches

(In Chapter Six we will use this and two other measurements to calculate bra size.)

Waist

Measure the narrowest part of your torso. (The average woman's waist is 8–10 inches smaller than the bust. Yours, like that of many other plus-size women, may vary considerably from the norm.) _____ inches

High Hip

Measure around your torso 3 inches down from your waist.

_____ inches

Full Hip

Measure the fullest part of your hip, which is usually about 8 inches below the waist. (Be certain to keep the tape measure level all the way around your body.) _____ inches (How far below your waist *is* your widest point? _____ inches) *Important!* If you are widest just

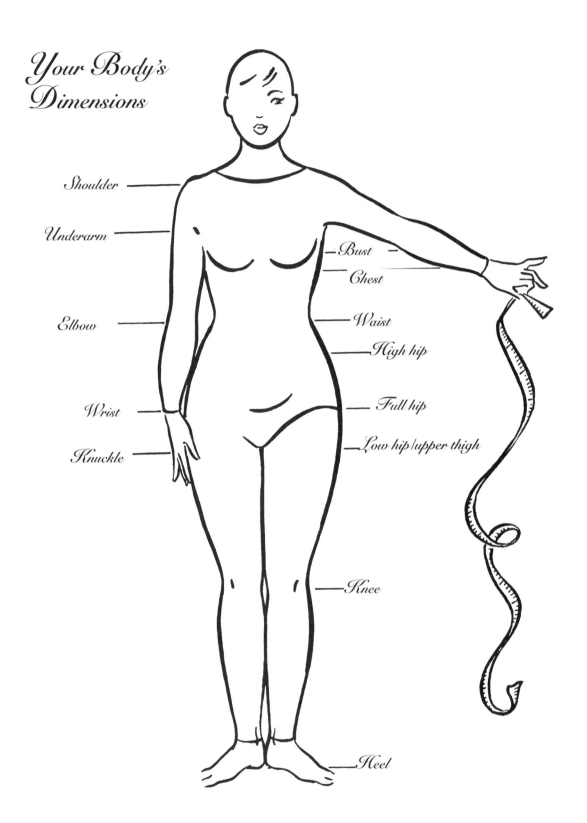

Your Body's Dimensions

Shoulder

Underarm

Elbow

Wrist

Knuckle

Bust

Chest

Waist

High hip

Full hip

Low hip/upper thigh

Knee

Heel

below the waist you are "high-hipped"; if widest farther down your torso or at the thighs you are "low-hipped."

Inseam

Leg break/crotch
to ankle bone. _____ inches

Hand

Measure around the widest part of the hand, at the base of the fingers. (This calculates your
glove size.) _____ inches

Arm Length

You may already know if your arms are short or long based upon how shirts and blouses fall.

Measure your arm from shoulder edge to the wrist break. _____ inches
The knuckle of the thumb usually hits

at crotch level and the elbow usually hits about even with the average waistline. If not, you probably have longer or shorter than average arms.

My arms are short _____.

My arms are long _____.

My arms are evenly
proportioned to my torso _____.

If you just skipped over this part because you don't want to be bothered or face the music, go back now and dig out the ol' measuring tape. Not wanting to know how big you really are is a part of the judgmental thinking that says large *equals* bad. The only way to change negative thinking is to make real, conscious changes, step by step. Step one, get out the tape. Step two, measure your body. Step three, begin to feel in control.

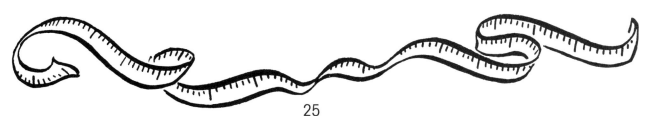

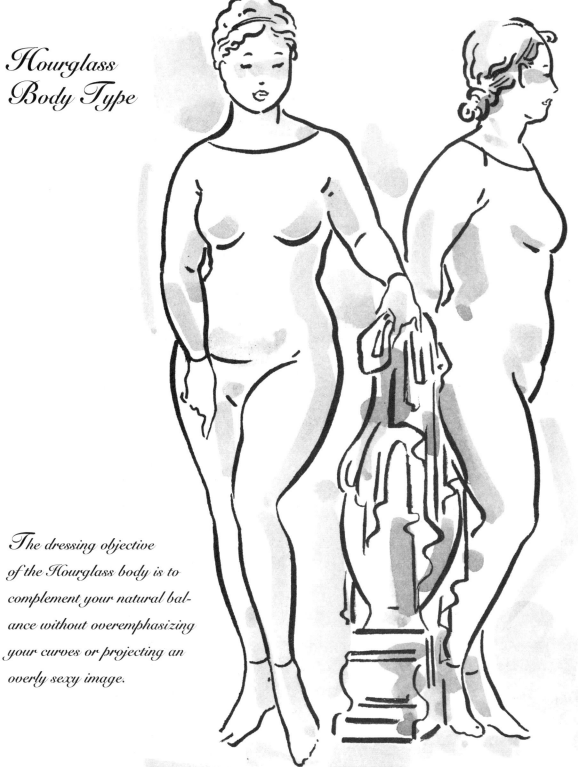

Hourglass
Body Type

The dressing objective of the Hourglass body is to complement your natural balance without overemphasizing your curves or projecting an overly sexy image.

Shape: Four Classic Body Types

Now that you have an understanding of your proportions and size, you have the tools to identify your body type. While every body is individual, most women's figures fit into one of the four classic body types. The explanations that follow will help you understand which type you are, and give you a summary of the fashion silhouettes that will flatter you most. Remember, you may not be a perfect example of your type. You could have a slightly different shape or dimension than the illustration—look for similarities rather than differences.

Hourglass Body Type

The Hourglass projects an overall curvy shape, with hips and shoulders about the same width. Even in profile your waist is well-defined—at least 9 inches smaller than your bust or hips. Your lower hips are usually wider than your high hips, and you may have a fairly round, full rear. Although your thighs are full, they are narrower than your lower hips (from the front view, at least), and your lower legs are relatively slim or shapely. Your Hourglass face, neck, and shoulders are probably proportionate to the rest of your body (though the hourglass body is prone to a double chin). You are blessed with the beautiful, natural, feminine shape usually associated with womanliness. Your even proportions and gentle curves make dressing easier than you might think.

With an Hourglass body you can call attention to your well-defined waist, but you may need to deemphasize your ample bustline in order not to appear top-heavy. You are flattered by soft, flowing, or "drape-able" fabrics and sophisticated lines that acknowledge your shape without adding bulk to your

Rectangle
Body Type

The dressing
objective of the
Rectangle body
is to suggest a
waist and use
gentle, fluid
shapes that rein-
force the vertical
and soften the
edges.

frame. Your only constraints are avoiding overtly sexy statements with clingy, body-hugging shapes, or confining your curves into tailored, boxy clothes that broaden you—the dreaded "refrigerator-box syndrome"!

Very full skirts are not a good choice for you since they add bulk where you don't need it. A slightly narrower skirt is necessary to balance your upper and lower torso. If very curvy, you can soften the line with long open overblouses, cardigans, and soft jackets that flow in a line from shoulder to thigh.

Good Ideas for the Hourglass Figure:

◆ Set-in waists and belts
◆ Vertical lines
◆ Tailored dresses

Bad Ideas:

◆ Form-fitting knits or tight clothes
◆ Boxy jackets
◆ Full skirts
◆ Cutesy looks

> Note: If your bust is more than about 2 inches larger than your hips you're an Apple; if your hips are more than about 2 inches bigger than your bust you're probably a Pear. See below.

Rectangle Body Type

You have an undefined waist, with similar bust, waist, and hip measurements. Your waist is usually no more than 8 inches different from your hips or bust—whichever is smaller. Your hips are more square than rounded, and are probably widest just below the waist. You may not be very large-busted, but you may carry some weight through your upper back or neck. Your arms and legs are likely slim in comparison to the rest of your body—and you probably aren't troubled by thigh bulges (also known as saddlebags).

Because your body tends to look large all over, and doesn't have a defined waist, you may feel less feminine than your more curvy sisters. Actually, you are easier to dress than some round bodies, since your body is very balanced.

Clothing that falls smoothly and gently over the midriff flatters the Rec-

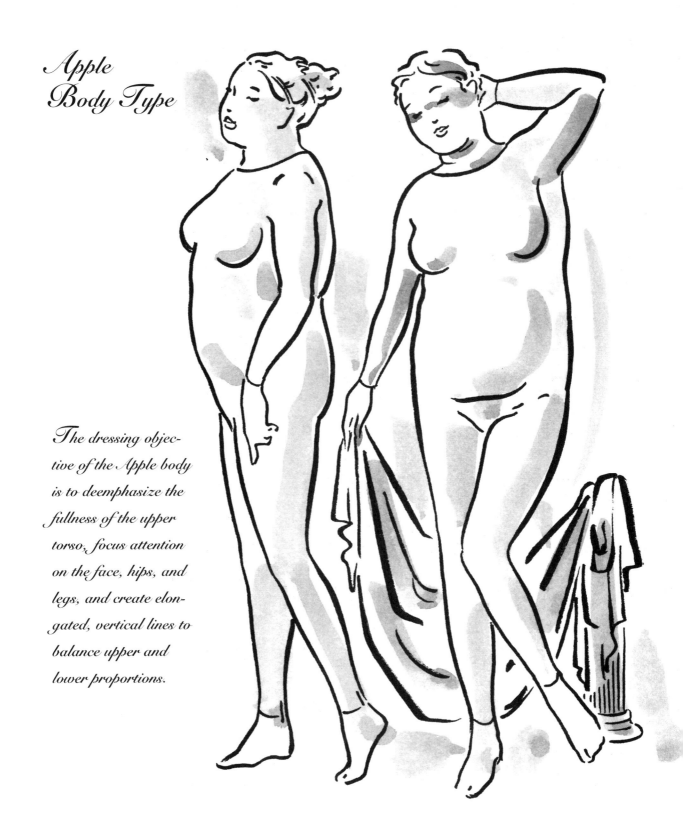

Apple Body Type

The dressing objective of the Apple body is to deemphasize the fullness of the upper torso, focus attention on the face, hips, and legs, and create elongated, vertical lines to balance upper and lower proportions.

tangle body most. You need to avoid boxy, stiff shapes that reinforce your straight lines. Look for styles that lend an illusion of an indented waist or flow past it altogether. Adjustable or hip-slung belts can work very well, as do dropped-waist styles, which give you a long line without losing body definition.

You should keep your necklines and shoulder area interesting, and reinforce the vertical line in soft fabrics and flowing lines. Knits are your best friend!

Good Ideas for the Rectangle Figure:

◆ Monochromatic looks

◆ Knits

◆ One-piece dresses

◆ Trousers

Bad Ideas:

◆ Boxy jackets

◆ Horizontal lines

◆ Full skirts & pants

Apple Body Type

Rounded in shape, you are full in the bust, waist, and upper back, sometimes with a prominent tummy area. Your appearance is top-heavy, usually with a pronounced midriff, and a flat rear. You are wider at the high hip than the low hip. As a natural wedge shape, your bust and/or midriff is larger than your hips, and you tend to be short-waisted, perhaps with a rounded upper back (or "dowager's hump"). Most Apples have a large face in relation to their bodies, and comparatively slim arms and legs (your thighs are the narrowest point of your torso).

You need to dress your body in shapes that work with, not against, your own natural wedge shape. To do that, you can focus attention either at the shoulder/neck/face area, or at your hip and thigh/leg area. This is a case of emphasizing what works (your face, your great legs), and ignoring what doesn't (you can't create a waist where none exists!).

As an Apple you have the most limited range of dressing options, but you

Pear
Body Type

The dressing objective
of the Pear body is to
de-emphasize your
hips and thighs, and
focus attention on your
shapely waist and
upper torso in order to
balance upper and
lower proportions.

can learn to make your natural assets work very, very well. Wedge-shaped dresses with shoulder attention and a narrow hem are made for you. The long-over-lean silhouette works perfectly for the Apple—you're best in long blouson tops and leggings or narrow skirts. You should avoid set-in waists and belts, fitted jackets and fitted tops.

Good Ideas for the Apple Figure:

◆ Verticals of all kinds

◆ Short flippy skirts

◆ Unconstructed jackets

◆ Scarves at the neck and around the shoulders

Bad Ideas:

◆ Fitted and tailored anything

The verticality created by monochromatic outfits are the best idea for your Apple shape. Prints and patterns are best worn all over or on the bottom half with a long jacket to cover. You should use necklaces or scarves to create long, vertical lines—but be sure that they hang against the body and don't cascade over your bosom into empty space!

Pear Body Type

As with all Pears, your hips and thighs are wider than your shoulders and bust; your curvy lower hips and rear are the biggest part of your body. Your waist is at least 8 inches smaller than your hips, and your bust and shoulders may be on the smaller side. Your legs are average to large in size, and your face and neck are slender in relation to your overall body size.

To flatter your shape, you need to emphasize your midriff and focus attention above the waist with color, line, and detail (and shoulder pads, of course!). Darker colors and softly pleated, flowing, or draped skirts will help to deemphasize your hips, thighs, and rear. Belts help to define your waist.

The Pear can wear print and pattern most effectively above the waist, along

Good Ideas for the Pear Figure:

◆ Shoulder pads

◆ Scarf around the shoulders

◆ Set-in waists and belts

◆ Separates

Bad Ideas:

◆ Short, or tight skirts

◆ Light, bright colors on the bottom; dark colors on the top

◆ Raglan or dolman sleeves

◆ Flat shoes

with light, bright colors that attract the eye. Softly pleated or flat-front pants work for you. You can wear long, softer overblouses, sweaters, and shirts—but they work best open over a belted or tucked-in top.

Everybody's Best

As we saw at the start of the chapter, there are three elements that reflect your body's basic design and therefore affect your strategy to flatter yourself in clothing, accessories, etc.: Do you understand your proportions? Did you measure yourself exactly to know your dimensions? Did you discover your body shape? Understanding your body is the first step in taking charge of your appearance and feeling good about yourself! And isn't it nice to know that you're unique but not alone—that there are others with your body type, and that you have assets that can be developed and highlighted? Now that you recognize its features you are ready to proceed with clothing your own body—perfectly.

The Elements of Design

◆ *Proportion:* Length of body sections

◆ *Dimension:* Body height and width

◆ *Shape:* Body silhouette

Sizes: Myths, Realities, and Strategies to Look Your Best

Sizing Up the Competition

In Chapter Two we examined bodies by proportion, size, and shape to illustrate how multidimensional and unique every woman is. By now you can see that your body has a definite pattern of proportion in your limbs and torso, measures to a specific set of numbers, and has its own particular shape.

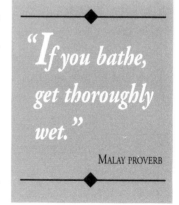

"If you bathe, get thoroughly wet."

MALAY PROVERB

When trying to find the right clothing size for you, remember that the mission is about great clothes—not smaller sizes. If you can recognize your body's proportions, shape, and relative size, you can judge the right clothes for you—without abiding by anyone else's size chart. It might help to remember, too, that not everyone, every culture, or every time in history revered thinness and a singular idea of beauty. As Francis Bacon noted in his *Essays of Beauty*: "There is no excellent beauty that hath not some strangeness in the proportion."

What does all of this mean when you go shopping? How do clothing designers interpret bodies into sizes? Why are you a smaller size in some things and a bigger size in others? Why do some clothes never seem to fit no matter what size you try? As we take a look at some of these questions, remember my mantra—*it's not you, it's the clothes.*

> **Myth #1:**
> *I don't have to try it on; it's my size and I can tell from the hanger how it will look.*
>
> **Truth #1:**
> *Every garment fits differently, even those from the same designer, same pattern, same group. The only way to know if a garment will flatter you is to try it on.*

Size is only a guideline for selecting clothes that suit the three-dimensional body. Some of the best-fitting clothes look awful on the hanger because the same delicate shaping that flatters your body can make them look limp and meaningless on the rack. On the other hand, there's the dress or suit that hangs there radiating personality and style—but can make you look as if you're wearing the very latest in refrigerator boxes. Now that's attractive!

Hanger appeal is a key issue for any designer's success because that's the first and often only connection most women have with their clothes. Unless someone hands you a garment in the fitting room, the only way you'll try something on is if it entices you enough to pull it off the rack—"Hey lady, over here! What about me? I'd look great on you—look at my color, my fabric, my design ..."

Of course that's not to say designers aren't concerned with you, your style,

36

or your body, but their top priority tends to be your wallet. Simply put, the designer is interested in four things:

1. Making clothes that you will buy.

2. Making clothes that will entice you to face a dressing-room mirror (see #1).

3. Making clothes that make you feel good (see #1).

4. Making clothes that are different enough from last season to make you feel out of style and in desperate need of a new wardrobe (see #1).

Consider how few clothes you would own if your only concerns were covering your body adequately to suit the weather and the available weekly laundry time. So let's not be coy—your concern is to find the best-fitting, most flattering clothes available considering the latest style, your lifestyle, and budget. A wise woman once said that people buy only two things: solutions to problems, and good feelings. So caveat emptor! Let the buyer beware of— and base decisions on—what constitutes size, style, fit, fashion, or need.

What's Size Got to Do with It?

Rest assured that your clothes wouldn't necessarily fit you any better if you were smaller, because proportion and shape are much more important in determining fit than actual size could ever be. Clothes have different shapes just the way people do, and recognizing your best clothing shapes is the key to finding clothes that fit and flatter your body. In Chapter Six we will explore the right silhouettes for you, but the first step in finding *anything* is to find the right size. So what's your size?

Since every woman has unique proportions, it stands to reason that clothes designed for every woman probably fit no woman perfectly, right? Yes, and no. Some of the body types are more evenly proportioned than others, and the women with those bodies can usually wear more clothing styles successfully than the rest of us. Fortunately for those figure types, most clothing is designed for a specific, well-proportioned Rectangular or Hourglass body. Unfortunately for the rest of us, we have to know what shapes to look for. Without universal sizing standards in this country (which means that we end up with a wide variation of sizing and fit from label to label) we have to know our bodies' dimensions and reinterpret sizing that works for each of us.

Myth #2:
I know what size I am. I've been that size a long time, and I know that size will fit me.

Truth #2:
Tag sizes sometimes have little bearing on the reality of what fits you.

Every day women ask, "What's wrong with me? I wear a different size in every label, and sometimes I need to go up or down *two* sizes. I just don't seem to have the right shape body." Well, nothing's wrong with you or your body, the problem lies partly with the fact that all bodies are unique three-dimensional shapes, partly with the way clothes are designed and made, and partly with the way you choose your clothes. Since you can't change the way designers plan their clothes, and you shouldn't have to change your body to suit anyone or anything just to get dressed, this chapter can help you adapt your own buying strategy.

Manufactured Sizes

Most manufacturers depend upon three simple measurements to determine garment sizing: bust, waist, and hip. While other dimensions (such as rise or back length) come into play, these three are the critical points that determine whether a dress, a skirt, a blouse, or a pair of pants fit or don't. Of course as a shopper you know that some labels shape their clothing in particular ways—some closely tailored and very structured, some loose and flowing, some shorter or longer, etc. This is an expression of their creative view of style and their interpretation of what's in fashion at the moment—and part of their approach to design. If the fit of one line of clothing isn't necessarily an accurate reflection of your body's shape, it doesn't mean anything is wrong with you! Michelangelo didn't see or paint figures the same way Matisse or Picasso did because all three were affected by their individual training and creative style. Likewise, every designer sees clothing (and fit) his/her own way. There is no master size/fit chart that manufacturers use, no governing body that sets standards of measurement. Each label invents its own.

Usually, the designer has an idea about how she wants to bring her clothing to life. Based on sketches or other tools, she makes a prototype according to her set of size guidelines, then (most) hire at least one fit model to try the garment on. In plus sizes this model is usually a "perfect" size 18 or 20 with an average rise, average leg length, average arm length, and is a Rectangle or Hourglass body type.

As the model moves around in the clothes, she reports on how well they fit her in every area, and gives direction on what should change and how. The armholes, neckline, bodice length, or hundreds of other details may be changed. A good fit model is worth her weight in gold to the designer, and may be the only connection she has between her drawing board and the customer.

Following this fitting, patterns are "graded" up or down from that sample for all the sizes to be manufactured, and the garments go into production. Manufacturers (cutters, sewers) analyze the specifications dictated by the designer and grader, and usually copy the clothes exactly. (Of course, sometimes they inadvertently cut things a little too small or too big, and if the flaw isn't detected, you end up with an odd—or marvelous—fit!)

This method works remarkably well in outfitting the most average, most well-proportioned women who share the same body type as the model. Unfortunately, if your body differs significantly from the fit model in size or shape, you aren't likely to get a perfect fit. Even "perfect" bodies vary in rise, back width versus bust width, arm length, leg length, etc. So the only way to guarantee that your clothes flatter your body is to try things on and choose those with the right shape, proportion, and size for you.

What Size Are You?

Women's large sizes have been described many different ways—most of them failed attempts to describe our bodies. "Half sizes" were developed more than fifty years ago for mature women who had large, low bust lines. (Corsets went out of style in the early twenties, and didn't reappear until sometime in the forties. My own grandmother had a bustline that, well, let's just say showed the effects of a lifetime free of constriction....) Half sizes were very short-waisted (probably because so many mature women suffered from osteoporosis),

Missy Sizes
Women 5´4" or taller

Size	8	10	12	14	16	18	20
Bust	35	36	38	39	40	42	44
Waist	25	26	28	29	30	32	34
Hips	35	36	38	40	42	43	45

Women's Sizes
Women 5´4" or taller

Sizes	14W	16W	18W	20W	22W	24W	26W	28W	30W
	L–1X	1X	2X	2X	3X	3X	4X	4–5X	5–6X
Bust	40	42	44	46	48	50	52	54	56
Waist	31	33	35	37	39	41	43	45	47
Hips	42	44	46	48	50	52	54	56	58
Nape to Waist*	$17\frac{3}{4}$	18	$18\frac{1}{4}$	$18\frac{1}{2}$	$18\frac{3}{4}$	19	$19\frac{1}{4}$	$19\frac{1}{2}$	20
Sleeve Length**	$23\frac{5}{8}$	$23\frac{3}{4}$	$23\frac{7}{8}$	24	$24\frac{1}{8}$	$24\frac{1}{4}$	$24\frac{3}{8}$	$24\frac{1}{2}$	$24\frac{5}{8}$
Inseam***	$29\frac{1}{2}$	$29\frac{1}{2}$	$29\frac{1}{2}$	$29\frac{1}{2}$	$29\frac{1}{2}$	$29\frac{1}{2}$	$29\frac{1}{2}$	$29\frac{1}{2}$	$29\frac{1}{2}$

*Nape, or the back of the neck to the waist, along the center back

**Sleeve is measured from the shoulder seam to wrist break

***Inseam is measured from the leg break/hip bone/inner crotch area to the anklebone, or just above the top of the foot

reflected a larger bustline, fuller waist, and were fashioned for the mature woman in terms of fabric, length, and overall design.

Sizing has evolved over the last thirty years. The numerical women's sizing system, in tandem with half sizes, was in use for many years. In this system sizes ranged from 34–46 for tops and 28–40 for bottoms. Neither seemed to bear any relation to bust, waist, or hips, but attempted to separate dress sizes from separates' sizes. Finally, in 1986 a new sizing system was introduced to revamp years of confusion over size designations. And as you undoubtedly noticed, Plus (or Women's) sizes replaced "half sizes." Although the actual measurements vary from one label to the other, the new Women's sizes (14W–26W) are scaled for the average modern woman over 5'4" tall, have slightly larger waist and hip proportions than their Missy counterparts (2–20), and allow for larger arms, legs, and tummy, as well as a slightly lower bustline. It's important to note that a Woman's or Plus size 18W, for example, is not the same as a Missy size 18. Look for the W designation to tell which is which.

In addition, many garments are sold in 1X–5X+. Every manufacturer has its own designation for these groupings, but our chart lists the most widely used size/measurement ratios. The retailer, manufacturer, or catalog will usually provide the specific measurements used to compute sizes—which can vary by as much as 6 inches, so check your own measurements before ordering. Where do you fall on the charts?

The system revamping also replaced Half sizes with Women's Petite (WP14–26), providing for the ultimate forgotten woman: those plus-size women under 5'4". The new system updates sizes to the reality of the world, including women proportionately short, but not necessarily short-waisted or having a

"mature" figure; the Plus Petite is simply the larger version of the Missy Petite. In most cases, the Petite Woman is cut an inch to an inch and a half shorter in the sleeve, pant leg, skirt length, and center back than the regular Plus sizes.

Women's Petite Sizes
Women under 5'4"

Size	14WP	16WP	18WP	20WP	22WP	24WP	26WP
Half Size	14½	16½	18½	20½	22½	24½	26½
Bust	40	42	44	46	48	50	52
Waist	31	33	35	37	39	41	43
Hips	42	44	46	48	50	52	54

You'll quickly notice that the Women's sizes and Petite Women's sizes have the same bust, waist, and hip measurements. The differences are in the subtleties—the width of the shoulders, the length of the waist and the rise—as well as arm and leg dimensions and lengths. Your body measurements should tell you if you are truly average, short, or long in each section, and guide you in which chart to use for you. Nothing replaces the best advice: Try it on, try it on, try it on!

Supersizes (28W–38W+) for women over size 26W is the largest group of newly designated sizes. Measurements for clothing in Supersizes vary tremendously from one manufacturer to another. Since they are primarily represented by custom catalogs, it's best to check the fit charts included with every catalog you receive to get the best fit.

Some manufacturers are also beginning to expand into larger Junior sizes to accommodate younger customers. Hooray! If you were (or are) a large-size younger gal, you'll really appreciate finding clothing styled for your age group that will fit you on the same sizing system your friends use. Traditionally the Junior charts are designed for smaller busts and fuller waists than Missy sizes and heights below 5'7":

Junior Sizes
Young women under 5'7" tall

Size	11	13	15	17	19
Bust	37	38	40	42	44
Waist	29	30	31	32	33
Hips	39	40	41	42	43

Size Strategy

If you're confused about the correct size or shape for your body, remember that the proportion of your clothes has to match your body's proportions. If you measure to a Petite height for example, but your proportions reveal that you have an average torso, you probably are just Petite in the length of arms and legs. In this case you would buy regular Plus-size tops and jackets, as long as they didn't fall too far down your thighs and shorten the arms. In pants, you would buy a Petite if possible, so that the thigh ease hits you in the right place, and the rise is correct for you. If your whole torso is long, including your rise, you would have

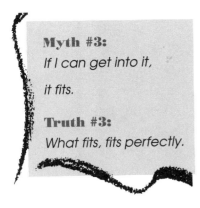

to buy a regular, non-Petite size to fit your torso proportions. Clothing is sized to fit the *average* body, which means that the fullness for the bust, hip, thigh, and upper arm should fall in the right place on *your* body to look your best. You can shorten or lengthen pieces, but basic shapes are more challenging to alter. It's worth the investment of time and money to find the right size for you.

Size Savvy

- Experiment with different brands, stores, and catalogs—size varies by several inches between brands.

- Try on sizes larger and smaller than you think you need. This is especially important when ordering by mail. I usually order a couple of sizes in most items, keep what fits, and send the rest back. What fits, flatters.

- Find a couple of labels that fit you well and stick with them. Ask when the new season's clothes arrive at your local department or specialty store and get there early for best selection in size and color.

- Catalogs offer a larger range of sizes than most retail brands. (See appendix for resources.)

- When shopping for suits and coordinated outfits look for brands that sell the tops and bottoms separately. (Most Plus-size women vary at least one size top vs. bottom.)

- Make sure that whatever garment you try has the right shoulder pads, worth their weight in gold because they finish off the shoulder line and balance the lower body. Resist the temptation to wear them too high or stacked up like a linebacker. Unless you have very sloped shoulders, the pad should retain the natural 2-inch drop from neck to shoulder edge. The secret is to find a pair large enough to cover the whole shoulder, which eliminates the lump effect and can square off a slightly rounded back or slouch. The best pair is covered in flesh-colored fabric and is Velcro™-equipped for easy removal and cleaning.

- Before deciding to buy a garment a size larger to allow for shrinkage, check the fabric content and care label. Many cottons are prewashed and won't shrink any further. Blends are also less likely to alter their original shape.

- More expensive clothing is often designed so that you fit a smaller size.

If you do nothing else, keep this in mind:

1. Size is relative to every manufacturer.

2. A size tag has nothing to do with how lovely you are, how attractive you are, or whether the garment is worth buying and wearing.

3. It's normal to own clothes in several different sizes that all fit perfectly and improve your silhouette.

4. Cut the size tags out of your clothes (carefully!) as soon as you get them home. I find this improves disposition considerably.

Understanding Clothes: Design, Fabric, and Color

Dressing-Thin Secrets Revealed: The Bottom Line on Inside Lines, Outside Lines, Vertical, Horizontal, Diagonal, Curved, and Straight Lines

In Chapter Two we discussed the elements of design as they relate to your body—proportion (length and ratio of sections to each other), dimension (body height and width), and shape (body silhouette). The clothes you wear add their own proportions, dimensions, and shapes *plus* another set of elements for consideration: style lines, texture, and color.

Choosing clothes with the correct silhouette for your body is the first step in dressing well, because they have the most flattering

> *"The art of pleasing is the art of deceiving."*
>
> FRENCH PROVERB

outside lines for you. The contours of clothes follow the contours of your body, so you need to choose clothes that don't bind you (by being narrow where you aren't) or add bulk to your figure (by being wider than you are). In addition, every garment has color, sometimes it has pattern, and it always has style lines based on its construction and ornament. These are a garment's *inside lines:* seams, button plackets, zippers, darts and tucks, pleats, lapels, pockets, fabric print lines, as well as the intersection of colors.

All of these design elements work together, and the trick to achieving your best look is in finding the right *balance* of these elements for your body. *The key to Plus-Style dressing is in manipulating and balancing your proportions, dimensions, colors, textures, style lines, and most importantly, shapes. Making your body look smaller is irrelevant.*

Style Lines: Vertical Is Beautiful

As a child I was amazed at the tricks my brothers could perform with their Hot Wheels™ cars on their bright orange tracks. Those agile little cars would zip through loop-de-loops, slow down to take the sharpest curves, and whiz like lightning through the straightaways! Your eye is a little like those cars, following lines like they are tracks; it dislikes wandering all over the place, and would rather trace a clean, straight line. But because your eye is naturally lazy, what it likes best of all is to rest on a horizontal line.

Because it travels fastest on them, *the eye perceives figures with vertical, straight lines as taller and slightly more narrow.* (Your natural vertical lines include the entire length of your body, each leg, and each arm.) Because

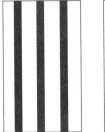 

Objects divided vertically appear taller, more narrow. Closely spaced lines enhance the effect.

 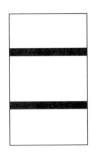

Objects divided horizontally appear shorter and wider.

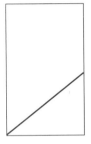 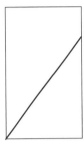 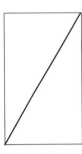 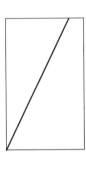

The longer, more vertical the angle of the diagonal, the taller and narrower the object appears.

they lead the eye back and forth, *horizontal lines make an object appear a little shorter and wider.* (Your natural horizontal lines include your shoulders, your bustline, and possibly your waist, hipline, and hemline.) When horizontal lines intersect verticals the lengthening effect is diminished. You want to avoid an obvious horizontal line at your widest point.

Following a curved line, the eye slows down to stay on track, and so *the eye perceives the size of items with curved lines as larger*, since they take longer to scan.

Diagonal lines move the eye along at an angle, and can broaden or narrow depending on length, direction, and where they lead the eye. The *longer, more vertical a diagonal line, the taller and narrower it will make an object appear.*

Lines divide space and can change proportions. A good example of the effect of lines can be seen in the cut of jackets—lapels are diagonals, closures might be vertical or diagonal, and hems can be horizontal or diagonal. A double-breasted jacket with only two buttons creates a horizontal line between them, while with four or six buttons, a new, stronger diagonal or vertical line is defined. When the jacket is worn open, as in the case of a cardigan, for example, two vertical or diagonal lines are created along the inside edge. If the jacket splays open over the hipline, a diagonal is created between the middle of the body and the outer edge of the hips. If the cardigan falls open without interruption, a more slimming straight vertical is created.

The eye also notices details from left to right, top to bottom (the same way you read English), so *you see horizontal lines first, then vertical ones.* Unfortunately, once the eye finds a horizontal line to settle on, it will keep zipping back and forth across that line until it finds something else more interesting to follow. Because horizontal lines will emphasize width, you will want to choose garments with strong vertical lines in order to direct the eye up and down, and reinforce the perpendicular.

Dressing Tip: Vertical lines lengthen a figure. Horizontal lines emphasize and broaden.

In addition, the eye will jump between lines, and so *you see a figure with closely spaced vertical lines as narrower than one with lines wider apart.* (A good example is a gored skirt; a six-gored skirt is more slimming than a four-gored skirt because the space between the gores is reduced.) You need to be aware of the style and construction lines of your clothing and accessories, and where they lead the eye. By manipulating the lines in a garment, you can change how that garment is perceived—its relative size, its dimensions, and its personality or fashion style. *Use focal points where you want attention,* and *use lines to lead the eye away from or toward critical points.*

The *primary point of emphasis* should be your center of communication and your best asset—*your face.* Beyond that, control the focus of the eye on your body. Have great ankles? Focus on them. Have pretty shoulders or need to place more emphasis there in order to balance width below the waist? Direct the eye there with accessories, color, or style lines. Want to downplay a large bust? Direct the eye away from its widest point (or avoid calling attention to it) with line, texture, or color. You have to direct the behavior of the eye as you would a two-year-old child, guiding it carefully lest it wander away and get itself right into the middle of where it doesn't belong. Keep the eye out of trouble—pay attention to the lines of your garments!

When a line is repeated it has tremendous impact. Our curved bodies are sensitive to line movement, so it's best to be cautious with curvy design elements. Our curves contrast with sharp angles, geometrics, and stripes, and are reinforced with curved lines. Choose clothing with details that have both curves and angles or straight edges. Contrast reinforces lines.

You're Only as Wide as Your Widest Line

A figure is perceived to be as broad as the line that defines it at its widest point. If you wear anything wider than it has to be, you add unnecessary bulk to your figure and make yourself look larger than you really are. Whether that line is at the shoulder, the hips, the knees, or the ankles, the viewer's eye will follow the horizontal line and perceive that width as your full width. Therefore you can look taller and more narrow by tapering your skirts, by not wearing palazzo pants wider than they need to be, and by avoiding full dirndl skirts. Remember my motto: *You're only as wide as your widest line.*

Curvy Is as Curvy Does: The Meaning of Lines

Another point to consider: Lines have style meanings. We associate very curvy lines like curls, ruffles, polka dots, and flowers as romantic, feminine, approachable, and less formal, while architectural angles and straight lines are seen as very powerful, formal, and masculine. Depending upon your preferred fashion style (we'll talk more about this later), you may or may not be comfortable with certain prints, patterns, and details. The lines of an outfit are as important as its color or fabric.

> **Dressing Tip:**
> Remember my motto: You're only as wide as your widest line!

Proportion

Proportion relates to fabrics, individual garments, and entire ensembles. It's the relationship of the parts of a whole outfit to one another, and the relationship of the sum of those parts to the body wearing them. While designers wrestle with these issues in every collection—manipulating hemlines, silhouette widths, design details, and color schemes—some general concepts on how to emphasize parts of the body always apply.

When creating their statuary masterpieces, the ancient Greeks thought that the most aesthetically pleasing proportions were those that were slightly uneven instead of being equally balanced. They considered a body divided roughly one-third/two-thirds to be perfectly proportioned. This theory is still true for most things, especially clothes. A jacket and skirt of the same length are not really as balanced or pleasing as a shorter jacket/longer skirt or shorter skirt/longer jacket. These long-over-short and short-over-long proportions will echo again and again in clothes (as well as works of art).

Hemlines and waistlines represent horizontal lines in clothes, and are proportional dividing lines that can change your proportions. A figure appears taller if horizontal divisions are created at or above the natural waistline, because the legs appear longer. While the human body's midpoint is actually around the hips, our eye perceives height based upon the leg length, or lower torso proportions. For example, wearing a long overblouse and pants shortens your legs and elongates your torso; a hip-length blouse would divide your top and bottom halves equally; tucking your blouse into your pants would make your legs look their longest, and you your tallest.

Knowing your body's vertical proportions helps to guide your selection of garments in order to balance your silhouette. If you have a short torso and average length legs and want to wear a long-jacket-over-a-short-skirt outfit, you know that you must find a jacket that is cut shorter than average, or the effect is wrong. An all-over petite would need to choose a shorter jacket *and* shorten her skirt. Other proportions to note:

- If you have long legs you can support a longer jacket (which can also disguise a short waist).
- A dropped waistline elongates a short waist.

- A raised waistline balances a long waist and makes your legs look longer.
- The shorter your jacket, the longer your legs look (so the longer the jacket, the shorter your legs can appear, too).
- The longer the skirt, the shorter the jacket should be (and vice versa).
- Matching your hose to your hemline adds length to your lower proportions.

Obviously most plus-size women are flattered by tops that are long enough to cover the hip and derriere; worn too short they cut you off and make you look wider than necessary. The trick, then, is to wear them just long enough, no longer. In order to maintain long proportions on the bottom, a good strategy is to wear a blouse or top tucked in or belted at the waist, with a jacket, cardigan, or overblouse open over that.

Your Most Flattering Fabrics— Textures and Patterns

Fabric Texture

In addition to line and shape, the texture of clothes adds a three-dimensional element to the way the eye perceives a figure. Since clothes are constructed of fabric, their texture makes a big difference in how they drape—that is, fit the contours of the body and reflect light back to our eye. This affects the way we see the proportions of garments and whether the effect is pleasing to our proportions. (Of course, when you accessorize you add color, texture, design, and focal points on top of those already there in the garments. We will talk more about choosing and wearing accessories in Chapter Nine.)

Generally speaking, *clothing with lots of texture, weight, and shine will make a figure appear larger.* So bulky, rough, thick, stiff, and sparkly or shiny fabrics will add size and volume. Clothes constructed from soft, matte (non-shiny), smooth, and medium to lightweight fabrics are minimizing because they fall into softer, straighter lines. Soft but highly textured fabrics such as velour, velvet, terry cloth, chenille, and corduroy do have a soft hand and can drape nicely, but they reflect quite a bit of light. Treat them as you would heavy or textured fabrics. Fabric weight and texture can be used to create focal points on the body because they can act just like style lines or color to attract the eye and maintain visual balance.

Pattern, Print, and Scale

Your eye is attracted to line and color, so it will find pattern quickly and linger there. In most cases, a space without a printed pattern is seen as smaller than a space with a pattern. A pattern that is regular and nearly fills the available space will generally make the covered area look smaller than a widely spaced pattern. So, *larger scale, widely spaced, high-contrast, light, or brightly colored prints make a figure appear larger.* Pattern is a good tool to use in balancing proportions and calling attention to particular areas. For example, a Pear body might use a patterned blouse to balance her larger below-the-waist proportions. Other things to know:

- Prints should be in scale with the body's size.
- An all-over print can disguise style lines in a garment.
- An all-over woven pattern or small print can sometimes have

the same effect as a heavier-weight plain fabric (tweeds, jacquards, moiré patterns, houndstooth, small dots, etc.), making the figure appear larger.

- Complex designs or prints should be worn on simple garments.
- Prints have personalities (bold, dainty, exotic, feminine, conservative, etc.); match their personality to the style of the garment and your fashion style.
- The smaller, more subtle, more muted the print, the more sophisticated, chic, and enduring it will be.

Dressy vs. Casual Fabrics and Patterns

In addition to their weight, texture, and pattern, the fibers used in fabrics have meanings in our culture associated with how they have historically been worn. One of the keys to dressing up or dressing down, whether for business or social events, is to understand how people interpret what we are wearing.

Shiny fabrics in fine weights and delicate textures like silks, satin, tapestry, velvet, crepe, faille, chiffon, lace, jacquard, etc., are most dressy. Traditional suiting fabrics, rough woolens, linens, cotton, challis, rayon, and medium to small prints are less dressy, more practical and professional. Heavy-weight cottons, cotton knits, denim, twill, corduroy, tweed, stretchy fabrics, large or bold prints, and brighter colors are generally seen as most casual.

Balance and Unity

A garment or outfit should have what the experts call "unity," which keeps a look balanced and aesthetically pleasing. The style and trim lines should be consistent, and the garment should share your natural shape or use its contrast dramatically. Lines have a rhythm and movement that should flow throughout an ensemble, and lead the eye in a direction that supports the balance and harmony of the outfit. Match similar fabric weights and textures, use similar lines, harmonize prints and patterns, be consistent in scale and proportion, and use colors that work together tonally—or contrast for effect.

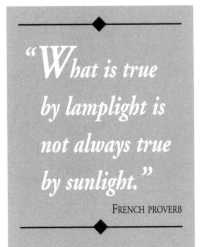

"What is true by lamplight is not always true by sunlight."

FRENCH PROVERB

When pairing separates, be certain that the details and proportions of each piece won't conflict and spoil the overall style or feeling you are trying to achieve. A jacket with piping on the lapels, for example, won't really work with anything but a solid-colored, smooth-textured skirt or pants of the same solid or accent color. Tweed, as a casual, rough-textured fabric, won't harmonize well with a silk charmeuse blouse which is very, very dressy.

The buttons of garments must also work together, and the textures complement one another. Brass, horn, plastic, bone, or wood buttons are less formal, while natural pearl, self-covered, complex design, and jewel buttons are more formal.

Work with Colors That Make You Look and Feel Happy

Color has meaning that goes well beyond superficial preferences. It evokes thoughts, feelings, and physical reactions based on everything from the toys of our earliest childhood memories to the colors worn by those we dislike. Color can relax, soothe, excite, titillate, amuse, reassure, and even heal. In fact, our color preferences and usage are personal, cultural, and perhaps even genetic. But to understand color and how to use it, start with the basics: *Hue, Intensity, Value, Contrast, and Temperature.*

Hue is what we think of as color—blue, red, and yellow are the primaries,

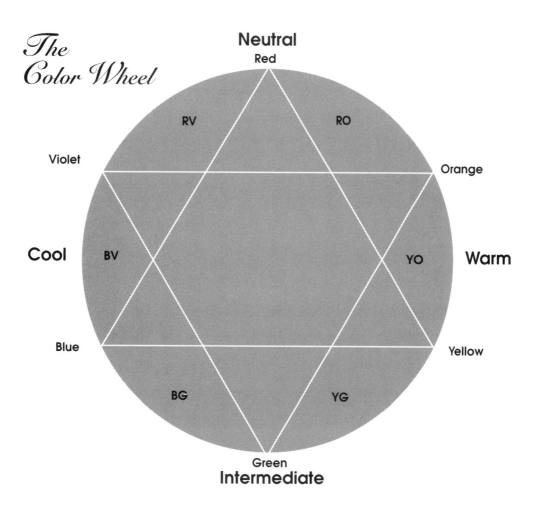

The Color Wheel

out of which all others are derived. Blue plus yellow equals green, red plus yellow equals orange, and red plus blue equals violet—these are the secondary colors. Endless variations of color exist based on combination of the primaries.

Refracted light, like a rainbow, starts with red and ends with violet. Wrapped around the color wheel, it's easy to understand how the hues relate. Low contrast (analogous) color schemes are those that lie side by side, like blue, blue-green, and blue-violet. High contrast (complementary) color schemes involve those that fall directly opposite each other on the wheel, like yellow and violet. Triadic (complex) color schemes involve three colors equidistant apart on the wheel, as in the case of violet, orange, and green.

Intensity refers to the brightness, concentration, or clarity of a color. A color's intensity can be reduced or *muted* by adding gray or by adding its opposite on the color wheel (which will eventually produce brown). An intense color attracts the eye and holds its attention, even though it's difficult to look at for any period of time. The primary and secondary colors are very bright and pure. (Think of true red, fuchsia, kelly green, lime green, magenta, cornflower blue, etc.) Generally speaking, we think of pure, clear, and bright colors as unsophisticated, associated with children or toys.

Value refers essentially to the lightness or darkness of a

0 White

1

2

3

4

5 Mid-Gray

6

7

8

9

10 Black

Value Scale
A scale of lightest to darkest by degree

color. Adding white to a color lightens its value, gradually making it a pastel. Adding black will shade, or deepen it until the original color is nearly obscured. The difference in color values produces *contrast*. The strongest contrast colors are black (the absence of light and color) and white (pure light, or all the colors combined). On a scale of 0 to 10, white, as the lightest "color," is in the first position, #0. Mid-gray is #5, and black is #10. All colors can be scaled this way, and although some are naturally lighter and some darker in their pure form, they all have a wide value range.

Other contrasts are presented by color intersections—the strongest of which are opposites on the color wheel: red and green, yellow and violet, orange and blue. When you wear these color opposites, an attention-grabbing contrast line is created that is stronger than design lines.

When it comes to people and clothing, we often talk about the *temperature* of a color, referring to its relative warmth or coolness. According to professional image consultant, instructor, and color specialist Carolyn Gustafson:

- Colors on the right side of the color wheel contain *yellow* and are considered *warmer*. (Think sun, gold, fire.) They seem to *advance* or appear larger (tomato red, oranges, yellows, yellow-greens).

- Colors on the left side of the wheel contain *blue* and are considered *cooler*. (Think moon, silver, water.) They seem to *recede* or appear smaller (raspberry red, purples, blues, blue-greens).

- Yellow is *visually dominant* over blue. Adding a small percentage of yellow to blue, or to any blue/red combination results in a *warmed* cool color (plum, turquoise, peacock).

- *True green* is 50 percent blue and 50 percent yellow, and is sometimes called an *intermediate*.

The Psychology of Color

The meaning of color has been studied by many people throughout the twentieth century. While some meanings seem nearly universal, others are hotly debated. The subtleties vary between cultures—it has been said that pink is the navy blue of India, for instance. But who can mistake the meaning of a red fire truck or a cool blue sea?

Darker colors are perceived to be more authoritative, bold, assertive, strong, dramatic, masculine. Lighter colors are perceived to be more feminine, soft, gentle, approachable. Brighter colors are interpreted as outgoing, energetic, fun, exciting. Dull or muted colors are thought to be shy, conservative, controlled, chic, and sometimes even boring.

Warmer colors such as gold, olive, orange, yellow, peach, rust, and most browns are perceived as warm, down-to-earth, friendly, approachable, and sometimes less sophisticated and expensive. Cooler colors such as blue, green, violets, pinks, and most grays are perceived to be more conservative, classic, businesslike, expensive. Neutral colors take on a personality of their own depending on situation, personality, and context.

Color Impact

In addition to style lines, color can have a big impact on proportions. Color places emphasis on the figure and changes the proportions beyond the style lines. The *lighter, brighter,* and *warmer* the color, the more it

Color Meanings and Messages

- **Red**—Exciting, assertive, stimulating, dramatic, passionate, courageous; sometimes domineering or sexual.

- **Pink**—Feminine, quiet, loving, approachable, sensitive; sometimes unimportant.

- **Brown**—Simple, responsible, comfortable, secure, earthy; sometimes downscale, unsophisticated.

- **Green**—Stable, balanced, fresh, soothing, friendly, sympathetic; sometimes predictable or boring.

- **Yellow**—Warm, cheery, creative, busy, optimistic; sometimes deceitful, impulsive.

- **Blue**—Peaceful, sincere, thoughtful, honest, patient; sometimes depressing, conservative.

- **Navy**—Enterprising, trustworthy, organized.

- **Violet**—Regal, artistic, unique, mystical; sometimes mournful.

- **Black**—Chic, formal, dignified, elegant, sophisticated; sometimes rebellious, negative, mournful.

- **Gray**—Reliable, conservative, modest, authoritative, controlled; sometimes too safe.

- **White**—Innocent, pure, clean, faithful; sometimes vulnerable, cold, aloof.

- **Orange**—Lively, enthusiastic, energetic, social, enterprising, networker; sometimes cheap or common.

will seem to move *forward* and appear *larger*—and the more *memorable* it will be. The darker, cooler, more subtle or muted colors tend to minimize a figure, and have less recall. So, if you want to invest in a suit or dress that will last a long time and flatter you through frequent or prolonged wearing, choose a neutral color. No one will remember they've seen it before (men use this to their advantage every day; the least memorable colors are neutral, medium tones like charcoal gray, navy, and men's suiting colors).

A figure tends to look tallest in a monochromatic outfit (or one of varying values of the same color) that presents an unbroken line of color—regardless of color choice. If you break up the values in an outfit, a darker color below the waist will "stabilize" a figure, minimizing the size of that area, and make the figure look slightly taller. A light color on the bottom will pull the eyes downward and shorten your vertical line, so it's a good idea to balance it with a touch of that same color on the top. Wearing the darkest value above the waist, paired with a medium value below the waist with matching hose will create the second longest vertical possible. Sharp color contrasts will break up a figure the same way design lines do, but can be even more noticeable. A darker or softer color head to toe will make you look slimmest.

When selecting color combinations, be aware of intensity and value, which create strong focal points and line intersections. In complementary color schemes, balance the contrast of the two colors by value and intensity or they will completely neutralize each other. One brighter or deeper than the other is always interesting. Analogous color schemes usually work best when both colors are equal in value and depth, but you should wear no more than

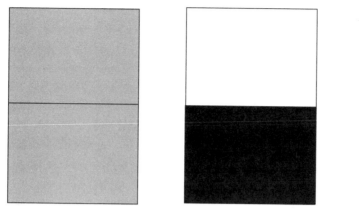

A monochromatic figure appears tallest. A dark-topped figure appears shortest.

two of them in addition to your main color. Monochromatic schemes are elegant whatever the color, and have the advantage of being either warm or cool.

When teaming up monochromatic ensembles or pairing same-color pieces, be cautious matching neutrals. Every black, navy blue, brown, gray, and beige is different—some are deeper, some are warmer, some cooler. Look at the combinations in natural light before venturing out. Also, be aware that when two colors are placed side by side they convey the message of the resulting color mixture!

Personal Color

Personal color analysis was pioneered in the 1940s primarily by Suzanne Caygill, based on the research and writings of artist and teacher Johannes Itten. Since then, personal color theory has developed into several schools of thought and practice, some of which use the seasonal color approach, dividing people by spring, summer, autumn, and winter. Other practitioners employ systems based on the three-dimensional aspects of color: value, intensity, and temperature. In the 1970s and 1980s, when women entered the workforce in great numbers, they embraced personal color typing and other image tools as a bridge to self-esteem and a means to help them develop a polished, professional presence. Carole Jackson's best-selling book *Color Me Beautiful,* which explained the seasonal typing system, launched the subject into the mainstream, and spurred millions of women to "get their colors done."

Knowing the best colors for your wardrobe is and always will be a marvelously helpful tool. Most women have some sense of what they like and dislike, and what colors garner them the most compliments. But so many women tell me that they can't wear certain colors, and have banished half of the spectrum from their closet. In fact, nearly everyone can wear some form of every hue—it's a matter of depth, temperature, intensity, and quantity. The chemistry of color is something even scientists are still exploring. There are no absolute rules, and many things affect how we see colors. The best hues for you should always be judged color by color, with room for exceptions and additions.

Every one of us has variations in value, intensity, and temperature in her skin, hair, and eyes. Each is colored by the same genetically controlled chemical soup of three chemicals with parallels to the primary colors: hemoglobin is red, melanin is blue-brown or orange-brown, and carotene is yellow. Your coloring can be warmer or cooler, brighter or more muted, no matter what value or depth (lighter to darker) it is. *When we wear colors that resonate on the same level as our natural colors, we look our best.* Essentially then, these are the keys to choosing the colors that harmonize with you:

- The right depth: How light or deep can you wear your colors?

- The right intensity or clarity: How bright or muted should your colors be?

- The right temperature: How warm or cool should you wear your colors?

You can determine whether warmer or cooler colors work for you by trying on lots of examples of each type and judging the apparent changes in your skin tone. But of course, the best way to find your most flattering colors is with the aid of a professional color consultant, who will drape you in dozens of color swatches to see how your skin, hair, and eye colors react. She will look for subtle changes in your complexion caused by the reflection of the color onto your face. Your best colors will make your skin look lovely, while a poor choice will make you look old, tired—or ill!

Discovering the level of contrast that flatters you best is perhaps even more important than temperature. Darks and lights contrast, as do brights and muted colors. A high-contrast person has a wide variation in the values of her skin, hair, and eyes. Some may have dark hair, dark eyes, and light skin. Others may have light skin, but medium depth to the hair with clear, bright eyes. Low-contrast people can be any color or temperature, but have limited variation in the depth of their skin, hair, and eyes. Medium-contrast people have moderate variation in the depth of their skin, hair, and eyes. Any one of their features may be lighter or deeper, but overall they are neither high or low contrast.

I have very light skin, light blond hair, and steel-blue eyes. On the value scale—white is 0, mid-gray is 5, black is 10—my skin is probably about a 3, my hair is about a 4, and my eyes a 6. My contrast range is 3–6, or medium to low. My eyes are a bright, clear blue, and my skin is bright neutral beige with lots of touches of red. I can wear brighter colors better than muted ones, but I use the brights cautiously to avoid emphasis where it doesn't belong!

Phylise Banner, the lovely wife of my illustrating partner Shawn, is a high-contrast, cool-toned beauty. She has pale skin (2.5–3), dark brown hair (about an 8), and cool, dark brown eyes (8). Phylise's value range is wide: 2.5–8. She is flattered by lots of contrast.

Image consultant Carolyn Gustafson recommends some tips for High-, Medium-, and Low-Contrast types:

High Contrast

Because you have a dramatic color pattern of hair, skin, and eyes, you can repeat the drama in your clothing colors.

- You will look best in combinations that combine very light colors with very dark colors, such as black and white, frosty pink and midnight blue, icy violet and charcoal, pale peach and dark brown.
- You will also look excellent in light or dark colors with a bright accent, such as white with royal, ivory with turquoise, black with red, navy blue with fuchsia. Or, you can wear two bright colors together, such as red and purple, hot pink with magenta, golden yellow and orange, violet and grass green.
- Avoid wearing muted colors.

Medium Contrast

- You have a wider choice of color combinations. You can combine light with medium or medium with dark to create medium contrasts. Instead of black and white, you would be better in medium pink and black, for example, or coral and camel, melon and brown, pink and gray, blue and taupe, yellow and red.

- You can even wear *high-contrast* colors by adding *medium* accent to reduce the contrast, such as raspberry with charcoal and white, or teal with pale yellow and dark brown.

- When wearing *low-contrast* colors, pastels, or light neutrals, add *medium-value* accents.

- Avoid wearing only very high contrast, or all pastel with no medium-value color accent.

Low Contrast

- Your personal color pattern of hair, skin, and eyes is very subtle. This *subtleness needs to be repeated in your clothing*. You will look best wearing one color in a combination of light to medium values or medium-to-dark values. This *monochromatic* technique uses various shades and textures of the same color family.

- For variety, try wearing *two or three subtle colors* together, or in a print such as pale yellow, aqua, and peach, or pale pink, light lavender, and silver gray.

Shortcuts to Your Best Colors

While a private color draping will reveal dozens of colors that will complement your body, you can easily come up with a short list yourself based on the colors that exist within your hair, skin, and eyes. For instance, your best white is the color of your teeth and eyes. If you have brown hair, that's probably the best shade of brown for your clothes and accessories—as long as you match the value and temperature. And everyone can wear red, since hemoglobin is an essential part of our makeup—you just need the right red. You'll find it in the color your cheeks turn when you blush, the palms of your hands, and the inside of your lower lip. Experiment with varying samples of warm and cool, bright or muted reds until you find the one most flattering for you.

Look into your eyes with a magnifying mirror in a bright light. What colors do you see? Most people have several—blues, grays, greens, yellows, and every shade of brown. If it's in your eye, you can probably wear the color wonderfully well. Also, the more intense your personality, the more intense your colors can be.

If you choose to wear a color that's the "wrong" temperature, intensity, or value, just wear it away from your face. *Color is less essential than fit, silhouette, and fabric.*

We can all wear neutral-temperature colors. In addition, color experts say there are ten "universal colors" that flatter nearly everyone. They are in the mid-range of value, intensity, and temperature:

Soft white	Bright burgundy
Medium gray	Teal (deep green-blue)
Periwinkle blue (blue-violet)	Watermelon red
Medium turquoise	Medium violet
(not too bright or too light)	Coral or warm pink

Neutrals are the foundation of any wardrobe. Some are warm, some cool. Your best hues repeat your hair or skin color. While black, white, and gray are neutral, so are these:

Beige	Navy	Brown	Taupe

When you use neutrals, be sure to add contrast, texture, print, or accessory focus for visual interest.

While there have been many books written on the subject of personal color, very few address the particular palettes of black and brown skins. To learn how to enhance the beauty of darker skin, I highly recommend the work of Jean Patton, a professional image consultant, color authority, and author of *Color to Color: The Black Woman's Guide to a Rainbow of Fashion and Beauty.* For women of every color and age I recommend Donna Fujii's *Color with Style,* and Mary Spillane and Christine Sherlock's *Color Me Beautiful's Looking Your Best.*

The ultimate test of a flattering outfit is whether others see us as we see ourselves. You get dressed and you think you look great, but does the world see you the same way? Can you tell if your clothes are really working for your body shape? Are the focal points working the way you want them to? Do you have on too much jewelry or not enough? Does the color combination work the way you think it does?

Jan Larkey, image consultant, trainer, and internationally known author and innovator of the Flatter Your Figure™ system recommends an ingenious, easy check she calls the "Blink Test":

The Blink Test:

1. Stand *at least 5 feet* from a full-length mirror.
   Close your eyes. Count to three.
2. Open your eyes. *Instantly:* What do you see first?
   Your assets? Your figure challenges? Do *you and all the*
   parts of your wardrobe look good together?

"What you see first is what others will also notice first.
If anything strikes a jarring note when you open your eyes, change it,
especially if it calls attention to a problem area. Repeat the Blink
Test, making changes until you see your positive points immediately
and a harmonious total image."

JAN LARKEY, *FLATTER YOUR FIGURE*

Understanding Style

Parlez-Vous Chic?

My dear friend and sister-in-law Ann and I have similar business backgrounds and attitudes, but she doesn't own a pair of jeans and I couldn't live without them. What we wear to the boardroom might be very similar (although she's probably six sizes smaller than me), but on a recent weekend at an informal family get-together she wore a pair of pegged gray fine-gauge wool twill trousers, a pale green cashmere sweater set, gray suede flats, and her grandmother's pearls. I was in a pair of black cotton/rayon straight-leg pants with a black leather belt, a white knit T-shirt, a big unconstructed purple sueded silk jacket, and black Italian calfskin loafers. We were both dressed appropriately, well-groomed and very fashionable, but our styles communicated very different things. She was more Elegant, I was more Dramatic—typical of both of us.

> *"Your own rags are better than another's gown."*
> HAUSA (WEST AFRICAN) PROVERB

Every woman has her own personal style based on her many roles, her background, her career, her hobbies, her age, how she feels about her body, and where she lives. It's also based, to some degree, on the prevailing styles when she emerged from her teens to womanhood—sort of like that soft spot you've got for the music that was popular when you first fell in love!

While fashion is a fleeting reflection of a cultural moment and of what designers feel they can sell based on what did or didn't sell last season, style is a personal expression of who and what we are, and how we relate to the world around us. To be called stylish is a compliment of the highest order; to be labeled a fashion victim is a true insult, suggesting you have no thought or creativity of your own. *Fashion is timely; style is timeless.*

Developing your own personal style isn't terribly difficult if you know how to approach your clothes. If you've ever felt that you were somewhere else when they were handing out the style genes, take heart. Developing personal style involves some examination of your lifestyle, your natural clothing style and color preferences, and some knowledge of what messages are sent by each style type. Once you have an understanding of your own style, shopping becomes a less daunting task, and you're likely to make fewer fashion blunders. Whatever style type you develop, it should make you feel comfortable and at ease. Having a firm grasp on your own style means that you have a style filter or lens through which you can view any new purchase. It gives you a tool for evaluation: Is it right for you? Does it integrate with the other things you own? Will you still love it in a year or two? What will it say about you to others?

In business situations I'm much more comfortable in traditionally tailored

Glamorous/Sexy

suits with a dramatic twist—like bright colors or unusual accessories. For personal or casual wear I like to be comfortable but somewhat elegant, with an eye toward new fashion details. I also enjoy styles that are an exaggeration or reinterpretation of classic styles, like nautical or military takeoffs and retro allusions (like my favorite but seldom worn leopard-print pumps—killer with my red suit!). My styles are a blend of Dramatic/Artistic with a tasteful dose of Elegant/Classic, and Natural/Sporty leanings in my private time.

To develop a comfortable style of dressing for yourself you will want to have a general awareness of the fashions of the times: the colors, hemlines, style lines, proportions, and fabrics being used today. It helps to keep current with what women are wearing on the street and in offices, restaurants, post offices, and playgrounds versus what the fashion denizens are showing us on the pages of the beauty magazines. Taking stock of the fashions other women are wearing helps us to recognize the shapes and colors that are typical, and what is considered appropriate where and when. Without that general awareness, every decision you make in every shop, at every clothing rack, is a new challenge, a new intimidation, and a new trial.

Have you seen anything lately that really caught your eye or made you take a second, admiring glance—even if you thought you couldn't wear it or knew it wasn't your size? Have you ever thought about the perfect suit, dress, skirt, blouse, trousers, coat, etc.? That's your inner style voice talking—the one that tells you the truth about who you are and how you want to be viewed. Listen to the voice and follow along to understand what it's saying about you.

Discovering Your Personal Style

Your natural style, the one that flatters you best, is one that evolves or develops—not one that you suddenly put on like a new dress. You shouldn't ever feel like you're wearing a costume in a play or some other person's clothes. You also shouldn't ever buy or wear something as a backlash to what you think you *can't* have. Whatever you wear should make you feel good and give you pleasure.

> *"She had a womanly instinct that clothes possess an influence more powerful over many than the worth of character or the magic of manners."*
>
> LOUISA MAY ALCOTT, *LITTLE WOMEN*

To figure out the style that's right for you, ask yourself, "What do I want to say about myself to the world? How do I want people to think about me? If a close friend were to describe me, what would she say?" Our clothes are always talking, but each style speaks in a different voice. To look your best you want to wear clothes that flatter your body and your personality. Also think about what people compliment you on—is it the color, the shape, the feeling of the clothing? Ask a close friend what she thinks about you in different clothes—not what she likes for her, but for *you.*

To begin, it helps to understand that most clothing falls into a particular style category that is reflected in its construction, fabric, pattern, and color—and is interpreted in a certain way by the rest of the world. Once you understand the style that works best for you, it's easy to identify and find other clothes in that category in the future. *If you know your style, you can avoid looking at clothes that don't match that style.* Voilà!

In the late 1980s, image consultants, authors, and speakers Alyce Parsons and Diane Parente drew on a large body of research and developed Universal Style, a detailed system of style evaluation and categorization that was among the first to fully explore the connection between clothing styles and the messages they send. Many consultants use similar style definitions, categories, and tools. By adhering to these principles, you can quickly understand the best style approach for you and your life.

To begin to understand the styles that best reflect who you are and how you live, look at the following questions and see if you find a pattern to how you usually dress—or would like to. What sounds right for you?

What's Your Style Type?

1. How would you describe your personality?

a. Energetic, friendly, casual, fun, spontaneous, unpretentious

b. Discerning, conservative, refined, efficient, reliable, dignified

c. Gentle, compassionate, caring, delicate, warm, soft, charming

d. Daring, exciting, sensuous, flirtatious

e. Independent, self-assured, flamboyant, unconventional, unique

2. How do you prefer your clothes to fit?

a. Comfortable and easy

b. Softly tailored

c. Loose, gentle, flowing

d. Body-defining or a little revealing

e. Structured, fitted, architectural

3. What kinds of fabrics do you prefer to wear?

a. Easy-care fabrics—cottons, blends, tweeds, khaki, denim

b. High-quality gabardine, twills, silk, cashmere, wool jersey

c. Fluid, lightweight silks, rayons, lace, challis, velvet, chiffon

d. Knits and jerseys with drape or stretch, or shiny and smooth textures

e. Medium- to firm-weight fabrics with body and texture, leather fabrics with unusual weaves

4. What's your favorite jewelry?

a. Simple, practical, classic

b. Elegant, simple but rich looking

c. Antique pieces, cameos, pearls, delicate items

d. Big, dangling, sparkling, shining

e. Striking, bold, ethnic, angular, unique

5. Which describe your favorite accessories and finishing touches?

a. Simple, casual shoes, bags, and belts that mix and match

b. Highest quality silk scarves, fine leather bags, belts, and shoes

c. Lace-trimmed pieces, ruffles, ribbons, bows, delicate colors

d. High heels or slingbacks, dramatic jewelry, perfume

e. Bold, unusual pieces, one-of-a-kind items, art to wear, dramatic wraps and hats

6. What are your favorite color palettes and strategies?

a. Neutrals, earth tones

b. Conservative, low contrast, and monochromatic colors in shaded or muted tones

c. Pastels, lighter and softer colors, and whites

d. Bold, bright, high-contrast colors in pure tones

e. Black and contrast mixes, metallics and brights

Did you see a pattern? Were you torn between one or two types? Individual style is nearly always a blend of styles based upon a dominant or core style. To find your core style—the one that defines how you approach clothing and your personality—look at your answers to these questions, and think about the type of clothes you are drawn to (whether or not they reflect those hanging in your closet at the moment). Compare that information to the style definitions.

If you answered mostly A's you're Natural; B's—Elegant; C's—Romantic; D's—Glamorous; E's—Dramatic. Here's a list of the styles in theory and in example.

A = NATURAL/SPORTY   **D** = GLAMOROUS/SEXY

B = ELEGANT/CLASSIC   **E** = DRAMATIC/ARTISTIC

C = ROMANTIC/FEMININE

Once you understand your style preferences and understand the messages each style sends, you can learn to adapt your personal style for other images, occasions, and moods while controlling how other people interpret what your clothes are generally saying about you.

For more detailed information on style, I recommend *What's My Style* by Alyce Parsons, with Allison Better (AMP Publishers), and *Mastering Your Professional Image* by Diane Parente and Stephanie Petersen (Image Development and Management).

Dramatic/Artistic Accessories

Natural/Sporty

The Natural/Sporty style woman is casual, informal, likable, direct, basic, warm, friendly, energetic, unpretentious, youthful, and sometimes outdoorsy. She's usually a people person, most comfortable dressed down in loosely tailored or layered clothing, natural fabrics with minimum care required. This particularly American style developed out of field and sports clothing into sportswear. The woman who wears this style usually prefers simple accessories that are functional, comfortable, and easy to wear with a variety of outfits. She avoids heels, and chooses totes and bigger bags that hold everything and don't have to be coordinated with each outfit. The natural woman almost always prefers (and looks best in) a nonfussy, easy-to-maintain hairstyle.

Some prominent Natural/Sporty women who fit this description include Martha Stewart, Meg Ryan, Lauren Hutton, and Katharine Hepburn.

Natural/Sporty

Natural/Sporty styles include: shirtdresses, loosely tailored suits, blazers, baseball and bomber jackets, T-shirts, safari looks, straight and pleated skirts, jeans, cardigans, men's influence in notched collars, shirts, trousers and boxy jackets or blazers, soft natural shoulders (minimum of padding), pullover sweaters, polo styling, trenchcoats, flat shoes and stacked heel pumps, and accessories in natural colored leathers.

Elegant/Classic

The Elegant/Classic woman is traditional, conservative, chic, sophisticated, formal, polished, consistent, respectable, poised, and timeless. She's impeccable in appearance, and never overstated or underdressed. Her clothes are perfectly tailored and maintained, and work together beautifully. She respects the mix and match theory, and uses it to expand her wardrobe. She takes the long view in clothing and accessories, and prefers classic, high-quality pieces that aren't subject to the whims of fashion and will last for years. She prefers a controlled, simple hairstyle and conservative makeup.

This style applies to a wide variety of women: Princess Grace, Margaret Thatcher, Diane Sawyer, Oprah Winfrey, Jackie Kennedy Onassis, and Audrey Hepburn.

Elegant/Classic styles include: sheaths, coatdresses, straight-styled (Chanel type) knit suits, matching suits in luxurious, natural fibers, jacquard and tone-on-tone fabrics, delicately shaped silhouettes with a minimum of details, straight-leg pants, jewel-neck and wrap-front blouses and sweater sets, pearls and real gold jewelry, and stones in "tasteful" settings.

Elegant/Classic

Romantic/Feminine

The Romantic/Feminine woman is soft, fresh, ladylike or dainty, youthful or refined. *Pretty* is her operating theory, and she likes to recall the lost grace and femininity of another age in her dress. She prefers delicate touches in color, shapes, textures, and patterns: ribbons, laces, bows and trims, high necklines, flowing skirts, small prints, and florals. She avoids suits, and conveys warmth, sensitivity, relaxation, and compassion. Women who typify the Romantic/Feminine image include Mia Farrow, Stevie Nicks, Andie McDowell, and Reba McEntire.

The Romantic/Feminine styles include: flowing, ruffled, lace-edged, bias-cut, trumpet, or gathered skirts; small prints and florals of every description; princess-styled dresses; empire- or dropped-waist styles; fitted or peplum jackets; peasant-style blouses; draped, ruffled, cowl neck, or scalloped collars; tucked, ruffled, or puffed sleeves; cameos, charms, marcasite, pearl, or filigreed jewelry.

Romantic/Feminine

Glamorous/Sexy

The Glamorous/Sexy woman is aware of her body and her effect on men. She can be provocative, exciting, flirtatious, and daring. She's full of confidence and enjoys revealing lines, body-conscious styles, open necklines, side-slit skirts, defined waists, colorful or intense makeup, and bigger or wilder hair-dos. (Any style that bares the flesh—any flesh—is considered Glamorous/Sexy.)

You'll recognize this style as the key to the public images of Dolly Parton, Delta Burke, Madonna, Whitney Houston, Heather Locklear, and Elizabeth Hurley.

The Glamorous/Sexy styles include: clinging, fluid, soft knits and smooth, shiny, or stretch fabrics in body-contouring shapes; open necks; strapless, off-the-shoulder, tank-shaped dresses and tops; leg slits; bare arms; wrapped-front blouses and dresses; sarong skirts; short shorts; leggings; cropped tops; bangle bracelets; drop earrings; high heels; cinch belts; strappy sandals; animal prints; and long, brightly painted or decorated nails.

Dramatic/Artistic

The Dramatic/Artistic woman is a creative, theatrical entrance-maker who prefers contemporary styling, striking designs, bold accessories, and avant-garde clothing and accessories. She conveys imagination, confidence, spontaneity, individuality, and power. She's usually cosmopolitan, commanding, resourceful, and eclectic. She's likely to indulge in a severe hairstyle and statement-making makeup.

Some notable Dramatic/Artistic types include Paloma Picasso, Whoopee Goldberg, Iman, Diane Keaton, and Jessye Norman.

The Dramatic/Artistic styles include oversized, hand-crafted, free-flowing or tapered, defined or exaggerated silhouettes—either loose and unconstructed or architectural and asymmetrical. Patterns are usually oversized or stylized prints, ethnic, mismatched, or abstracts and geometrics. This woman is rarely without a stunning pair of sunglasses or a significant piece of jewelry.

89

Dramatic/Artistic

What Your Style Says About You

You'll note that each of the styles is distilled to its essence, which you will probably find a little too limiting. Some suggest "costume" much more than others, and may or may not be appropriate to particular occasions. For instance, Glamorous/Sexy in its pure form wouldn't be an appropriate choice for business wear, and Dramatic/Artistic would have to be modified to be appropriate for formal situations such as the courtroom. Thank goodness most of us aren't one-dimensional personalities, either. If some days make us feel like expressing a little more drama, others call for a touch of romance, and some nights are pure glamour.

In the same way that every personality is a result of varying environments, experiences, preferences, and habits, your personal style can be adapted to take on the characteristics of the style types that say what you feel, by varying the colors, fabrics, textures, and silhouette combinations. Glamorous/Sexy, for instance, becomes more Elegant/Classic by wearing subdued colors, minimal jewelry, and more controlled hair. Natural/Sporty can become more Dramatic/Artistic with unusual or eclectic jewelry, high-contrast colors, or intense hair or makeup. Likewise Romantic/Feminine can be more Elegant/Classic by wearing traditional suiting in pale colors or with lace touches, etc. The possibilities are endless in the same way that personalities are endlessly varied and unique.

> *"The subjective actress thinks of clothes only as they apply to her, the objective actress thinks of them only as a tool for the job."*
>
> EDITH HEAD, *THE DRESS DOCTOR*

91

The Five Styles of Modern Lives

Romantic/Feminine   Natural/Sporty   Elegant/Classic

Glamorous/Sexy   *Dramatic/Artistic*

Elegant/Classic

Accessories

The easiest way to modify our clothing and express our true nature is to vary the accessories we choose to punctuate our style statements. These final touches pull a look together, give it context and tone, and often are the standout elements of first impressions. Accessories are a great place to start in

To Get That Style—Here are some quick tips for achieving a basic style look:

- ***Natural/Sporty:*** Layers; non-serious accessories; minimal makeup, hair, and nails; fun but neat mixable pieces; bright colors.

- ***Elegant/Classic:*** Coordinated, classic outfits; restrained, quality accessories; limited pattern and toned-down colors.

- ***Romantic/Feminine:*** Soft lines and gentle, flowing fit; delicate touches of color, pattern, and texture; old-fashioned or floral patterns and accessories; gentle, wavy hairstyles.

- ***Glamorous/Sexy:*** Tight or revealing garments, strong or dark colors, exaggerated accessories; bold makeup and hair.

- ***Dramatic/Artistic:*** Bold colors or high-contrast patterns, textures, or style lines; unusual or exaggerated accessories; high-fashion touches.

changing or adapting your wardrobe. If you want to make some new statements, it's easier to start to build a new look with scarves, shoes, belts, jewelry, gloves, bags, and hats than with suits, dresses, or entire outfits.

Shopping for Your Style

Your own style is a billboard testifying to your personality and lifestyle, so you want to get it right and find it easily. The average department store or boutique contains dozens—if not hundreds or thousands—of garments of every description, so how do you find the ones right for you? Elimination, not consideration! When you browse the racks, you're looking for four things:

- The best style to express your personality and suit the occasion
- The right silhouette for your body
- The right size to fit
- The right color

Each element is vital to you looking your best, so if you compromise on any one, you and the rest of the world will see and feel the difference. To evaluate a garment, run through your checklist: Is it the right shape or silhouette, the right size, a color that flatters you? No? Keep moving because there are always alternative choices, if not in one store or catalog, then another.

If it is the right shape, size, and a color that appeals to you, take a close look at the style. Is it a new fashion look or something that looks familiar? Is it the same kind of thing you've been buying and wearing for years? Do you want to look the same or different? What impression does it give you—does it feel formal or informal, wild or reserved, happy and exciting or quiet and indifferent, creative or straightforward, businesslike or dressed-down, young or old, etc. Try to identify the style or combination of styles at play. Look at the overall design as well as the details for clues. Is it you? Could it be? Will it make you happy?

Can't decide? Nothing looks right? Feeling ambivalent? Ask yourself why—are the clothes too expensive, too cheap, too unlike your personal style, too much like what you already own? It's possible that the buyer let her own strong tastes heavily influence her purchasing so that nothing suits *your* tastes.

If you are still uncertain, maybe you're just not ready to shop, or are feeling too negative about yourself to get excited about clothes. Give yourself a break and try again another day.

Women who instantly recognize the best styles for themselves are those who have thought a lot about their personal style and what pleases them. Clothes talk; what do you want yours saying about you?

Elegant/Classic

getting Dressed

It's been said before, but it bears repeating: The key to choosing clothing that will flatter your body is to select garments that are shaped basically the same way you are shaped so that you aren't adding bulk or cinching your body. Beyond that, you need to look at the design lines to see where they lead the eye, and evaluate whether that focal point is correctly placed for you. The classical proportions that look correct and balanced to the eye are long over short or short over long. The eye isn't always pleased with an evenly balanced proportion. That's why shorter tops over long skirts or pants look right, and a longer jacket looks better with a shorter skirt.

"Seek advice but use your own common sense."

YIDDISH PROVERB

In Chapter Two you measured your body to discover whether your proportions were average, short, or long. Now you know whether you're short- or long-waisted, if your arms are short or long, if you are long or short in the leg, etc. Knowing this, you can choose clothes that will either fit you off the rack, or will be better suited to you after only minor alterations. Remember, if you can't find a garment right away that works for you it's not your fault—the designers have just not created a silhouette perfectly suited to you. Keep looking until you find the right thing—don't settle! But be sure to tell the buyer at your store what you want.

When evaluating a garment, look at its elements and see if you can "take it apart" from a design point of view, and compare it to your needs: neckline, sleeve, and shoulder type and placement, length, pocket, and design line placement, etc. This way you learn what to look for in clothes, and learn what can easily be fixed—or not. When you find the best shapes, repeat them!

On the following pages you will find some garment suggestions for each body type. But since I can't list every conceivable garment, and no two bodies are truly alike, it helps to know what to look for *in theory*. Try the clothes that seem right, but don't be afraid to reject them if they don't work. The lists include basic garments that should work for each of the four body types based on their *horizontal* measurements (bust, waist, high hip, full hip, etc.). But for many women's bodies, vertical measurements (torso length, leg length, etc.) will be more important, so you need to use a critical eye and be willing to experiment.

Underneath It All—
Foundations Are the Key to Dressing Well

The Right Bra Size and
Other Essential Mysteries Revealed

A properly fitted bra is one luxury you can't afford *not* to have. These beautiful large bustlines of ours are one of our key assets, so they deserve the best treatment possible. The fringe benefits of caring for them with properly fitted bras include better fitting clothes and reduced back and shoulder pain. One of my best friends used to complain that though we could send a man to the moon, map the bottom of the oceans, and conquer other unimaginable scientific and medical limitations, we couldn't seem to design and construct comfortable bras to fit and flatter every woman. Then she got herself fitted for new bras by a professional and it changed her life. It made her look at science—not to mention her clothes—in a whole new light. Are you having trouble with your bras, too?

According to the experts, 85 percent of women wear the wrong bra size. That's a staggering figure, but it reflects the fact that so few of us know what to expect from a bra. Here's what a good bra should do for you, according to S&S Industries, makers of the best bra underwires:

- Contain all the breast tissue inside the cup.
- Shape, separate, lift, contain, conform, and support breast tissue.
- Not dig in at the shoulder.
- Fit close to the breastbone and not stand away at the center.

- Not ride up in the back or the front—regardless of how you move your arms.
- Be comfortable enough for you to slip a finger underneath the band at the base of the cups.

The best way to get a good fit is with the help of an expert. Lots of department stores and lingerie/foundations boutiques can help (check your local Yellow Pages). Part of the challenge in fit is in finding the brand or brands that fit you best. Bras, like other garments, have no size standards. One manufacturer's C cup is another's D cup, etc. Furthermore, even the experts tell us that experience and trial and error are often the best fit guides, but they all agree that you start with your tape measure!

There are two fit measurements to bras: body, or brand size, which represents the size of your rib cage and makes up the body of every bra, and cup size, which represents the actual breast tissue. Since every woman's body is different, not every measurement technique works for everyone. The following guidelines should help you get the best fit, but remember, these are general guidelines. Depending on what bra style you choose, sizes will vary.

How to Measure for the Right Bra

1. While wearing your own best-fitting non-minimizer bra, measure your rib cage under your breasts. Then add 3 inches to this figure. The total is your *body*, or *band size*. (If the total is an odd number, like 39, go to the next highest even number—in this case 40.) Another way to measure for band size is above the bust, directly under the arms. Compare these two numbers; if they are different, use the larger number.

2. To determine cup size, measure gently across the fullest part of your bust-line. If this measurement is 1 inch more than your band size, your bra cup size is an A, 2 inches is a B, and so on.*

Once You Determine the Right Size, Here's the Correct Way to Try On a Bra:

1. Slip the bra straps over your shoulders and grasp both sides of the bra. Lean forward, letting your breasts ease into the cups.

2. Straighten up, and without letting go of the fabric, slide both hands to the back of the bra and hook it on the middle hook, making sure the band is low in the back.

3. Adjust the straps to smooth out the top of the bra cup. Your breasts should be at a comfortable height, about midway between your shoulder and your elbow.

*Measuring guidelines courtesy S&S Industries, Inc.

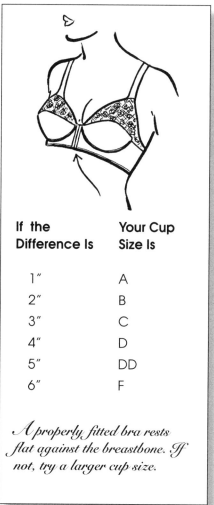

If the Difference Is	Your Cup Size Is
1"	A
2"	B
3"	C
4"	D
5"	DD
6"	F

A properly fitted bra rests flat against the breastbone. If not, try a larger cup size.

Wearing the right bra can take years off your figure and add immeasurable confidence. I strongly recommend an underwire bra for most women over a B cup. It lifts and shapes the breasts, keeping the bustline high. This is especially important to shorter-waisted women who need as much torso length as possible. When trying on underwire bras, make sure that they fit flat against your breastbone, and don't cut into you anywhere.

Keep in mind that you need a wardrobe of bras, not just one or two. If you wear anything cut low in the back, off the shoulder, or low in the front, you may need a special bra—thank goodness manufacturers are finally making beautiful bras in all types. And now they even make sports bras in larger sizes, which are critical for exercising, because lots of bouncing isn't good for your breast tissue, the muscle wall behind it, or your back and shoulders.

I've recently seen quite a few women at my shows and seminars wearing sports bras with their regular clothes. They can't seem to figure out why their clothes aren't fitting them correctly and come out of the fitting room for advice. It could be the bra, ma'am. Sports bras are excellent at protecting your sensitive breast tissue during activity, but are not designed to shape and mold you naturally under your clothes. A good bra lifts and shapes.

Minimizer bras are an option for the very large-busted woman who is having trouble fitting clothes over her ample bosom. They work by transferring tissue sideways under the arms instead of out front. If you aren't having trouble with the fit of your clothes you may not need a minimizer.

Even if you find just one bra that fits and flatters, buy it in multiples—don't wait. Bras are one garment that really makes cost-per-wearing practical.

Women complain to me all the time that special bras can cost them $40 or more. But these same women aren't fazed by blouse prices higher than that. I don't understand—a bra is essential, you wear it every day, and it lasts a long time if you care for it well. Why shouldn't it cost more than a pair of jeans? You just need to be practical when shopping and planning your wardrobe. If you have a choice of color, you only really need beige. No matter what your skin color, beige will work well under the widest range of colors. White tends to stand out under light colors, and black will show through most lightweight fabrics.

Naturally, if you wear a teddy over your bra you can indulge in a whole wardrobe of colors and patterns. I wear my favorite beautifully patterned and colored bras under dark or heavyweight fabrics where they won't show. They make me feel feminine even in my blue jeans.

Undercover Essentials

Do you have at least one beige half slip to wear under light-colored skirts? Do you have a full slip to wear under dresses? Do you have at least one light-colored camisole to wear under blouses to keep them from revealing too much and clinging? If you don't own them now, you may want to get them. Those simple items are the true basics of lingerie that most every plus-size woman should own. Of these, the most important are the half slip and camisole.

Don't you just hate to look in the rearview mirror and see a lumpy back peeking out from under your bra? A simple solution to this problem is a camisole between your bra and the blouse. An all-in-one teddy with a snap

crotch will stay in place, but a simple camisole will work just fine (I tuck mine into my hose for a smooth line). They also put a little distance between you and your clothes—which is important when wearing white blouses and other lightweight materials that can turn transparent in the wrong light.

Some women find a full body briefer to be a convenient smooth solution to the lumpy-body effect. If you are comfortable with them and don't mind working around the crotch closures in the ladies' room, there are some terrific new styles on the market made from Lycra and nylon. Look for one that fits your bust perfectly, and is long enough to accommodate your torso. Lots of women find a control brief and a wider-banded bra to be a good solution for upper and lower torso without the constriction of an all-in-one.

The other essentials I can't live without are foam shoulder pads—to wear

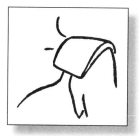 

The pad on the left is perfect for set-in sleeves and will create a clean line from shoulder to wrist. The one on the right is best for soft, knitted fabrics and raglan, dolman, drop sleeves, and those without a sharp seam at the shoulder edge.

under everything. I have two kinds, and they live in their own little cardboard "cans"; one has a more rounded curve to the shoulder, the other set is straighter. Depending on the type of shoulder/armhole I wear, I simply slip these foam friends on, tuck the little tabs under my bra strap, and voilà! I have a squarer, more balanced shoulder line to compensate for my large arms and "dowager's hump." I also confess that I've successfully used them to add a little padding to my bra to create a more balanced look above the waist for an outfit that put too much emphasis below the waist. Since I'm large through the back and shoulders but not in the bust, I sometimes need a little assistance to get my clothes to hang correctly.

Another secret from my closet that gets me through the warm weather: Cotton/Lycra bicycle shorts worn under long skirts prevent thigh rash when you forgo hose. They are a cool and smooth alternative to polyester tap pants or a split petticoat. It's a great solution—but don't try this with a short skirt!

The bottom line to foundations that work is this: For a great look in all you wear, start with a good bra that fits you well and accommodates the design of your garments, and wear a slip and/or camisole to smooth out your body under clothes that are the slightest bit revealing or close to the body.

Separates: A Myriad of Choices

Start at the Bottom: Skirts, Pants, and Shorts

A lot of plus-size women find that they depend on separates to make their wardrobe run. Indeed, if you adhere to the capsule wardrobe concept, you can get tremendous mileage out of judiciously chosen jackets, skirts, pants, and tops. The drawbacks include the risk of looking not quite put together, and having to work hard at coordination, but they are easily overcome with a little planning and organization. The Natural/Sporty style type (primarily) and the Elegant/Classic style type (secondarily) will find themselves most easily accommodated by separates. The big consideration when perfecting your separates wardrobe is to select pieces that work well with those you already own, and that are shaped perfectly for your body type.

Occasionally women tell me that separates are difficult for them to deal with because they have so little time to get ready in the morning, and figuring out what to wear is too time consuming. My advice is usually this: "Getting dressed" is really about dealing with putting together an outfit that you feel good about, and good in. You can spend time organizing an outfit each time you wear it, or just once—and wear it that same way each time. Some women actually enjoy assembling their outfit each day. They vary the tops, bottoms, and accessories to suit their needs, and in so doing their outfit becomes an expression of their creative nature, reflecting their feelings of that moment, that day, that event. Others would rather save time by organizing their clothes once, and know that their outfit looks good no matter what their current mood. They keep entire outfits—including pins, necklaces, earrings, hose, and shoes—together, and exclusive to that outfit (or they hang a little card on the hanger with notes on which accessories and tops or blouses work with that skirt, pants, jacket, suit, etc.). There is no right or wrong method, so take your pick—less time each day but less variety, or more variety but more time spent on your clothes each day. Recognize that whichever organizational method suits your personality and time, having some system or guide will make the difference between looking well dressed and, well, dressed.

Skirts

As old as time, and as fresh as ever, skirts are a mainstay to every wardrobe no matter your age, occupation, or lifestyle. It's all in the shape—narrow, wider, widest, long, shorter, shortest, simply constructed or complex in design. But basically, skirts divide into narrow types and wider, or full, types. The key to finding skirts that will flatter your shape is this (where have I heard this before?): *Choose skirts that are shaped the way you are shaped.* However, in order to remain balanced, take care not to wear your skirts either too loose or too tight for your figure. You don't want to overemphasize the curves of your tummy, hips, or derriere, or add bulk—and therefore perceived width—to your lower half. Remember, *you are only as wide as your widest line!* If you choose a flared or wide skirt, select one made from the softest fabric that will fall into lovely folds close to the body.

The other important point to remember is that a skirt must be longer than it is wide to look correctly proportioned, so *taper your skirts slightly when you raise the hem.* Too many plus-size women wear long, wide skirts because the style is reassuring, covering the tummy, derriere, hips, and legs. The truth is that we are flattered by skirts that are shorter and narrower than you might expect. In fact, although some designers insist on creating a variety of *A-line skirts* for plus-size women, if it's too full, too bulky, or stiff, it's one of the worst shapes for a plus-size body because it adds bulk where it's not needed. To work well, an A-line skirt should be modified to supply just a slight fullness or ease across the hips. Similarly, the *dirndl* and *flared* styles can flatter a fuller hip if modified to give you ease without bulk and executed in a soft, drapeable fabric.

For guidelines on the best skirt styles for your body, bear in mind that vertical lines break up the large expanse of a skirt, and will tend to lengthen and narrow a figure. The closer together vertical lines are, the more slimming effect they tend to have on a figure. Take note of design details that create horizontal lines that will lead the eye back and forth and tend to broaden the figure—borders, pockets, seams, or pattern lines.

If you have a high hip (the widest part of the hip is just a few inches below the waist), you will be flattered by straighter, narrower skirts. The low-hipped figure (widest 6 or more inches below your waist) is flattered by skirts with a little more fullness and drape. *Hip-yoked skirts* (which drop the fullness of a skirt down a few inches below the waist with a horizontal seam that runs completely around the body) tend to work better on low-hipped women with a significantly defined waist and flatter tummy, but can flatter nearly every body with the right fit across the hip. If you're low-hipped, wear the yoke just above the fullest part of the hip. High-hipped women can wear the yoke at any comfortable point that doesn't pull the fabric horizontally. Yokes that dip into a V in front are generally a little easier for most women to wear. To balance the yoke, choose slim, non-bulky tops.

Pleated skirts are a perennial favorite in a variety of widths and lengths. Done correctly in the lightest- and finest-weight fabrics with a gentle drape, they've a feminine grace that is very flattering. If you are high-hipped, you will need to fit the skirt at the waist and make certain it's not too tight across your hips. If low-hipped, you may need to wear the pleats stitched down all the way to your widest hip area to ensure the skirt falls correctly. Either way, you need to move around and sit down in a pleated skirt before buying it to make sure it doesn't ride up or split open at the pleats. Keep in mind that:

- The pleats have to lie flat across the hips, tummy, and derriere whether they are stitched down or not. Stitched-down pleats are neater and generally more slimming.
- The free-falling pleats have to be longer than the area that is stitched down in order to make the skirt appear visually balanced.

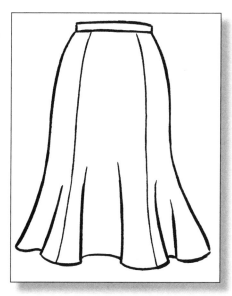

Trumpet Skirt

Another great option for plus-size women is the *trumpet skirt*—but only if you have long enough legs to allow the long, straight fall of fabric to the knee. The flutter of fabric is a feminine, lovely look that balances the plus woman's hips. The best have six gores and are slim without being too body conscious.

No matter which style you choose, consider skirts made from the finest lightweight fabric with a soft drape. This will minimize the bulk on the lower half of your body and lend you a clean, fluid line. No matter what your shape or body type you will most likely be flattered by skirts with elastic inserts in the back or sides. This nifty design feature keeps the waistband flat but gives you room to move. Likewise, we are all flattered by a skirt that falls smoothly at the sides. If your pockets gape open the skirt's too small. But even on a well-cut skirt they can pop open when you sit or move. Try stitching them closed. Also, look for skirts with a quality lining, even if they are meant to be lightweight summer garments. Lastly, bear in mind that it's always more flattering to wear your hem even all the way around, even if that means a few dollars in tailoring. Most plus-size women's skirts ride up in front or back.

Pants and Shorts

Thank goodness for pants and their nearly complete acceptability everywhere—backyards to boardrooms. They are comfortable, practical, and when carefully selected, an attractive alternative to skirts for every body type. Frankly though, without a little care pants can have a sloppy feel, so plus-size women need to work a little harder at looking pulled together in pants to avoid looking less than their best.

As curvy women, our pants need to be tailored to fit both our narrow and widest sections. So given the choice, choose a pant that conforms to your hips, thighs, and derriere, and have the waist tailored (a fairly simple and straightforward procedure that any seamstress or tailor can easily execute).

A nearly impossible fix, on the other hand, is a crotch that is too low. Buy your pants with the correct rise, with enough ease to make sitting, standing, and bending comfy without extra material getting in your way. A crotch that's too long is most unattractive, will make your legs look shorter, and can get bunched up when you move, promoting thigh wear. The only possible solution for "droopy drawers" is to turn, or roll the casing of an elastic waist pant. If you have your seamstress do this fairly simple procedure make absolutely certain you have enough length in the leg to keep the proportions correct.

Speaking of which, thigh wear is a real problem for nearly every woman—even those below size 14W. The best solution is to choose pants that fit well, and are constructed of sturdy, quality fabrics with a soft or smooth hand to minimize friction. A good-quality wool gabardine is least likely to pill and wear. Nubby, textured, knitted, or ribbed fabric will wear fastest. A lined pant usually falls better and holds up longer. (Lining can be replaced when worn.)

Pants give the wearer a long, vertical line that is a smashing look for all of us. To complete that look *it's important to wear socks or hose the same color and tone as the pants*—better yet, choose a shoe in the same range, too. This keeps the eye moving vertically and makes your legs look longer. The idea is to avoid horizontal lines that break up the effect—crotch folds, cuffs, stress wrinkle lines, etc.

The proper length for pants is determined by your leg length and the pants width; as with skirts, *the wider the pant, the longer it's worn.* Short wider-cut pants make you look cut off, or "dumpy." The best look is a clean, unbroken line from your waist to the top of your shoes. Women's pants, unlike men's, should be worn without a "break" at the top of the foot. With stirrup pants, the fabric should come all the way down and rest on the top of your foot—none

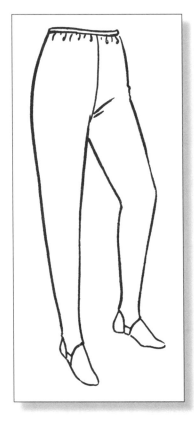

Stirrup Pants

of your ankle should show. Too many designers execute this look wrong, and it makes you look sloppy. If you are longer than average in the leg, buy Tall Women's stirrups (see Resources for catalogs that carry Talls). Many plus-size women find that stirrups with a sewn-in center crease is a great way to reinforce the vertical, and give the pant some body in its design. Stirrups, by the way, should be worn with a high-vamp shoe or bootie, and *never* with heels.

All front creases should fall in a straight line, away from the body, from waist to foot. (A back elastic can help the waist fit, and allow the pant to fall correctly.) As with the fall of your skirts, you can correct the hem of the pant leg to maintain the cleanest line even if your legs are proportionately heavier on the inside or outside, or you are a little bowlegged.

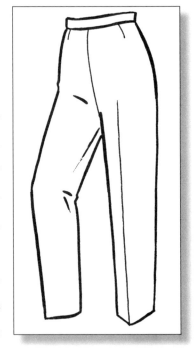

*Straight-Leg Pants
(flat front)*

When fitting straight-leg pants, look for those that taper slightly toward the ankle. This keeps the bulk to a minimum, and will make you look a little taller. This is especially important with wider pants. (Rectangle and Apple bodies may have to have the thighs tapered slightly to maintain a longer, leaner silhouette.)

In shorts, look for styles that fall below the widest part of your thigh without adding bulk to your lower body. *Jamaicas* are the longest, then *Bermudas*, then *boxers*, then *tap pants/short shorts*, etc. *Walking shorts* are a fairly long style, but aren't very practical for many plus-size women because of the horizontal line created by this style's cuff. If you have thin legs (like most Apple bodies), walking shorts can be an acceptable alternative. A lot depends on the length, color, and fabric.

Jeans, one of the greatest inventions of the twentieth century, are not the most attractive style for most plus-size women because they tend to emphasize the obvious curves. And contrary to what the world seems to think, don't you find them just a little uncomfortable? Not exactly bedroom slippers, unless they're made with Lycra to give you stretch where you need it. But personal thoughts aside, many manufacturers are striving to fit every plus-size body type—and some are actually succeeding. Just be certain the style you choose doesn't add bulk in the leg or thigh, is the right length for your leg, and that the curves are where you want them to be and lie flat everywhere else. What looks like a clean, smooth line when those indigo devils are new can turn into a tummy-tugging, derriere-draping, hip-hugging, all-too-real reflection of you after a few wash cycles. As the most evenly proportioned plus-size body, Hourglass figures may find the classic five-pocket styles easiest to wear.

For suggestions on the best skirt and pant/short styles for you, look for your body type on the following charts:

Hourglass:

- Emphasize your waist without overemphasizing the curves of your bust and hips.
- Choose skirts with soft drape—but not cling.
- Skirt styles to try:
  Straight (works well if you are high-hipped)
  Wrap
  Trumpet
  Pleated
  Gored
  Inverted front pleat
  Kilt (stitches on pleats should end above the widest part of your hip)
  High waist (unless you are short-waisted)
  Modified flared
  Modified A-line
  Modified dirndl
  Gathered
  Hip yoke
  Golf skirt
- Pants and shorts should be cut well so they neither cling, exaggerating your curves, or add bulk to your body and throw off your natural balanced silhouette.
- Pants and shorts styles to try:

Straight leg
Tapered baggies
Pleated front
Culottes (short)
Jodhpur
Jumpsuit
Harem pants
Jamaica shorts
Bermuda shorts
Boxer shorts
Tap pants/short shorts
Walking shorts
Leggings
Stirrups
Skort

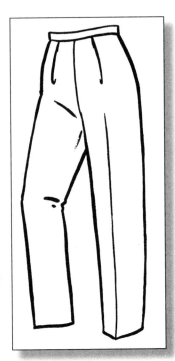

Pleated Pants

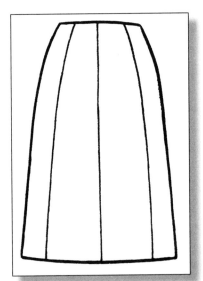

Gored Skirt

Rectangle:

- The Rectangle needs to define the waist and soften her lines.
- Slim skirts and those with an easy drape will give you verticality.
- Elastic waists—either full or partial—are a good solution to your full waist.
- Skirt styles to try:
  Straight
  Tapered baggies
  Inverted pleat
  Pleated (narrow pleats are best)
  Wrap
  Bias cut (only drapes well without
    a tummy bulge)
  Trumpet
  Gored
  Hip yoke
  Modified A-line
  Golf skirt
  Narrow/knitted straight skirt
- Pants/shorts styles to try:
  Straight-leg
  Legging
  Stirrup
  Pleated front
  Hip yoke
  Jumpsuit

Overalls
Culottes (short)
Boxer shorts
Tap pants/short shorts
Jamaica shorts
Bermuda shorts
Narrow cuffed walking shorts
Skort
Elastic waists

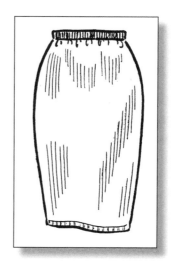

*Knitted Elastic-Waist
Straight Skirt (tapered)*

Apple:

- The Apple is least flattered by clothing with defined waists; avoid them whenever possible. You need to redirect the eye to the face, hips, thighs, and legs.
- Reinforce your wedge shape with narrow silhouettes below the waist.
- Look for pants that are narrow through the thigh, or have them tailored to a more narrow silhouette.
- Skirt styles to try:
  Straight
  Trumpet
  Inverted pleat (if it falls straight without a flare)
  Narrow pleat
  Hip yoke
  Golf skirt
  Narrow/knitted straight skirt
  Any slim skirt with enough elastic or ease to accommodate your waist.
- Pants and shorts styles to try:
  Stirrups
  Leggings
  Narrow straight-leg
  Flat-front
  Hip yoke
  Overalls
  Boxer shorts
  Tap pants/short shorts
  Bermuda shorts
  Jamaica shorts
  Narrow cuffed walking shorts
  Skort (soft fabric)
  Elastic waists

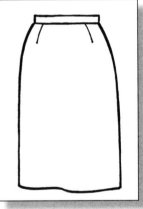

Straight Skirt/Modified Dirndl

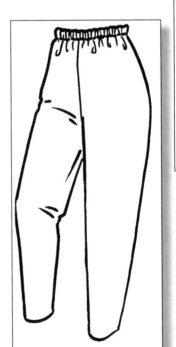

Elastic-Waist Pants (tapered leg)

118

Pear:

- Broaden the upper torso with brighter, lighter colors, design details, and patterns at the shoulder and bust area.
- Deemphasize the hips and thighs with darker colors and soft skirts (but be sure that the skirted suit has visual balance above the waist).
- Try maillot, wrap, sarong, strapless, French-cut leg, wrap, skirted, and simple strapless styles.

fabulous Fit:
The Ultimate Flattery

The Horizontal Challenge

Nothing says elegance more than a garment that fits you perfectly. People will think you paid a fortune for your clothes if your fit is flawless. Unfortunately, fit is such an elusive quality in plus-size clothing, you may not even be aware it's missing. Certainly you want to be able to sit, stand, and walk easily, and we know that nothing marks a woman as insecure with her body like tight, bulging, wrinkling, or overly large clothes. The difficulty for plus women is maintaining the tight versus loose balance because we're trying to drape our curves (which as any sculptor would tell you, is where the genius lives). Clothes look great on the hanger and very thin models because they only have to deal with the vertical, never the horizontal. For my money, that's the real challenge!

> "*Stupid solutions that succeed are still stupid solutions.*"
>
> YIDDISH PROVERB

Most of us tend to buy our clothes loose enough to guarantee our comfort, but a little ease turns into *way too big, way too fast.* While the plus woman needs to focus on the vertical lines in her clothing in order to compensate for her extra width, she can't overwhelm her body with garments that are too big. Clothes that are too large will emphasize a figure challenge, not minimize it. Remember, you are only as wide as your widest line. Here are three nasty realities:

1. Clothes that are too small for you will make you look larger.
2. Clothes that are too large for you will make you look larger.
3. Ain't no justice in this world....

Once upon a time women wore more formal clothing designed to fit closer to the body (and we all wore the undergarments to support the look!). As styles changed we gained comfort but lost knowledge of our bodies and how clothing can be used as a tool for flattery. In previous generations, before women in the workforce had a radical effect on how the garment industry designed and sold us clothes, women had more personal knowledge of sewing, or hired dressmakers to alter or design their selections, or at the very least bought their clothes in smaller, local boutiques where they got lots of individual attention from a professional sales staff. Talking with an expert about the best fabrics, textures, designs, silhouettes, and dimensions to flatter her body was an invaluable education that most women today are denied.

(*Note:* Interestingly, custom-made clothes are still widely available. Nothing—absolutely nothing—beats the fit of a garment constructed just for you. While it may be a bit more expensive, it can be well worth the price in durability and flattery. If you love a garment and it loves you, you will choose to wear it all the time. In doing so, the actual price, or *cost per wearing*, is much less than that of a garment that was a "real bargain" when you bought it, but never leaves the closet!)

Without adding clothing construction techniques to your information overload, you can easily learn what to look for in garment fit. You can save money, aggravation, and guilt by accurately judging clothes in the fitting room, before they become space-fillers in your closet. *So what is fit? It's found in clothes that flow smoothly over the body, don't cling or pull in any area, and allow you to move unrestricted.*

The Elements of Fit

Ease and Stretch

Ease is the difference between the size of the body and the size of the garment. Certain styles incorporate very little ease into the design, while others are based on lots of ease delivered through flare, pleats, or other fullness. The typical design uses minimums of about 2 inches at the bustline, 1–2 inches at the waistline, and 2–3 inches at the hips for ease of movement.

It's important to understand how a garment is designed to fit in order to flatter your body with the right size. Plus-size women sometimes make the mistake of buying a size too small because they don't allow enough fit ease. Likewise, wearing a garment much larger than necessary adds too much ease, and throws off the balance of fit throughout the silhouette.

Everyone feels differently about how much is enough to make them comfortable, but the trend in popular clothing is toward loose vs. body-conscious. Regardless of trends, clothing should fall in the proper manner without either constriction or a surplus of fabric that adds bulk without flattery. Tops and outerwear are designed to fall gracefully from the shoulder, and skirts and pants are designed to fit the hip and waist. *Remember, just because you can get into the garment, doesn't mean it fits.* Check the shoulders, bust, seat, crotch, arm and leg allowances, etc. Does it fit everywhere? If not, a size up or down may or may not correct the situation. The garment has to be the right silhouette for your body.

Closures

Closures should hang correctly, and hit your body in the location intended. Front-button garments should have a button that falls in the center of the fullest part of the bust in order to keep from gaping open when you move.

I have no patience when it comes to buttoning and unbuttoning blouses—I'd rather open them just enough to slip over my head without getting any makeup on them. I find that this not only saves me time, it keeps the buttonholes tight. On the rare occasion of finding a button-front blouse that gaps but otherwise seems to fit fairly well, I sometimes sew the front pocket closed from the inside, using a blind stitch that won't show through. It's not a perfect solution, but it can turn a "7" into a "9"!

Armseyes and Shoulders

Some garments (especially cheaper cuts) use very deep armseyes (or armhole openings) to compensate for inadequate fit. They are a tempting shortcut because blouses and jackets cut this way can *sort of* fit a panorama of body types without more elaborate and precise darting and cutting techniques. Naturally, women differ in back size and bust size, with various combinations determining where they require the most ease. A large armseye will pull to the back or the front to accommodate these shape differences instead of staying put in the middle.

A good rule of thumb is to look for an armseye that allows ease of movement without cutting into your arm, gapping, or pulling at the bust area. The lowest should fall not more than 1½ inches below your armpit—unless the design purposely calls for more. One advantage to a high-cut armseye is the longer, cleaner line it affords your torso from armpit to waist and hip, which in turn makes you look taller. This is especially important to petite or short-waisted women.

Shoulders are a key area for plus-size women because they define your upper body and balance out your lower half. While it's important to wear at least a little padding, you need to retain the natural 1- to 2-inch drop from neckline to shoulder. If you wear shoulders too square or too large you risk looking like a fullback or dominatrix. Too droopy and you look sloppy all over. Experiment with pads.

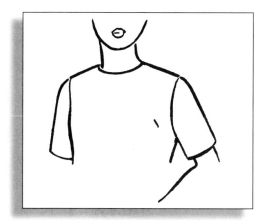

Set-in Sleeves

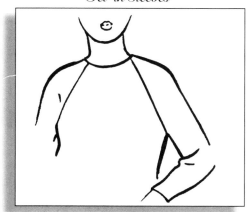

Raglan Sleeves

Dolman Sleeves

Sleeves

Set-in sleeves are the most common and generally the most flattering. They provide excellent range of movement—especially when cut well and fitted with a good shoulder pad. The top seam should sit at or just outside the shoulder bone, not inside.

Raglan sleeves, which attach to the garment body in a diagonal seam from the neckline, are an adequate solution for large busts, as long as your shoulders are broad, and a good shoulder pad is used.

Dolman sleeves are formed as a single unseamed piece with the sleeve, bodice, and shoulder. They can work well with some wedge-shaped dresses and for women who are much larger on the top than the bottom. On the negative side, they add a lot of unnecessary bulk to your body and are hard to fit under coats or jackets, so freedom of movement is somewhat limited.

I recommend you avoid the ever-popular *dropped sleeve*, which adds another horizontal line on the upper arm right where you don't

157

want one, and widens the upper body. But since so many designers choose them for plus-size clothing they may be difficult to avoid. If your upper arms are heavy, you may already look slightly rounded through the shoulder, so it's even more important to choose a pad that will square off the shoulder and present a clean fall of fabric.

Sleeves should hit just at the wrist bone or you look sloppy no matter what the cost or quality of your garment. If you are full-hipped, avoid long sleeves that end at the jacket hem. Wear your hems just above or below the wrists. But more important, perhaps, is sleeve width; the best sleeve fits your arm with enough ease for free movement without extra bulk, and tapers from armseye to wrist. A too-wide sleeve is the hallmark of a badly designed garment or one that has been crudely graded up from a Missy pattern rather than being designed and cut for the plus-size body. You should be able to pinch about 1½ to 2 inches of double fabric at the underarm seam when your arm is held out straight.

Be cautious in wearing short sleeves that end before the elbow. The saggy or plump underarm peeking out of the bottom of a short sleeve can spoil the most attractive look. However, a full short sleeve can highlight your arms and hands. They're best used to balance full hips and derriere.

Hemlines and Skirt Lengths

Hems should fall evenly all the way around. On most plus women, skirts rise higher in either the front or the back and need rehemming. There is no way to construct a skirt to accommodate every body, so you need to alter to fit you.

Consider the alteration of every skirt as part of its price.

Hem length also affects the perceived height of the body, leg length, and leg shape, so the hem should fall at a narrow part of the calf for ultimate flattery. The classic length is about 2 inches below the center of the knee.

To find the best length for you, I recommend the scarf method. Stand in front of a full-length mirror in just your hose. Hold a scarf straight before you like a curtain, and starting at your feet, raise it up little by little until you find the most flattering point on your leg, which will probably be just above or below the widest part of your calf. (If you have a helper, have them measure from that point to the floor and record the results for future alterations.)

The most important key to skirt length is taper, taper, taper. *When you shorten a skirt you need to taper it in at the same time to maintain its proportions—*

> *"I think every woman would be well advised to discover her own length and never shift too far from it."*
>
> GIORGIO ARMANI

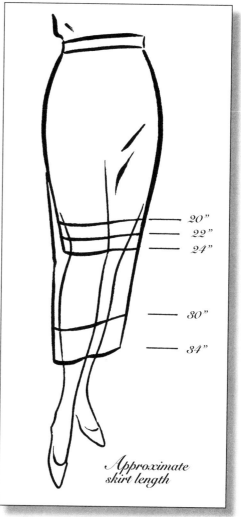

20"
22"
24"

30"

34"

Approximate skirt length

but not so tight that you can't easily turn the entire skirt around your body. (Since most designers use fit models about 5'7", you may need to alter skirt proportions to flatter your body.) A skirt must always be perceived as longer than it is wide to best flatter a figure.

Some Other Details

Crotch. The crotch should have enough room for comfort without riding up or hanging so low so that it gets in the way.

Waistbands. A perfect-fitting waistband doesn't gap, dip down in the back, grab you, bind you, force your body into odd shapes, or otherwise embarrass you. There should be about two-fingers width ease at the waistband.

Pocket Position. Pockets should lie closed without tugging or pulling, and are generally designed to fall where your hands need them. If they gap, are too high or too low on side seams in skirts and pants, you probably need a different size garment. If you are broad through the hips you may want to avoid hip pockets, which can add bulk, or else keep them sewn shut.

Seams. Simply, seams are designed to lie flat. If they shift, pucker, show stress, or tear, your garment is too small or large.

Darts. Darts are a marvelous device for fitting the bustline and other curves. The best run toward the curve, and end about 1 to 1½ inches from it, with no wrinkles or bubbles.

The Construction and Fit Checklist

Happy days! You've searched the racks, found the best shapes and silhouettes for your body, found the right size (you think), considered the colors, and have a few choice selections in your price range to take in the fitting room. It's easy to be swayed by price, color, or the ol' cute factor. If you're shopping on a deadline for a special occasion, it's even easier to be sucked into a bad choice. There are a few things to know about quality construction:

- Seam allowances are $5/8$ inch. They should be finished off with a zigzag or other finishing stitch, and should not fray or show loose threads anywhere. Seams should look smooth and hang straight, without wrinkles or puckers.

- Interfacings shouldn't wrinkle or pull. The best are sewn, not fused to the fabric.

- Buttons should be sewn on tightly, without loose threads. The best buttons are bone, shell, leather, or covered; plastic buttons are a sure sign of shoddy construction. Buttonholes should be straight, without loose threads.

- Fabric patterns should match at the seams. Natural fabrics or blends are *generally* better than synthetics, although the new microfiber polyester looks, feels, and acts like silk, and blends can make delicate fabrics wear better. Rayon has wonderful drape but must be dry-cleaned.

- Hemlines must hang straight and even. Stitching should not be visible, and the inside should be finished with tape.

- Pleats and vents should lie flat.

- Collars should lie flat.

It's Too Big When...

◆ The sleeves extend below your wrist bone.

◆ Blouse or shirtsleeves hang more than ½ inch below jacket sleeves (may need to just tighten wristband of blouse).

◆ The shoulder pads slide down your back or front.

◆ It bags in the seat or the crotch.

◆ There is too much fabric gathered under the fastened belt.

◆ Your bra straps show at the neckline.

◆ The neckline gaps open, or won't lie flat.

◆ The waistline falls below your waist.

◆ The pants are so full at the thigh they resemble jodhpurs.

◆ The straps fall off your shoulders.

◆ The skirt or dress turns 'round and 'round on its own when you walk.

◆ Darts pucker.

◆ You can grab a handful of fabric where you shouldn't be able to.

◆ A wrinkle or bulge appears below the collar across the back (the back waist is too long or the collar sits too high).

◆ It still fits you when you're eight months pregnant.

It's Too Small When...

◆ The crotch rides up.

◆ Pants cup under your tummy or posterior or don't fall straight from the hip.

◆ Dresses or tops gape open (even slightly) at the closing.

◆ You don't have full range of motion in the arms.

◆ The sleeves bind uncomfortably when you raise your arms.

◆ Long sleeves reach well above your wrist bone.

◆ You can't bend your arms easily with wrist buttons closed.

- The armseye is pulled toward the front to accommodate your bust.
- The front button placket gaps or pulls open over your bust or tummy.
- The blouse pulls out of the waistband when you bend, sit, or lean over.
- The skirt rides up several inches when you sit.
- The skirt rides up at the waistband (too small in the hips or thighs).
- The skirt cups under your tummy or posterior.
- Side pockets gape open.
- Undergarment lines show through.
- You can't button a jacket's buttons easily and still have room to move.
- Tension wrinkles appear anywhere.
- It pinches you anywhere.
- The front zipper shows signs of stress.
- The side or seat seams start to pull apart or show signs of stress.
- It's difficult to breathe, or you can't sit down.
- The dress waistline falls above your natural waist.

When a Wrinkle Is More Than a Wrinkle

Wrinkles usually mean you have a poor fit—either a garment is too small or too large. Tight horizontal wrinkles mean there isn't enough fabric to fit around you comfortably, so the garment slides up or down to a smaller area. Tight vertical wrinkles are usually a sign that your garment is too short and needs to be lengthened. Diagonal wrinkles are a bigger problem—they usually mean you need to let out both horizontal and vertical seams.

Garments that wrinkle because they are too loose are just as unattractive. Horizontal wrinkles can form because the garment is too long; loose vertical wrinkles are a sign that the garment needs to be narrowed. Droopy, saggy wrinkles are a sure sign you are losing weight and need to consider buying at least one size smaller in clothes.

Alteration Checklist

Alterations should involve minor adjustments made by a qualified individual. In the right hands, any garment can look custom-made. In the wrong hands you can easily destroy a garment and uselessly spend a lot of money. Not every garment is suitable for alterations—knowing which is which is very valuable.

Follow this checklist before paying for a garment or any alterations, and find a good tailor or seamstress to perform them. Ask friends for recommendations, and talk to the person who will be doing the sewing to find out about their qualifications. They should have plenty of experience in constructing and altering all types of garments. Never let a store salesperson or anyone other than the one doing the alterations conduct the fitting. (And never leave the store without trying on the altered garment!)

1. Before buying, size up the garment—how's the width, length, shoulder fit, bustline, waistline, armhole, sleeve dimension and length, neck design, and general fit? If a garment doesn't fit you well off the rack, it may be either the wrong size or the wrong silhouette for your body.

2. Can you grab an extra handful of fabric anywhere? If so, can it be taken in easily at a seam, or will the alteration be a complex process of taking it in a little here, a little there, etc.? The more complex an alteration, the more costly and risky it is.

3. The easiest fixes are hem lengths, sleeve lengths, tapering or taking in the side seams, shortening straps, and altering elastic waistbands.

4. The most difficult fixes involve alterations at a point in the garment where other details occur (pockets, button tabs, pleats, lining, cuffs, darts, multiple-seam cross points, etc.). I generally don't recommend alterations that involve the neckline, collar, shoulder, or armhole, because they are pivot points that affect a host of other fitting challenges. Likewise, changing the basic design shape or proportions of the garment is usually too complex a job to be successful.

5. You can only let out the seams where there is enough fabric to add to the allowance while retaining a secure seam.

6. It's impossible to take up a crotch that's too low without adding gussets of the same fabric.

7. Some fabrics are too delicate to endure structural changes; leather, vinyl, very sheer, textured, and shiny fabrics are all difficult to work with, are weakened by repeated sewing, and leave punch holes from the stitches. Bulky knits can also be difficult to manipulate.

8. Stained clothes must be cleaned before altering so that the pressing steps during alterations don't set the stains permanently.

For detailed excellent advice on how to, why to, and when to alter garments, consult *Fabulous Fit* by image consultant, author, teacher, and designer Judith Rasband (Fairchild Publications, 1994).

Bonus Advice: Consider how much you will have to spend to alter a garment to make it right for you. That, plus the original cost, is the real price of that or any other garment.

Managing Fit for Weight Fluctuation

Nothing looks worse than clothes that are too tight or too loose. But since most of us are known to vary our weight occasionally, how to cope? This is always a problem for dieters who want to look good without spending more than they have to on clothes that they won't be in for long.

The bad news: Clothing can't be altered more than about one size before the basic shape is compromised. If a tailor or seamstress claims they can take a garment up or down more than one size, they're lying—or inexperienced. The good news: Several styles will look good through weight fluctuations of many pounds. The key is to avoid tightly fitted or tailored pieces if you know you're likely to gain or lose a few pounds. Instead, look for these:

- Raglan sleeves
- Full (vs. tapered) set-in sleeves
- A-line gathered or gored skirts with elastic waists
- Wrap skirts
- Chemise dresses
- Some coatdresses
- Trapeze dresses
- Some blouson dresses
- Some sheath dresses
- Surplice dresses
- Jumper dresses
- Boxy or unconstructed jackets
- Drawstring or elastic-waist trousers
- Boxer shorts
- Knits

Fit by Mail—Catalog Buying

Catalogs contain some of the best values and fashionable options in casual, business, dressy, resort/beach, or active wear for plus-size women. When people ask me whether they should take a chance on catalog buying, I always answer with a resounding yes! I don't have the time to go to every store and see all the seasons' selections, so I rely on catalogs for lots of things. The keys to shopping smart are to know the return policy and general reputation of the company, read the sizing chart and apply it to your measurements (see why that's so important?), and to consider your body shape and proportions when ordering.

Ask yourself if the garment is the right shape for you:

Does the dress have a straight silhouette, is it a wedge, or is it balanced in width top and bottom?

Does the dress have a defined waist, or is it a straight chemise?

Do the pants have a straight front, or are there pleats?

Is the waistband elastic or set in?

What is the inseam of trousers?

Does the shoulder extend beyond the arm or lie flat at the corner?

How high or low does the armseye sit?

Will the skirt need shortening, and if so, will you have to reshape it to do so?

Never, ever believe one size fits all. One size means that it will cover, or *accommodate*, many sizes, which has nothing to do with fit or flattery.

And above all: *Just because you can get into it doesn't mean it fits.* Plus-size women don't always expect (and sometimes aren't even familiar with) real fit, but it pays to understand, appreciate, and acquire clothes that really fit and flatter. Fit's the difference between looking good and looking perfect—and perfect isn't necessarily easy to come by. But it's worth every penny.

face Shapes and Other Pertinent Mysteries

Face Shapes——Who Cares?

If you understand your face it's easy to determine which accessories, hairstyles, necklines, collars, and makeup techniques will improve and complement your appearance. Since your face is (hopefully) the focal point of communication and central to your identity, it's important for you to *put your best face forward.*

Earlier I talked about the research numbers that show that people are more aware of what they *see* than what they *hear.* Other studies have shown that subtle, nonsurgical changes in a person's face—such as changing the shape of an eyebrow, replacing eyeglass frames with a more flattering style, or a different hair arrangement—made an enormous difference in the way others perceived and reacted to that person. As visual animals, we are accustomed to using nonverbal clues to analyze people,

> *"Even children of the same mother look different."*
>
> KOREAN PROVERB

decide if they are friend or foe, and predict behavior. (Do I like them or not? Will they hurt me or help me?)

No matter the shape of your face or figure, the pursuit of beauty is an exercise in achieving a balance, or symmetry, of your features, not in trying to achieve a specific shape. While it's been widely reported that the "perfect" face shape is oval, and that all other faces should be contoured to resemble that shape, oval is the "perfect" face shape only if you are limited to a singular idea of beauty. If you can't be yourself, you can't be happy, and if you're not happy, you're less than your best.

In one landmark, often-quoted book on image for women, the author's expert on makeup recommends starting with "a pure white base under the foundation. This acts as a primer to block out imperfections and even the skin tone...." He goes on to describe how to apply one foundation to match the natural face tones and another two shades darker to use in shading. His "ultimate objective is to create the illusion of the oval face...." Good grief! What about beautiful skin as an asset? What about the beauty of variation? No amount of paint will change some shapes to oval—and why would you want to? No woman's face should ever be viewed as something to be reconstructed, as a piece of canvas ready to receive someone else's "artistry." You're terrific as you are—you just need a little information to know how to make the most of what you've got.

Makeover Magic——Hocus Pocus?

Did you ever watch a makeover on TV or read one in a magazine and wonder how they make such a change in a woman's look so quickly? Here are four good explanations:

1. They start with someone who has the most potential for change, someone who "breaks the rules" with the wrong hair shape, hair color, makeup, or clothes for her face, figure, and hair type.

2. They convince her to relinquish control, which allows them to make radical changes she might not have tried on her own.

3. They follow some basic guidelines: (a) choosing hair shape based on face shape and body type; and (b) choosing makeup application colors and technique based on face shape, skin coloring, and hairstyle; and (c) choosing clothes that work for that body type.

Myth #4:
Women are born with beauty and style genes. Just like the natural instinct for nurturing or singing, you either have 'em or you don't.

Truth #4:
Choosing and wearing clothes, accessories, makeup, and hairstyles are learned, not genetic talents. Anybody can learn to look better.

4. They are professionals, with the right tools, skills, and training—which really only means that they take these sort of things somewhat seriously.

You, too, can have a makeover by applying some basic information about body types (you already know all about that), face shapes, your taste preferences, and today's current looks. With the right professional for guidance and the desire to be flexible in your thinking (and doing), you can achieve a full makeover without waiting for a formal invitation from a magazine or television show.

Here's How to Start Your Own Makeover

It helps to understand your face shape and get some guidelines for the type of hairstyle, eyeglass frame, and makeup that will work for you. The world generally reveals five or six different face shapes, but in reality the possibilities are nearly as endless as the differences in people. Your face, like your body, is three-dimensional. It has length, width, and depth. Those three factors in conjunction with your skin, hair, and eye color determine whether your configuration resembles your mother, your sister, your Great Aunt Zelda, or no one else on Earth.

Identifying the shape of your face requires a few minutes (maybe the help of a trusted friend), a good mirror, a headband to hold back your hair, a ruler, a length of string about 20–30 inches long (or calipers), and your imagination.

Starting with a clean, makeup-free face, pull back your hair with a headband or wrap it in a towel so that you can see the full outline of the face and hairline. If it helps, you might want to outline on your mirror what you see in lipstick, grease pencil, or Magic Marker (be sure it washes off). Look straight into the mirror—not up, down, or from the side. Let your face and all your chins hang out where you can see them!

Look at the outline of your face, comparing length versus width, distances between features, and note the relative size of the features themselves. *When evaluating your facial proportions, the scale of your features in relation to your head and face size is important, not the actual size of your nose or any other feature compared to that of a friend or anyone else.*

How does the length of your face from your chin to the bottom of your nose compare with the distance between your eyebrows to the tip of your nose? What about the length of your forehead from hairline to your eyebrows? On a proportionally even face those three are about the same length. Where are you long vs. short? That's key to your face shape and how you wear your hair.

Is your face vertically proportionate? Look at the width of one eye from inner to outer edge. Is that space wider than, more narrow than, or about the same width as the bridge of your nose? Can you fit five of those lengths across your face? If not, your face may be quite thin. Did you notice that your face is not even from one side to the other? (No one is perfectly even.) This affects where you put your makeup, where you might want to part your hair, and how your glasses sit on your face. (I have to adjust my specs by a half inch so they fit across my face straight!) To see how different people are from right to left, choose a full-face photo of anyone in the closest magazine, and cover the right half, then the left. Some people actually look like two different faces entirely!

Look at your nose, your eyebrow length and width, your mouth length and width, the size of your eye opening, your nose length, tip width, and bridge width, etc. What do you see? Are they small, medium, or large? This scale will translate into the size of your accessories, prints, etc. Use your face type to find the best accessories and makeup tips that follow.

Next, you should look at the shapes you see. Can you tell if the lines that define the edges of your features are straight or curved, horizontal, vertical, or diagonal? Look again at your eyebrows, eyes, nose, the tip of the nose, your mouth smiling and still, your hairline, the sides of your face, and your jawline. You will probably see a pattern of curves or angles, and a general direction of lines. Most plus-size women have more curves than angles, which means they are more flattered by clothes and accessories with curves vs. angles.

Lastly, does your face and hair have a lot of detail or texture? Is your hair curly or very smooth? Are there visible lines or uneven texture on your face? Do you have patterns—freckles on your skin and highlights or shade variations in your hair for example? These features will influence how you wear your patterns, textures, and clothing lines. Having some natural pattern and texture to

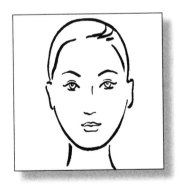

Oval Face

Round Face

Square Face

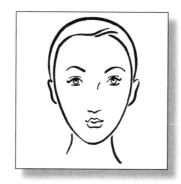

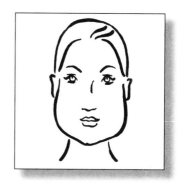

Oblong Face   *Heart/Diamond Face*   *Triangular Face*

your face and hair will allow you to wear fabrics and accessories that are highly patterned and textured.

Now find your face type based on what you see in the mirror and the descriptions that follow. Be sure to make a note of your face shape classification because you'll want to correlate it to accessory and hair information later on.

The Oval Face

This face is noticeably longer than it is wide, resembling an egg. It's widest at the cheekbones, with a slightly rounded chin. The forehead is balanced with the rest of the face. This is the most common face shape.

The Round Face

The cheekbones of the round face are much wider than the jawline and brow bone. The width is usually two-thirds the length, or more. The chin is usually full and the forehead moderately broad.

The Square Face

The forehead, cheeks, and jawline are about the same width. The face appears somewhat short (width is more than two-thirds the length), with a square or angular jaw.

The Oblong Face

The forehead, cheeks, and jawline are about the same width. The face is noticeably longer than it is wide.

The Heart/Diamond Face

The Heart forehead is equal to or wider than the high and sometimes angular cheekbones, and is significantly wider than the narrow, somewhat tapered jawline. The Diamond face has a more narrow forehead, but with wide cheekbones like the Heart shape. Both faces are nearly as wide as they are long, and may or may not have a "widow's peak."

The Triangular Face

The jawline is significantly wider than the forehead. The cheekbones may be wider than the forehead, but are narrower than the jawbone. The face width is usually two-thirds or more of the length.

Did you find your face shape? If not, look again at the width of your face compared to its length. Is it much longer than it is wide, or only moderately so? Try to accurately assess the width of your face at the temples or forehead, the cheekbone, and the jaw. Some faces are broader at the top, some at the middle, and some at the bottom—just like bodies! If you know where your face is wide and where it narrows you can easily decide what type you are. Go back and read the descriptions after you have measured. Keep in mind that your face doesn't have to match the illustrations exactly. Still puzzled? Ask a friend or your hairstylist for help!

As we'll see, the shape of your face will affect the eyeglasses you choose, how you wear other accessories, the best hairstyle shapes for you, and how to make up your face for maximum flattery. Think of it as a road map for beauty. Anybody for a drive?

accessories:
The Finishing Touch

Pizzazz and Polish, the Easy Way

When I was just out of college and starting life in the professional world I didn't have much money for good clothes. But hats and colorful touches were big, so I added a few spectacular chapeaus, some lovely colorful leather kid gloves, and some pretty scarves to my wardrobe and immediately established a reputation as a stylish dresser. Women with many more years of experience and a lot more money engaged me in conversation about clothes in order to pick my brain and get free fashion advice. Considering that I was at least four sizes bigger than these svelte, stylish New York advertising grande dames, I was flattered. I knew one thing: Assembling an outfit was like creating a work of art, or like decorating a room.

> "*Don't ignore the small things—the kite flies because of its tail.*"
>
> HAWAIIAN PROVERB

Choosing and Wearing Accessories— the Rulebook

Rule #1: *Whatever accessory you wear must be in proportion to your body.*

- Choose items that are medium to large scale, depending on your height.

Rule #2: *It must add some pizzazz.*

- If an accessory doesn't add to the effect, it takes away from it.

Rule #3: *Accessories can provide the needed style and panache to balance your dramatic larger body.*

- Go for color interest, unique style, classic style, etc.
- Accessories chatter more loudly and expressively than your clothes. Yours can say many things—romance, drama, spontaneity, creativity—but make sure they are all complimenting you!
- Take a risk with new looks and new items to stay current, and periodically evaluate a new approach.

Rule #4: *Accessories must be appropriate.*

- Be certain your clothes and your accessories are going to the same place—casual, business, or formal—together! The accessory must suit the personality of the garment, as well as you.
- Choose enduring styles for your professional wardrobe.
- Choose function first, form second for watches, briefcases, umbrellas, snowboots.

Rule #5: *KISS (Keep It Simple, Sister)*

- Wearing accessories is like talking to a child—simple, clear, precise statements are always better.
- You are not decorating a Christmas tree—add pieces slowly and don't overdo it. Understatement is often pure elegance.
- Evaluate the overall picture, the way people will see you—not piece by piece. Use the Blink Test (p. 72) as a reality check.

Rule #6: *Place accessories at your focal points to direct the viewer's eye.*

- Place focus on the face and neckline (see p. 184).
- The viewer's attention will be drawn to wherever you place the accessory, so be cautious.

Rule #7: *A single colorful accent is an afterthought; repeated it's a theme.*

- If you wear a color not found in the fabric or trim of your outfit, use the new color at least twice in your accessories to balance the overall look.

Rule #8: *Buy quality leather belts, bags, and shoes.*

- It's better to own only one or two high-quality leather belts than a variety of cheap ones. Remember, people only see what you have on, not your whole closet. You don't get extra points for owning things you're not wearing!

Rule #9: *If anything is broken, soiled, inappropriate, or out of place, someone will definitely notice.*

- Clean it, fix it, polish or adjust it before you wear it. Don't ruin an otherwise terrific outfit through sloppiness or carelessness.

Since I couldn't buy just anything off the rack (because of both size and budget), I had to think through my wardrobe and add those pieces that would give me the most effect for the money. Accessories allowed me to update my look to the moment, instead of having to rely on the slightly out-of-date plus-size looks of the time. The lessons I learned then have served me well since.

For very formal occasions, black is basic. The sophisticated beading and sequins on the top complement the rectangle torso, while the chiffon handkerchief hem adds verticality (without bulk), movement, and feminity.

For less formal occasions, a monochromatic, light-colored, elegant suit, with the right shoes and bag, is an excellent feminine option that never goes out of style.

The classic safari suit is (and always has been) a great monochromatic casual look for most plus-size bodies. To wear the jacket open, tie the belt behind you to provide back waist definition.

This soft taupe casual suit is just right for the model's coloring. Worn closed, it's more formal; worn open over a silk T-shirt, it's flexible dressing at its best. The rounded collar lends a feminine attitude.

Poolside is easy with classic suits that fit the torso and are comfortable to move in, without a lot of visual detail. The coverup and a great hat are key.

A fun casual "cottage-dress" jumper that adjusts at the shoulder to fit as high or low on the hip as you want. A drop-waist dress is a great look for many plus-size bodies, and the center front buttons perfect the look by reinforcing the vertical. The hat balances the width below the waist.

Photograph by Michael Keel

Photograph by Michael Keel, courtesy of Cynthia Carver

A classic Chanel-type short-over-short suit that easily dresses up or down, depending upon your accessories—and your attitude!

A perfect Tomatsu rendition of the long-over-long formal suit. The fabric is soft and drapes well, with the skirt tapering at the lower calf. The contrasting blouse ends at the waist, while the monochromatic hose, shoes, and skirt highlight the lower-body length.

My favorite Dana Buchman suit: this is a classic big-over-small proportion. The jacket is cut with just the right amount of flare to ease past the widest part of the hips, and the skirt is cut short and narrow to taper at the knees, reducing the width of the silhouette. The V neck and black buttons draw the eye in a verticle line to the face.

The same big-over-small look in a different fabric and hue suitable to the model's coloring. The dark hose and shoes flow together to elongate and narrow the legs.

A terrific example of casual comfort—the V-neck sweater highlights the neck/shoulder area and flows gracefully past the hips. The pants are comfortably loose but drape without adding bulk.

A great way to indulge in fun, ethnic prints—a big shirt with an exaggerated, open neckline over narrow, dark leggings.

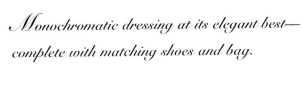

Monochromatic dressing at its elegant best— complete with matching shoes and bag.

Separates give you the most wardrobe flexibility and allow you to choose pieces that resolve particular figure challenges. The vest elongates a short waist, the fitted jacket complements the small, pear-body waist, and the dark pants disguise wide hips and force the focus upward. The shell-colored jacket flatters warm coloring.

The marvelous thing about today's plus-size fashions is that they can flatter a complete range of shapes, sizes, ages, and personalities.

Jewelry

You can wear silver or gold no matter what your coloring—although some strict seasonal color theorists will tell you otherwise. Whichever you choose, remember that your jewelry arrives visually before you do. When you put something on, check the whole body view as someone else would see you. It may be a lovely piece, but if it's not right for you, or if it doesn't substantially add to the overall effect, leave it at home. Here are some points to consider when buying and coordinating outfits:

- God invented necklaces to add vertical lines—but forgot to compensate for large busts and midriffs that get in the way, so use discretion when deciding on necklace length. If it cascades off your bosom into the air, you may want to wear one that ends an inch or two above the fullest part of your bustline. Also, if you have a midriff roll you may not want to emphasize it by wearing your necklace right at that point.

- Earrings are the most important piece of jewelry because they focus attention on your face.

- Scale is key—wear earrings, pins, etc. at least as large as your eyes, but not larger scale than necessary.

- Heavy, full, square, or round faces and heavy necks are flattered by flat earrings in complementary shapes.

- The shape of the earrings should reflect your lines. Since most plus–size women are slightly curvy, choose jewelry with gentle lines and softened angles. Perfect circles emphasize your curves.

- Round or mounded earrings can make the face look wider.

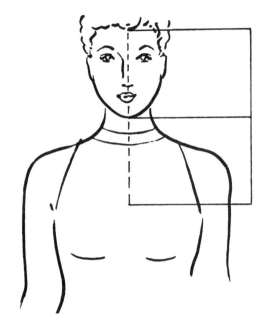

Your best looks balance the proportions of head, neck, and body—a challenge for plus-size women. The "balance point" concept developed by Carla Mason Mathis and Helen Villa Connor in The Triumph of Individual Style *is a great tool to decide the best placement of collars, necklines, details, necklaces, pins, etc. To find yours, measure your face length and drop down that same distance from your chin to your chest.*

- Drop earrings will shorten the neck.

- Bracelets should be worn in multiples or be fairly substantial to balance your larger body, but on a naked arm they create a distinct horizontal line, so be cautious.

- Bangles and other jewelry that make noise are not appropriate for business.

- An overly decorated wrist makes a strong visual impact and can be unflattering to women with very wide hips.

- Graduated pearls or beads are not the best choice for narrow shoulders or a full bustline because they draw the eye to the center. Bigger-scale beads (9mm+) of uniform size are the best choice.

- Bracelets and some necklaces create horizontal lines that can shorten, widen, and accentuate, so be sure to check the overall effect (few plus-size women can easily wear chokers, for example).

- More than two rings is considered very fashion forward. Rings on the forefinger and thumb are extremely daring and communicate sex appeal.
- Pins are best when larger or worn in multiples. Use your focal point and place them high to call attention to your face and away from the bust.

Scarves, Belts, and Gloves

Scarves are a fabulous way to inject color, boldness, and movement into your wardrobe, lend a little soft-ness to your ensemble, and establish focal points for the eye. Worn around the neck, they can be tied to emphasize the vertical. Of the three basic shapes—oblong, rectangle, and square—a very large square pro-vides the most flexibility. They can be worn simply or folded into complex designs and used to fill spaces and direct attention.

Scarf quality is determined by the fabric type and weight, the delicacy or complexity of colors, and the manner in which the edges are finished. The best scarves are hand rolled and meticulously stitched by hand. The following fabrics will flatter any wardrobe and last for years if you take care to have them dry-cleaned:

- Chiffon—sheer silk or polyester. The look is ultrafeminine.
- Charmeuse—silk or polyester satin-finished fabric. Fluid and elegant with a wonderful drape.
- Crêpe de chine—luxurious heavier silk crepe with a sheen; plain and patterned.
- Satin striping—lightweight silk chiffon/crepe or charmeuse with alternating woven stripes.
- Jacquard—magnificent brocades, damasks, and tapestry weaves of patterned silk or wool, often overprinted.
- Twill—a strong silk or wool weave with diagonal lines.
- Wool or rayon challis—lightweight weave, often with a paisley or floral design.

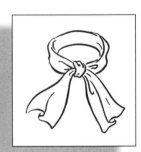

Tying the Perfect Square Knot: Hang a long scarf around your neck. Cross right over left, bringing that end under, up, and over the top of the other. Then in the same way, cross left over right. Adjust the knot evenly. (Confused? turn the book upside down so the scarf appears as it would around your neck!)

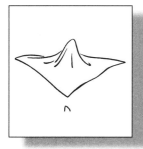   

The Perfect Ascot: Spread out a large square scarf, right side down. Grab the center and tie a small knot. Flip the scarf over, right side up, knot underneath. Tie the opposite corners behind your neck.

Here are some tips on how to tie and wear scarves:

- Lightweight scarves that flow and move lend grace to the plus-size body.

- A large square thrown around the shoulders looks great on every body type. Wear it draped over one or both shoulders for added panache or as a light wrap on a summer evening. The heavier wools are a terrific substitute for a jacket in cooler weather.

- Neck and shoulder treatments look best on the Pear and Hourglass because they balance the bottom half of the body.

The Ascot

- Long, vertical scarf treatments work best for the Rectangle and Apple bodies.

- Avoid scarf treatments that hang free-flowing off the bust (particular problems for Hourglass and Apple bodies).

● Twisted, scarves can make dandy belts or decorative headbands. Twist a small square scarf to desired width. Holding the ends, center it at the back of your head. Knot at your crown, leaving the two ends out (fluff them up), or tuck them in for a little knot effect. Give the whole scarf a turn so it's off-center.

or

● Center an oblong or large square at the back of your neck. Wrap the ends around the top of your head. Twist the ends once in front and bring them around the back of your head and tie with a square knot. You can easily turn a square into an oblong for more options: Spread it out, right side down; fold in two opposite ends, overlapping in the middle; fold the same sides in again to vary the desired width.

- Scarf clips and tubes are indispensable accessories that allow you to join the ends together without knotting—plus they're pretty!

- If a scarf isn't large enough to tie a comfortable knot, try using a rubber band. (Fluff to hide the band.)

One caution in wearing scarves: If you have a short neck or a heavy chin, a scarf may take up too much room at the neckline opening.

About Belts

Here's the best advice about belts: Find 'em, buy 'em, wear 'em—but only top quality. Most everybody can wear them in some form (except the Apple body who needs to obscure her waist as opposed to focusing attention there). Nothing polishes your look more effectively—especially the classic styles. The most flattering way to wear a belt is under an open jacket, cardigan, or big shirt. Then the full width of your waist is hidden, but the waist curve is highlighted.

Belts are a perfect example of the wisdom in choosing quality over quantity because wearing a good smooth or embossed leather belt for years will make you well dressed, not boring. It's always a good idea to replace the cheap belts that come with trousers with your own leather belt, and some-times even the fabric-covered belts attached to dresses.

If you have trouble keeping a belt at your waist, invest in a good gold chain belt which will find its own level. Remember, a wide belt is only appropriate for the long-waisted and is the most difficult for plus-size women to wear—it tends to cut us in half and emphasize our curves. The narrower the belt, the more formal the look.

Be aware that the color contrast of a dark belt on a lighter outfit (and vice versa) will create a strong horizontal line that widens your form. However, you can lengthen your torso by matching the belt to your top—or lengthen your legs by matching the belt to your trousers or skirts. Also, remember to blouse your tops gently over the fastened belt for your most attractive silhouette.

Glamorous Gloves

Gloves are some of my favorite accessories. I have an entire hatbox full of them—fuchsia, green, royal blue, navy, black, and four pairs of red ones! Living in the Northeast, I wear wrist-length (or longer) leather gloves from October until April. Encased in a somewhat heavy wool coat for that same period, colorful gloves in combination with wool scarves are the only way to brighten an outfit. I wait for the best prices at midseason sales and stock up in multiples for the two

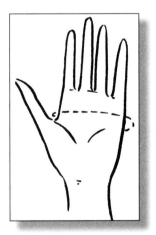

Your glove size is the same as your palm.

colors I know I'll wear out—black and red, and a new pair of driving gloves for weekend panache.

I recommend that you measure your hand around the widest part of your palm to get your size, then buy true to that number (your size is the measurement in inches). Leather stretches like crazy, so don't buy too big. If you have a large hand like I do, try the Speigel catalog for high-quality, fair-priced varieties in sizes above 8.

The best etiquette is to match your gloves to your bag, shoes, coat, or another color in your outfit.

The Best Bags

I confess I dragged around my share of briefcases, purses, and totebags before becoming enlightened. A permanently lopsided back and its associated ache have convinced me that the key to carrying the right bag for your image and your health is to carry less. I now make the extra effort every day to sort through what I need for the bag of the day, and carry only one bag—purse or briefcase or tote (I use one of my trusty ziplock baggies stuffed with makeup and other essentials inside the bag). I don't buy a lot of bags, but I insist on high quality because I think it's cheaper in the long run, and a good bag is a hallmark of quality and style. Here are some tips on choosing the best bag for you:

- The best bags are soft and not solidly structured with sharp angles. Although many good brands are out there, some women swear by Coach™ bags for quality and durability. The price is high, but the guarantee is forever. I once sent one back ten years after acquiring it to ask about repairs to the worn-out edges. It was returned to me two weeks later fully repaired, looking like new, with a personal note of apology for my inconvenience(!) and simple care tips to extend the life of the bag for another twenty years. *That's* dedication.

- Carry a bag that's in proportion to your body. A small bag will make you look larger by contrast.

- A sloppy, round, or very unstructured bag is the least complimentary for your proportions—especially if it sits on your hip where it adds to your width.

- Stay with lighter tones and neutrals in summer, darker colors in winter.

- When evaluating a bag, picture it in the context of the total outfit. Too many women buy bags that are overdecorated.

- For evening, a clutch bag is perfect—shoulder bags will tug your finery askew. Look for a slightly larger than usual formal bag.

- True elegance is matching your shoe color to your bag!

Hats

Come on, admit it, you love the panache of hats. They're glamorous, chic, often charming, sometimes even mysterious. Besides being a great way to

hide on a bad hair day, they lend height to your silhouette and a certain je ne sais quoi to your image. So if you are a little stymied by choosing the right one for your wardrobe, face, and head, here's what you need to know:

- Measure your head circumference at the center of your upper forehead, about an inch above your ears where the hat will rest. Women's hat sizes range from about 22" to 24", the average being about 22½" to 23½". Most won't be sold by size, but it helps to know if your head is small, medium, or large so that sales associates can assist you in choosing. The best advice is always to try it on—with your hair arranged the same way you intend to wear it with the hat on.

- Make sure your hat fits *gently* or you'll be wasting your money. You won't wear a hat that doesn't fit.

- Examine the actual shape and scope of the hat, don't be swayed by its ornaments.

- Straw and silk hats are worn in summer; felt in fall and winter.

- Choose a hat that you can wear with at least one outfit you already own. Everyday hats should be not too unusual, or you limit the times you can wear them.

Face-to-Face: The Face Type Guide to Eyeglass Frame Shapes, Hats, and Earrings

The Oval Face

Eyeglasses. You can support the widest variety of frame shapes. Rectangular shapes work very well, but avoid low or elaborate earpieces. Rimless usually look great on a short oval face. Be careful to choose frames that are as wide as your face, and avoid extreme cat's-eye shapes or anything that curves upward too much.

Hats. Large brims work well. Keep the brim proportionate to your height (shorter women will be flattered by smaller brims and shorter crowns).

Earrings. You have the widest selection of flattering shapes of any face. If you choose a shape on a diagonal it will call attention to your cheekbones. Avoid long dangling earrings if you wear glasses.

The Round Face

Eyeglasses. Your frames should be no wider than your face. Softly angled, squared, elliptical, or octagonal and combination shapes work well. If you choose an oval, be sure it tips up at the outer edges. Avoid repeating the shape of your face with round lenses, and don't wear overly small, thin, delicate styles like Granny or Ben Franklin or decorative or wide sidebars that emphasize your face width. Frames that enhance the cheekbones are very flattering.

Hats. A high crown and an asymmetrical brim will add to your face length.

Earrings. Choose earrings that are longer than they are wide.

The Square Face

Eyeglasses. Curved and large oval styles nicely offset your angles. Avoid square shapes that emphasize your squareness. Choose frames that are no wider than your face, but look for decorative earpieces that draw attention to your temple area. Attention should be high on the frame to give your face some lift.

Hats. Irregular brims and prominent crowns will narrow your face. Cock your hat at an angle to offset your angles.

Earrings. This face requires curved earrings that are longer than they are wide.

Eyeglass Frames

Eyeglasses are an opportunity to enhance your features and draw attention to your center of communication: your face. Image consultant and optician Dolly M. Wilson and I advise that you find a qualified, experienced fitter to help you select frames according to your prescription, face shape, personal coloring, and color preferences. The important things to remember when selecting them are:

- Frame shape and overall size should be in proportion to your face shape and overall size.
- A low or contrasting color bridge will make your nose appear shorter; a high (and clear) bridge will lengthen it.
- A clear bridge in a plastic frame will balance eyes that are small, or close together.
- If your eyes are wide set, a darker bridge may be better for balance.
- Center your eye horizontally in the middle of the lenses.
- The upper part of the frame should reflect the natural curve of your eyes and eyebrows.
- The frames should not extend above your eyebrows (double brows!).
- Eyeglass frames should balance your color patterns in skin, hair, and eyes and the intensity of the colors you most often wear. They should enhance and harmonize with your hair color but not necessarily match it.

- The lowest part of the frame should not extend down to the widest part of the nose. Frames should never cover more than one-third of your face.

- With a few exceptions, low placed earpieces will tend to drag the face down; high placed earpieces can add lift.

- Eyeglasses can emphasize dark shadows and bags under the eyes, so pay attention to your concealer. If you have either problem and wear bifocals, look for vertically narrow frames that sit above the undereye area.

- Lipstick color to balance the top and bottom halves of your face becomes more important when wearing glasses.

- Remember that lenses for nearsightedness make the eyes appear smaller, while lenses for farsightedness make the eyes appear larger. Use your makeup to balance these illusions.

- Be sure that the earpiece cuts a straight level line from the frame front back to the ear. There should always be more space below the earpiece than above.

- Avoid tinted lenses for business or wearing sunglasses inside—when people can't see your eyes they feel disconnected from you and are more likely to be suspicious or treat you less warmly. It's a sign of respect to be as open with people as possible—sunglasses close you off.

- Your earrings should not be larger than your lenses.

- Never repeat your face shape in eye frames.

The Oblong Face

Eyeglasses. Glasses often complement this face, breaking up the length and adding width. Choose a frame wider than your face, but don't cover too much cheek area. Upswept outer corners often flatter, and ovals will nearly always work well, but avoid rectangles that repeat your face shape.

Hats. Try hats with full brims to soften and widen your face. Interest at the brim will draw the eye up. Avoid tall, narrow shapes.

Earrings. Avoid long drop earrings. Choose shapes that are wider than they are long, such as round shapes, squares, fan shapes, etc.

The Heart/Diamond Face

Eyeglasses. Look for frames that are slightly smaller than the widest part of your face, but avoid a narrow-length lens. Try rectangular shapes and asymmetrical ovals with the broadest part toward the outer edge of your face, below the corner of your eyes. Look for generally thinner frames that are slightly heavier on the bottom edge, but stay away from frames that are bold. Curved shapes soften a sharp jawline, and simple eyepieces balance the width of your face.

Hats. A small hat worn high on the head will draw attention upward. Try a wide brim, but avoid overly large or tiny shapes.

Earrings. Earrings should add width to this narrow jawline. Look for shapes that are wider at the bottom than the top—like pears, teardrops, etc.

The Triangle Face

Eyeglasses. Glasses balance your bottom-heavy face. The best are slightly wider than the broadest part of your forehead, with a lower edge that curves upward and narrows. Details on the sidebars draw attention to the eyeline, away from the jawline. Rectangular shapes and cat's-eyes work well, but avoid ovals and very bold designs. Choose a thin-rimmed frame.

Hats. An upswept brim will draw attention up to the eyes, as will some small-brimmed, high-crown hats. Turbans and toques can work well.

Earrings. This face requires earrings that are longer than they are wide, worn above the jawline.

Hose and Shoes, Glorious Shoes

Who was it who said that clothes are the measure of a man? The same applies to shoes. Have you ever noticed a woman with run-down lifts? Or worse, with no lifts at all, just the frayed leather that once covered her heel, scraping along the ground as the naked metal heel spike hits the pavement with every step—*clack! clack! clack!* Not very elegant. I once read that people notice you from the ground up, ending at your eyes.

If that's true, shoe polish is a much better investment than mascara. Besides, shoes are expensive and they last much, much longer when you clean, polish, and preserve them.

Heel height is measured at the heel front.

The Ultimate Checklist— Shoes That Fit

- Shoes, like clothes, vary in size by brand. Buy what fits, not by size.

- Measure both feet. Buy shoes that fit the larger foot and ask for a pad to adjust the space in the other shoe.

- Shop for shoes late in the day or when your feet are at their widest width or most swollen.

- You should have about a half inch of space in the toe box beyond the end of your longest toe.

- The widest part of your foot should fall at the widest part of the shoe or they will wear unevenly right from the start.

- If the shoe gaps when you walk they're probably too wide.

- If your feet force the sides of the shoes to extend beyond the soles, you need a wider width.

- Except for minis, your skirt should cover the top of a boot.

The key to shoes are finding ones that fit but flatter. The American Academy of Orthopedic Surgeons reports that more than 43 million Americans have trouble with their feet, usually from wearing the wrong size shoes! In their recent study, they found that 88 percent of a group of 356 women evaluated wore shoes smaller than their feet. Another study shows that 64 percent of those who gained weight had an increase in shoe size. In fact, most of us go

- If the shoes slip off your heel when you walk or stand up on tiptoe, they are too wide in the heel for your foot. If the problem is minor, a special pad may fix your heel in place.
- For the most comfortable, coolest shoes, look for leather lining (and preferably suede quarter lining for the heel), and leather soles as well as uppers.
- Heel balance is critical. When standing in a shoe, the heel should feel firm under your foot, not wobbly or off center. If the shoe isn't comfortable after standing for a few minutes, it definitely won't be comfortable when walking.
- A "rolled topline" (the joining of the outside leather and inside lining) that starts an eighth of an inch inside the shoe is indicative of good quality, good fit, and comfort.
- The shorter you are, the shorter your foot, the shorter the heel.
- Choose natural materials for the upper.
- The most flattering dress style is the traditional pump with a U- or V-shaped vamp.

up in shoe size as we age. When was the last time you measured your feet?

Experts recommend you buy for fit, not for size. Since, like clothes, there are no uniform size standards for shoes, fit is relative. The best way to get the right size is to be fit with the proper instrument at a shoe store. Or, measure your foot yourself by outlining it on a piece of paper; cut it out to take shopping with you.

In addition to size, it's important that your shoes are in proportion to your body. If they're too small or too big, you risk looking like a cartoon. Generally you're safe with a 2-inch heel that isn't too narrow or too wide. Even your flats will look better with a little bit of a heel—say, $\frac{1}{2}$–1 inch. Remember that the shorter you and your feet are, the shorter your heel height should be to keep you in balance.

Larger women should avoid heel straps, Mary Jane straps, and other high-vamp styles that close up the foot with a horizontal line. The more traditional V- or U-shaped vamp opens up the space on the top of the foot and presents an unbroken line from the leg all the way down, which will make your legs look longer and more graceful.

Be cautious with strappy sandals, which are hard for any foot to wear. Little piggy toes poking through the straps at odd angles are downright unappealing, and the small straps may be out of balance with your larger body. Also, before you opt for sling-backs (a much more formal and sexy look than pumps), be sure to check the rear view. Pudgy heels might be better off in closed pumps.

Boots are finally being offered for wider feet and calves. There are two things to keep in mind to flatter the larger woman: Always wear your skirts or pants long enough to cover the tops of your boots, and remember that the thicker and heavier the sole, the more informal the boot.

The very best advice for flattering your legs and feet with the longest possible line is to match the tones of your hemline, your hose, and your shoes. For business, shoes should be the same color as your hemline or darker, never lighter. Hose should be the same shade as your shoes or lighter, not darker. Avoid excessive contrast, which breaks up your leg.

Hose

Of course you know that darker colors will slim the leg, but the most flattering look is one single color or shades of the same color from hem to toe. This is the rule of hose for appropriate dressing: *Hose must be a nude shade, or the same shade as your shoes or lighter, never darker.* Avoid too much contrast. If your skirt is a bright color like red or blue, wear nude or match your hose color to your shoes. Black is usually a good choice.

Pay attention to the hose you wear with pants, too! Remember that light-colored hose at the bottom of a dark pantleg (and vice versa) will cut you off short, and draw attention to your feet. You will look taller and slimmer in hose that match the hemline.

Opaque and most textured hose are for winter wear only. Stay with lighter shades and textures in the warmer months.

Socks go only with trousers. Period.

Never wear hose with runs. Period.

As with all clothes, choose the size that fits, not the one that flatters the ego—even with the latest advances in micro-fiber technology, there is nothing worse than a tight pair of pantyhose.

Whether you're looking for a classic set of pearl earrings, need to get a new pair of glasses, or have found that perfect hat, think of your accessories as the punctuation for the conversation your clothes are having with the world.

Makeup Magic Made Simple

The Magic of Makeup

Makeup should redirect attention to where it does the most for you. Think of cosmetics as you would eyeglasses that bring you into focus for the rest of the world. Likewise makeup should help you look better, but some of us like to look better more dramatically, and some want to look better more softly.

The ultimate beauty goal is to bring your features into a pleasing balance that highlights your eyes and your hair, and counterbalances your larger body, not to reconstruct your face cosmetically or otherwise.

If you invest a few minutes to apply a little makeup the right way you can make a big improvement in your overall image and positively affect the way the world interprets you. Dark under-eye circles, for instance, tend to draw the onlooker's gaze away from the

> *"Hold short services for minor gods."*
>
> NEPALESE PROVERB

eyes, which are central to the expression of our individual beauty and our personality. The wrong lip color or a heavy mustache can also redirect the eye or
throw the balance off. Likewise, if you choose strong makeup colors that are
out of fashion and that don't play up your assets, you're expending energy
needlessly. Why bother, when you could skip it altogether and get more sleep,
which would probably do more to enhance your beauty than wearing your
hair and makeup wrong. Why go to the effort to apply makeup that doesn't
improve your looks?

What Every Woman Wants to Know

The important lesson, of course, is that the purpose of makeup is to
enhance, not detract. As in dressing, you have to look at the overall effect
you're making instead of looking at features or colors one at a time. When you
think about it, we're lucky to have the options of camouflage and enhance-
ment to help us improve our appearance and highlight our assets. A little too
much and you look obvious and not at all improved; too little, and you miss
out on the opportunity to look your best. The outcome is all that matters, and
you don't want your makeup to send out the wrong messages and undo all
you've achieved with your voice, your body language, your clothes, and your
hair. This is the golden rule of makeup application: *If you* affect *a change,*
make sure the effect *is pleasing.*

Cosmetic questions rank among the top three things women want to know
more about. But some of us feel badly about getting to the age of twenty or
thirty or forty or more, and still not really knowing how to use makeup to

achieve the best look for us, or feel a little shallow for focusing on something so, well, *female*. Relax. Anybody can learn to work with makeup—and nobody says you have to spend a lot of time on your face every morning in order to look presentable. It just takes a little practice and a little patience.

Get Your Look

The best advice is to get lessons from an expert. Since makeup is an interpretive, or subjective art, you may need several opinions, but the basics are easy and the investigation could be fun. Think of it this way: You'll make a significant investment of time, money, energy, and pride in purchasing and using cosmetics in your lifetime. Every woman cares about her appearance because, like it or not, the world judges us on it. Simply put, you are worth the investment of time and patience, even if you choose less expensive products. So learn from the best how to achieve your best look. You'll have greater control over the superficial judgments the world will make about you.

Go to one of the exclusive makeup counters in the department stores and ask for a makeover from their most knowledgeable artist/sales associate. Make an appointment with Christian Dior (who does great training for their associates), Chanel, Lancôme, Clinique, or one of the other high-end companies. MAC (a professional line just getting into department stores in major cities) also teaches seminars on makeup and will give you private, thorough lessons with a professional artist for a small fee. Some of the companies offer special promotions a couple of times a year using professional makeup artists—theirs or an independent artist. If you get a chance for a consultation with a professional, grab it. Plan to do this at least three times with three different artists before you make a major investment in products. Get the technique first—ask questions, take notes, get them to write down what they used (colors, shades) first, second, third, etc., and *why.*

Before you sit down with any of these artists/sales associates, be honest. Tell them that you want to learn the best look for you, but that you won't be making a purchase immediately because you need to walk around with the makeup on your face to see how it feels and how your skin will react. Tell them that if you like the look and feel at the end of the day, you'll consider a purchase. Even experienced, talented, knowledgeable, nonfashion-oriented women may do this once or twice a year to keep up with the latest looks and color palettes. Besides, it's fun.

Makeup Must-Haves

If you're like most women, you want to get the most improvement in your appearance in the least amount of time. You don't want to spend a lot of time at the mirror every day, nor should you. Fortunately makeup has improved a lot in the last few years, so products are easier than ever to work with. *Here are the things you absolutely must own, if nothing else:*

- *A good mascara* that won't smudge off. Brunettes should choose black; blondes and redheads should wear brown. Many in-the-know women use supermarket brands; others can't live without brands that cost fifteen dollars or more. It's up to you—find one that goes on easily and comes off when you want it to.

- *The right oil-free foundation for your skin tone.* If you buy them pre-wrapped in the drugstore you won't know if they match until you get them home. Shop around at a department store or beauty supply store that will help you test them. The experts blend them on the spot for the perfect color, but you'll have to just keep looking until you find a brand just right for you. You must test foundation at the jawline to know if the color is right. Check this in *natural* light. *Key: Sheer is better.*

- *Concealer in the same shade as or just a half tone lighter than your skin.* Avoid concealer that's too light or too pink or you can get the opposite effect you're looking for.

- *Blush color in your natural shade.* What color do your cheeks turn when you blush deeply? That's the color you should choose, but avoid one that's too dark. Take care to select one that's warm if you are warm, a cooler color if your skin tone is cool. (Hint: Pink is cool; peach is warm.) If you want, another lighter, more delicate color on top of your natural deep blush can look great—done well.

- *Eyebrow powder or pencil to match your hair color.* Eyebrow powder is very natural, but best if you use a clear mascara over it to "set" it. If you choose pencil be sure it's sharpened to a fine point. Some professionals swear by supermarket brands.

- *Eye pencil to line lids.* Brown, taupe, smoky gray-blue, work on most. Choose black if you have very dark hair and eyes.

- *A couple of complementary shades of eye shadow* (soft brown, taupe, or smoky gray-blue) *for the crease,* and *a light shade* (palest pink or cream, etc.) *for accent* in smooth, pigment-rich formulas. (African-American women need to be cautious choosing very light shades—you want to avoid an overly "powdery" look.) Never try to match eye shadow to your eye color or the color of your clothes. It's *shadow*. Use it that way. If you're over sixteen, avoid iridescent eyeshadow because it emphasizes skin imperfections.

- *Lip pencil.* Match your lipstick or get one just a half tone darker—not too dark! Some of the best I've tried sell at the drugstore for under $3.

- *Translucent face powder—loose or pressed.* Some like it expensive, some like it cheap. I like it oil-free, without a heavy scent, in a natural sheer shade. Rice powder is a good option.

- *Makeup sponges.* Buy them by the bag cheaply at drugstores and beauty-supply stores. Ideally you should have two kinds: the little triangles to apply and blend most everything, and the large, round powder-puff type in foam or velour for loose and pressed powder.

- *Eyelash curler.* Don't forget to change the little rubber liners occasionally. Cover Girl and Maybelline are popular choices.

- *Good-quality natural-hair makeup brushes.* The best natural sable, badger, squirrel, goat, and pony hair brushes will be gentle on your delicate eye skin and hold the powder well, and not retain bacteria-breeding moisture. (If makeup sponges or brushes remain moist they provide a perfect breeding ground for bacteria. Keep yours clean and dry.) The brushes you should have are: powder brush, blush brush, angled eye-shadow brush, fluffy shadow brush, lip brush, eyelash comb, a baby toothbrush for eyebrows, and a velour powder puff. Don't scrimp here. Buy top quality and you'll have them for a lifetime. *Resources:* Nordstrom's own S.A.N.E. brand, MAC, Shiseido, Body Shop, Chanel, Il Makiage, Bobbi Brown Cosmetics, Shu Uemura Cosmetics, others at quality beauty-supply stores, etc.

- *Tweezers.* Use the style most comfortable for you, but clean them with alcohol after every use.

- *Pencil sharpener.* Try metal duos with openings for two different-size pencils. Clean them thoroughly as well.

Seven Minutes to Your Best Face: A Routine You Can Live With

If you have seven minutes—and you can't argue that seven minutes will throw off your schedule—here are the basics:

- Working with a lightly moistened makeup sponge, apply a *very sheer* coat of foundation over your face to even your skin tones, blending into the neckline.

- Lightly enhance your eyebrows with powder or an eyebrow pencil. This step is very important. Eyebrows define your face and "anchor" your lip color.

- Line your upper eyelids very lightly with a brown or taupe-color eye pencil.

- Brush some translucent powder over your whole face with a very large, fluffy brush. (If you use powder foundation, skip this step.)
- Apply a little bit of blush.
- Apply mascara to your upper and lower eyelashes.
- Line your lips with a pencil that is just a half shade darker or more intense than your natural lip color, then lightly fill them in. (This is especially key for older women to prevent lipstick from "bleeding" into the creases.)

If you get good at this, you can add the following step and still meet the seven-minute deadline:

- With your eyes open, add a little light brown, dark gray, or taupe-color eye shadow at the outer corner of your eyes in a small V shape—to emphasize the crease. Use a lighter color on the lid and brow bone for highlight. (Avoid creme eye shadows which turn to nasty oil slicks in the creases.) Blend with a small, fluffy brush. Follow with mascara.

Also, right after applying foundation you can add a step to disguise skin imperfections and dark circles with a little concealer. But keep it concentrated just on the needed area. If your eyes are more intense, wear your lips less intense, and vice versa. If you do both, your look may be much stronger than you intended.

That's it. That's all you need to enhance your features.

Some women can do it in under five minutes, some a little longer. But if you spend more than about ten minutes, you're probably doing it wrong or you're doing too much.

Technique

You will need practice to get it right. Let me repeat that: You will need practice to get it right. But make sure you don't wear your practice face in public! Think of your practice time as skill development, like learning to type. I have total faith that with a little research, the right products, and some practice, you will be beautiful.

Foundation and Concealer: Start with a Prepared Canvas

Good skin care not only preserves the color and texture of your skin for the future, it sets up the best surface for makeup application. First, start with clean, lightly moisturized skin. (If your moisturizer doesn't disappear into your skin in two minutes, you've put too much on and it needs to be blotted.) I always do my makeup in my underwear because powder has a way of getting away from me, and it stains!

The trick to liquid foundation is to dab dots around your face—forehead, cheeks, chin, nose, etc. Using a clean, slightly moistened makeup sponge, blend the dots. (If you mist the sponge with a water bottle you can control how wet it is—but be careful to use only fresh water or you add bacteria to your face.) For creamy foundations or combo powder foundation compacts,

The Ultimate Beauty Tip: *The less makeup you can use to achieve your best look the better.*

213

you want to apply just enough to cover the face in a sheer layer. Avoid the Kabuki mask look—it ages you.

Contrary to what you may think, less is more with foundation, especially with the new formulations. Once upon a time you might have needed more, but not now. The idea with foundation is to even out skin tones, not to white-out the skin. Pancake is rarely even used for TV anymore, so you certainly don't need it for walking around! Professional artists say that you should use just enough for light coverage, and no more.

Some women hate foundation because it irritates their skin. I urge you to try a few before giving up. These days there are water-based, oil-based, and everything in between. Dermatologists recommend oil-free or water-based foundations that don't clog up your pores, or sweat and oil glands.

To hide imperfections you can use a little concealer. Work with your make-up sponge and dab just a little, then blend, blend, blend. The trick to concealer is to use it only on the blemish or dark area, not as a base, and to blend by blotting with a sponge, or if you don't have one, your ring finger (your weakest finger).

To set liquid or semiliquid foundation, dip your large powder brush into loose powder, and shake off the excess. Brush your face in short, downward strokes. This gets all the little facial hairs lined up the right way.

I happen to have smooth, even skin with a few broken capillaries from sun damage as a kid. I like to use some of the dual powder/foundation compacts. But if you use them, I find that once you get them wet it's hard to get them to loosen up to use dry. So I keep one for each. A word of caution here: Some of these products are very drying, so use them sparingly—especially around the eyes. I've learned to keep them away from the undereye area or the powder shows off every line and crease! Otherwise, they're terrifically easy and fast, and a cinch to carry with you in your bag for touch-ups.

Pencil-Perfect Eyes

When using pencils, be sure to sharpen them a little before each use to get the bacteria and dust off, then wipe them on a tissue when you're done. Don't press too hard on delicate skin. If they don't go on smoothly, the formulation might be a little too stiff for your skin and you might want to find a softer brand. But to loosen them slightly, warm them in your hand before you sharpen the tip.

To draw the best line around your eyes, get down into the lash line, and use short, light strokes—don't try to draw a single, straight line nonstop. If your skin is without lines and creases, you can line the outer third of your lower lashes very lightly also, then smudge with a cotton swab, thin eyeliner brush, or your ring finger. For a soft look, invest in a flat eyeliner brush and use shadow for liner. (The darker your hair, the darker your eyeliner can be.)

A word of caution: A hard line of eyeliner under the eye will age you by calling attention to the skin under the eye. It also tends to close in versus open up the eye—which is what you want, right? Before any woman incorporates under-eye liner into her routine, I encourage her to do one eye with, one eye without, and compare. If you must use it, be sure to make it a smudgy, soft line—never a hard, dark, straight edge. *Never, ever* line the inside of your eye .

Lips

For lips, use a soft line to define the edge and prevent lipstick from "bleeding." Look straight into the mirror to draw the line, then turn your face up and down and side to side to see how the shifting light looks on the edge. Lip edges define the angle between the smooth plane of the face and the curve of the lip, so they create their own shadow line by breaking the flow of light. Is the line natural looking? Try connect-the-dots rather than attempting a solid line in one continuous motion.

Eyelashes

To apply mascara right, be sure you don't have any globs on the wand when you pull it out of the tube (wipe them off on a tissue if you do). Holding it like a pencil can help, but go with whatever is comfy for you. Stroke evenly from the base of the lashes to the ends. Go lightly over the lower lashes—some women use the wand straight on, others use just the tip. My friend Debra's favorite trick is to fold a tissue over and place it up against the lower lid just under the lower lashes so if she presses too hard with the wand on those little lashes it hits the tissue and not the delicate undereye skin (which has to be treated very gently at all times—especially when removing makeup).

When dry, run an eyelash comb through your lashes to separate the little hairs. I've actually seen women try to do this with a *pin*! Please don't use this method. My dad always told me the key to doing anything well is to use the right tool for the job, and whether you're painting a house or putting on makeup, it's still great advice. Be careful with your eyes.

Eyeshadow

The very best eyeshadow is pigment-rich powder that goes on smoothly, retains its color, and stays in place all day. Learning to use good brushes is critical to achieving a professional look and keeping your makeup fresh for hours. (Those little sponge applicators can't apply powder smoothly and evenly like a brush, and they tend to hold onto moisture, which is a breeding ground for bacteria.) Hold your makeup brush like a pencil and "draw" with it, using the same delicate motions you use to write on paper.

Remember that wherever you place your brush first will be the strongest point of color. As is the case with all powders, start with a little, and add more if you need to.

Eyebrows

Kevin Aucoin, the most well-known make-up artist of today, says that changing brows is the most significant thing a woman can do to her face, short of having a face-lift. Don't ignore yours. Brush them upward and fill in or extend them with short, quick strokes of a pencil. If you have to shape them, pluck only from underneath, eliminating stray hairs. Mom was right—they don't always grow back, so be

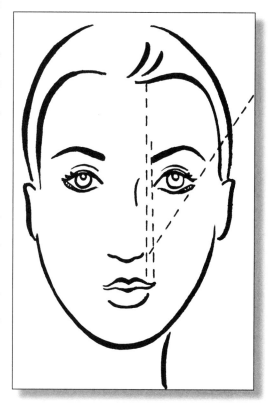

The Perfectly Proportioned Eyebrow

cautious. It's worth it to have a professional shape them once, then you can manage maintenance yourself.

The brow should begin at a point about even with the inner edge of your eye. The peak of the arch should more or less line up with your pupil. To judge where the brow should end, lay a pencil diagonally between the corner of your nose and the outer corner of your eye. The upper end of the pencil will hit your brow bone at the best point for your eyebrow to end.

If you lighten your hair, your eyebrows should be a little lighter, too. A dark brow on a blonde may look dramatic, but it can also look unpolished. This is important for ladies over sixty who may be getting naturally lighter or turning gray. You must always update the colors you wear on your face to stay in tune with the changes in your coloring. As we women age, our estrogen level drops and we become "cooler" in coloring. Even if you were once very flattered by very warm-based colors, you need to reevaluate how they look on you every few years.

Cheeks

Find your cheekbones by gently feeling down with your fingertips from your eyes to the center of your cheek. The bone runs under your eye and ends about even with the tip of your nose. Place blush *just under that bone*, starting with the center of the bone directly beneath your eyes. Blend up and out in short, light strokes. Cheek color selection is critical for most African-American women. You are generally more flattered by reds, pinks, and burgundy shades than by more orange tones.

Contouring

Every makeup and image book I've ever read has pages and pages of text accompanied by beautifully illustrated images of how and where to contour the face to make it look: more slim, more oval, more angular, more *something*. Bah humbug! You are whatever face shape you are, and all the contour powder in the world won't change it. If you pressed me I would tell you that with skill you can minimize the effect of a double chin by applying a darker foundation and powder around the edge of the chin area, and to narrow a very wide nose you can use a little darker makeup along the sides. But the truth is that contouring works in photography where you get to manipulate lighting and focus attention; it doesn't really work that well in person. For the most part, you'll be far more successful working with your natural looks, not against them.

General Genius

All makeup should start lightly and build in intensity, coverage, and color. It's harder to take cosmetics off the face than it is to add them.

This is the key to all makeup: If your natural skin, hair, and eye color is more intense, your makeup can be, too. If you are lighter or less intense, you should wear your makeup lighter in coverage, intensity, and value (light vs. dark).

This is also key: The first place you touch down with a color-laden brush is the point of color intensity. Keep the concentration of color on the outer corner of the eye and at the apple of the cheek.

Touchups

No woman I know wants to run around checking and redoing her make-up constantly. If you feel compelled to add pencil, blusher, concealer, mascara, etc., throughout the day, chances are you are responding less to reality than to the auto pilot in your mind that's telling you you're not good enough.

 # Makeup Do's and Don'ts:

- Do put your makeup on in sunlight—or at least do the final check in sunlight. This is critical because different light sources actually change the apparent color of makeup—and objects.
- Do use a lighted, magnified makeup mirror.
- Do put your makeup on while undressed or wearing something white so that color doesn't reflect back onto your face and obscure your perspective.
- Do try to use real cotton balls instead of synthetics.
- Remember, the darker your hair and eyes, the darker your eye makeup can be.
- Blend, blend, blend.
- Blend up, not down.
- Keep makeup within the perimeter of the eye and brow lines.
- Use sponges.
- Less is more.
- Your objective: shiny hair, matte makeup.

Hit the pause button.... If you do it right the first time, the only thing your make-up needs through the day is a little lipstick and some powder—unless you decide to head out for a hot date and want to turn up the intensity. But frankly, if you wear colors too intense or draw lines that are too dark, you risk looking outrageous, unfeminine, or "hard." Go with a little brighter lipstick and a tad more blush for an evening out, and you're lovely.

Tip: *On the go? Baby wipes are great as make-up removers—non-greasy, disinfecting, unscented.*

Biggest Makeup Mistakes Women Make:

- Ungroomed eyebrows. Brush them up, fill them in, extend the line to the right point or pluck it back.

- Ignoring facial hair. Bleach your upper lip to lighten your mustache, or remove it with wax—quick, easy, effective for weeks. Many hair and nail salons offer this service at a very reasonable rate. When finished with your makeup, brush translucent powder over your whole face with a large brush *in a downward direction* to redirect all your face hairs in their natural path.

- Selecting the wrong shade of foundation for your complexion. Test it on your jawline to find the right shade. This also prevents that nasty make-up line where your face and neck meet.

- *Too Much Makeup.* Less is always more—especially in foundation. Blend, blend, blend.

- Not curling eyelashes. Curling makes them look longer, more prominent, and gives you a little lift.

- Overdrawing the lip line by more than a *smidgen.*

- Wearing iridescent eye shadow. Unless you are flawless, it will emphasize every little imperfection.

- Rimming the inside of the eyelid with color. This actually closes in the eye—I promise!

- Wearing eye shadow the same color as your eyes. Actually, browns for warmer skin tones and grays or cool browns for cooler skin tones will work just fine. You really don't need a lot of shadow, you've just seen too many cosmetic company ads.

Skin Care

Beautiful skin is more important to real beauty than any makeup or cosmetic you can buy—and it's really, really painful to replace, so you should take care of it. Dermatologists tell us that sun exposure is much more damaging to our skin than anything else we do or don't do, and more critical than our natural genetic makeup (pardon the pun). Dr. Setrag Zacarian, internationally renowned dermatologist and pioneering cancer specialist, advises that nearly all the wrinkles, lines, creases, or folds we see after a certain age are attributable to sun damage, so sunscreen is essential all the time, starting when we're babies.

The first step to beautiful skin is to drink at least eight glasses of pure water (not soda, not juice, not tea) a day. In addition, you need to gently clean and moisturize your skin to keep it looking and feeling good—and to create the best surface for your makeup. "Water," Dr. Zacarian reports, "is the universal moisturizer. Using a simple, over-the-counter skin moisturizer (with a sunscreen) after you bathe locks the moisture into your skin." Actually, the outer layer of the epidermis is composed of dead skin cells, which are shed continuously. So a moisturizer softens the dead-skin surface layer, giving it a smoother look.

Here's what you should do to keep your skin at its absolute best now and in the future:

- Take off your makeup before bed or you irritate your skin and eyes, and give bacteria a fertile breeding ground!

- Use a gentle cleanser or mild beauty-bar soap twice a day. If your skin is very sensitive or dry, you can use a mild lotion or cream like Cetifilin. All soaps and cleansers have the same function, which is to clean off the excess oil, dirt, dust, etc. (As you get older, the skin gets more fragile and dry because your oil glands secrete less, so use cooler water and don't scrub.) Whatever kind of product you choose should remove eye make-up and everything else in one step. Some very savvy ladies have been happily using Dove for years.

- If you have oily skin, you can use a simple low-alcohol toner to remove excess cleanser, help exfoliate the skin, and (theoretically) set it up to absorb the moisturizer. If your skin isn't oily, a toner is optional. Use clean 100 percent cotton balls, and stroke up—not down.

- Apply a light moisturizer with an SPF (sunscreen protection factor) of at least 15 to your damp skin (damp is key—if you want to trap as much moisture in the dermis as possible). If your favorite one doesn't contain sunscreen you can spray your face with sunscreen first. (See your drug counter for pure sunscreen.)

- Before bed, clean your face and apply an Alpha Hydroxy Acid creme. These magical fruit-based formulas work a little mysteriously, but constantly, to help the skin speed up the replacement of surface cells with healthy young things—a process that tends to slow with age. Try Alpha Hydrox, Clinique's Turnaround Creme, Estée Lauder Fruition, Avon's Anew, etc., *and* a heavier moisturizer (unless the product is both an AHA *and* a moisturizer). Special eye creams are a great idea, but AHA cremes are the best thing to happen to skin care since artificial detergents replaced lye in soap. They speed up the replacement of dead skin cells at the surface of your skin, make it look softer and younger, and can reduce uneven skin color and smooth out its texture. Need I say more?

Facials? Some women swear by them; others have beautiful skin without ever experiencing the luxury. Personally I think they feel great, but hands that are less than professional stir up my skin and make me break out. If you have skin eruptions, very oily skin, or unusual skin challenges, see a dermatologist for advice rather than spending time and money on questionable treatments that could do more harm than good. (Your dermatologist can prescribe wonderful products available only by prescription.) Remember, masks and facials can't do anything to permanently add moisture to your skin or otherwise change it substantially. Moisture is water, which comes and goes—and can be sealed in only temporarily by the right moisturizer.

There are a whole range of new treatments and procedures available that really can make a discernible difference in reducing the signs of aging—lines, creases, uneven coloration, and dry patches of skin. Over the counter, Dr.

Zacarian recommends the daily use of an Alpha Hydroxy Acid creme. If your skin is irritated by the formula you try, you may need a weaker concentration (read the label), or simply a different brand. Good news—the drugstore brands work every bit as well as the more expensive ones.

Retin A, chemical peels, and other new treatments can make you look years younger and are terrific for treating acne as well as evening out your skin color and texture and reducing superficial wrinkles. As with other treatments and many drugs (including some antibiotics), Retin A will make you photo toxic—you'll burn like crazy, without tanning, in sunlight. So careful! They're not for every face, and shouldn't be taken lightly. Consult your doctor, who has these treatments and others to deal with pigmentation irregularities, unevenness, wrinkles, and other problems (like broken capillaries, which can be easily fixed with electrodessication—a treatment using a mild electrical current or laser).

Demon Sun

The most important skin care issue is sun damage. Those little brown spots that develop on your skin aren't from age, they're from sun exposure. While they generally aren't cancerous, they are harbingers of concern for the state of your skin generally. These "tingenes" are more prevalent on lighter-skinned people. Actually, Dr. Zacarian warns, the lighter the color of your skin, hair, and eyes, the more you need to be concerned about sun damage. Tinted glass in cars and in buildings doesn't guarantee protection from the ultraviolet rays, either, so you should always wear a PABA-based SPF (Sun Protection Formula) of about 15 under your makeup. Be sure to apply the sunscreen before you head out into the sun to let it absorb into the skin layers, and reapply often if you plan to be in direct sunlight on the golf course, at the beach, etc. If you're one of the 10 percent allergic to PABA, look for one of the PABA-free formulas.

About Nails: And Now, Another Word from My Soapbox...

Your hands are an expressive part of your communication. You should keep them groomed and trimmed. Chipped nail polish is an even bigger no-no than run-down heels! Some plus-size women like to grow their nails long and paint them bright colors, hoping it will help them feel more feminine. They want their hands to appear longer, more delicate and slender, but they may create the opposite effect. Bright polishes and unusual ornaments accentuate your full-figured fingers. Nails that are longer than about half the length of your nail bed are way too long to be chic, especially if you are in business. People won't take you seriously. Decorated nails may be works of art, but they rank right up there with paintings on velvet—they are never seen as a class act. You will always look well turned out and be socially acceptable in every circle with a sheer light polish or a "French" manicure.

While it's true that nail wraps with silk and acrylic allow you

Tip: *I pull the silica gel packets out of my empty vitamin pill bottles and throw them in my travel cosmetics bag to keep it free from bacteria-breeding, makeup-melting moisture.*

to wear your nails at any length, you must be careful to maintain them or water can get underneath and cause fungus problems that are very difficult to cure. Over time these artificial surfaces can affect your natural nail bed and weaken your own nails substantially.

You can strengthen your nails with several new products that really do make a difference over time (but a patch test is essential; if you are allergic to any of these you can't wear them): Avon Strong Results, Nailtiques, Develop 10, Mystic Nails, others. The best thing you can do to grow stronger nails is to preserve your cuticles and never cut them! Just like my high-school cheer— push 'em back, push 'em back, way back!... And of course, moisturize, moisturize, moisturize those hands. I have tiny tubes of hand cream in the car, at my desk, next to my bed, and at every sink. You may think it's silly, but I've had manicurists compliment me on my soft, smooth skin. Water weakens nails, so use rubber gloves for chores.

Feet? You must! The best way to take care of calluses is to file them down with a pumice stone or foot file. Shaving is useless since it makes them grow thicker. For a real treat get yourself a professional pedicure once a month or so, but be sure to ask for clean tools (and if you must shave your calluses, demand a fresh blade). Better still, get your own tools and take them with you each time. Don't allow the operator to cut your nails too short (especially at the edge) or you risk cutting into the cuticle. Infections are nasty on your toes.

Arguably, one of the best things in life is a foot massage, and there's no better way to keep your tootsies moisturized and soft!

hair!

Size Doesn't Matter, Darlin'——Really

What's the line about the crowning glory of a woman? For us, it's true. Brains and beautiful hair are possible no matter the size of the body. But the perceived size of the body is definitely affected by the shape and size of the hair! To balance these larger bodies it's necessary to pay closer attention to face shape and body proportions in determining the right hairstyles. Studies show that while people notice you from the feet up, they *remember* you from the top down. If you want people to remember you fondly and remember you in proportion, remember your hair. Drama attracts the eye, so you have the opportunity to use your hair to make a bolder, more elegant, more chic, more *whatever* statement than your body.

> "*Begin with an error of an inch and end by being a thousand miles off the mark.*"
>
> CHINESE PROVERB

Above all, your hairstyle should flatter you, be easy to care for, and reflect your personality and style—just like your clothes. Most plus-size women look better in hairstyles that add a little volume or height across the width of their head at the crown. Everything depends on your body/head/hair ratio, but generally you want to *choose a hairstyle shape that is in harmony with, but does not exactly repeat the shape of your face or body.*

My talented hairdresser, Julian Petrocelli, cuts and coifs many famous heads quietly and beautifully. Who knows how much public confidence is created by those hands? He does!

Julian's top ten hair do's and don'ts for plus-size women:

1. *Do wear your hair above your shoulders.* Wearing your hair longer than shoulder length creates a single mass silhouette with your head, neck, and shoulders running into your body. The best lengths are about a half inch above your shoulders or shorter, which adds neck length.

The exceptions: If, on a regular basis, you wear your hair swept off your face with height on top, as in a French twist; or in a Gibson Girl–type arrangement with the hair piled softly on top of the head with falling tendrils around the face.

2. *Do try to create a little hair volume.* Don't pull your hair back in a severe ponytail or knot. This places tremendous emphasis on facial size and the proportions of the face and head to the rest of the body, thereby creating the "pinhead" effect.

3. *Do wear your hair in a style that works for your hair type.* Geometry counts! If your hair is curly, a good cut is essential to balance your natural roundness with some angularity. The round "halo" effect is not flattering to a full face because the round curls, the round cut, and the rounded face reinforce each other. Wavy hair, on the other hand, is easier to work into a wide variation of shapes and 'dos, since it can be coaxed into curls or straightened relatively easily.

Stick-straight hair requires special attention. You need a good cut to establish some volume in the right places for your face shape, or you may want to consider a body wave for a little lift, but don't wear your hair one length without bangs, layers, etc. This is difficult for any woman to wear well, but if you have a full face that requires definition, it simply won't flatter you. Shorter to longer layers that frame the face are a better idea.

The exceptions: If you back-comb (or tease) the top for added height, and wear a headband; if you pull the front sections of hair off or away from your face artfully with combs or barrettes.

4. *Do keep most of your hair off your face.* Don't try that short pixie haircut with the hair brushed forward, toward, or onto your face and forehead. Although I see this recommended in a lot of how-to books, this look makes even a thin face look full and tends to squash all your features together. Whatever the style—long, short, medium—a fuller face will always be more enhanced by hair directed up, off, and away. Generally, wearing it with a little height on top and directing it up and back away from the temples works well.

5. *Do keep your hair in proportion to your body and head.* Don't try to overcompensate for your size with hair that's *too big.* Big hair doesn't always dwarf what's underneath it, and it can wreak as much havoc with your head and body silhouette as its opposite—the pulled-back, pinhead look. Big hair also calls attention to a large hip/derriere by making your shoulders look small! So don't hide under your hair—it's not camouflage.

6. *Do wear styles that frame the face without closing it in.* Don't wear full bangs that can square or close off a full face and make it look even more full. Wear your bangs wispy or brushed to one side.

7. *Do take the time to style your hair on a daily basis.* Sadly, people do judge a book by its cover, and as the odds may already be stacked against you for being larger in size, it's imperative that hair and makeup be perfect. Some people are born with great hair, but most are not. If color or body wave will enhance your skin tone or hair texture, do it! If your hair needs the aid of rollers or a curling iron, use them! If you're not adept at styling your hair or using tools to achieve the look you want, schedule one or more appointments with your hairdresser for styling instruction. Persevere until you get the hang of it.

8. *Do find a hairstylist you can relate to and whose style sense you trust.* If you're not connecting with your hair professional, chances are you're not going to come out looking your best. Cultivate a rapport and together experiment with your hair to come up with your best style and look. There are exceptions to every rule of matching hair shape and face shape, and they are all affected by your body type, your neck length, your personality, your hair type, etc., so you need to be able to work together to find the real you.

9. *Do take some chances with your hair and embrace change.* No one should be sentenced to the same hairstyle for life! You, your hair, and the fashions of the times change constantly, so you will need to rethink your style and color periodically, too. As you get older your skin tone changes, and if you're coloring your hair you may need a slightly different shade. If you don't ask, the colorist may just stick to the color formula in your file.

10. *Do communicate your style preferences to the hairdresser.* Show up at your first few hair appointments (until he or she gets to know you) wearing clothes that are indicative of your style personality and how you spend most of your time. Tell your hairdresser about what you do for a living and how you see yourself, and about how much time and skill you are capable of putting into your daily hair routine.

Working with a Stylist

To find a new stylist, Julian suggests you look for another woman with a cut that you like, and find out who her stylist is. Or, he says, interview stylists at recommended salons and see what they suggest for you. For African-American women this is particularly important, since working with black hair takes special skills that are not common to every stylist. A word of caution: If stylists are sitting around with nothing to do, waiting for customers to come through the door, you should keep walking. Your hair and your image deserve the best cut and color, so find a good stylist who's in demand.

Kim Lépine, Madison Avenue hairstylist extraordinaire and owner of the very chic Kim Lépine salon in New York, advises that when choosing a stylist or colorist you visit the salon prior to your appointment to see if you relate to the person and the environment. If you don't have a referral, talk to the receptionist about which stylist would be right for your kind of hair, and ask who they recommend in your price range. If you're comfortable, make an appointment.

Occasionally, the beauty magazines like *Allure*, *Elle*, *Self*, and others will do a story on the top stylists and colorists in each market across the country. They do use references for proof of results, so if you can get an appointment with a professional they have positively reviewed, go for it! (The problem will be getting to them early enough to get an appointment. When someone is included in a story like that their phone usually rings like crazy, so don't delay—and save the article in case they are booked up for a few months. You might get to see them down the road when all the hoopla dies down.)

Freebies and Other Secrets

Julian points out that going to the salon-of-the-moment doesn't always get you the time and attention of the best talent, so ask about a person's experience, training, etc. If you can't afford the best salon but are interested in making a big change in your haircut or coloring, you may be a good model for instruction at one of the top teaching salons. At periodic sessions the most senior stylists and colorists instruct the novice employees. In certain cases you might be cut or colored by the instructors themselves in order to illustrate a cut or color technique that they want everyone to see, but either way you won't leave the salon until your hair meets the highest standards.

For these teaching sessions you usually pay a nominal fee which varies from free to $50 or so for a $75 and up process. You will need an appointment, which may be hard to get, and you may not have a lot of say in what is done to you—within limits, but a cut-and-color class of this nature is guaranteed to be better than any quick-cut-joint clipping or unsophisticated coloring you're likely to get. Call the better salons in your city for information.

Getting What You Want

Julian, Kim, and Antony all point out that if a hairdresser criticizes your current hair color or style or makes you feel uncomfortable in any way or displays arrogance, it's a good indication that they don't have a code of ethics that you will value. Your stylist/colorist should be gentle with you, and understand that your hair is a deep connection to your sense of self.

They advise you to bring pictures of styles you like along with you to the consultation. The hairdresser can tell you if those styles will work for your face, body, and hair types. If not, they may give him/her a good indication of the feeling you're looking for. Also, Julian points out, you should always see your new stylist or colorist with dry hair first, so they can see and feel what your hair is like before getting it wet. If a salon wants to whisk you off to the sink before a face to face, you may want to consider whether they have your best interests, not to mention styles, at heart.

Until you get to know each other well, feel free to point out the nature of your hair. Does it shrink a lot when it dries, perhaps, or is it really very curly and looks a lot longer when wet, etc.? Some fine hair looks very straight but takes a curl really well, for example. Don't forget—you know your hair better than anyone.

The Style's the Thing—Your Best 'Do

Kim suggests that you discuss your ability to work with your hair before deciding on a new style. Show up with your hair styled in the usual way so you can explain what it is you want to change. If you are thinking of a perm, you should be good at handling your hair because a perm won't necessarily make it any easier to style, it just gives you more styling options. Keep in mind that hair grows nearly half an inch a month, but you can't perm the same hair more than twice—at the most.

If you have a question while your stylist is cutting your hair, speak up—but don't interrupt in mid-snip or you could throw off the cut. While a pleasant dialogue is nice and can help you to get to know each other, don't feel obligated to keep up the small talk. A hairdresser's silence may be concentration. One cautionary note: Don't smile while they cut your bangs because they could be too short when you relax your face!

Before you leave the salon be sure to check the style from all angles with a hand mirror to understand what your style looks like when they "finish" you. Don't ever leave a salon with a wet head after a cut since hair shrinks when dry, and it may need a little final clip to assure the shape. If you have any maintenance questions about your 'do, that's your last chance to get clear, so fire away.

Tip: *If you think you may not fit into the smocks provided by your salon, bring your own. (See the Appendix for details.)*

The Right 'Do for you

Just as your clothes and accessories are most effective when you work with your natural shape, so too is your hairstyle. Here are some things to consider when deciding on the right look for your face.

The Oval Face

Nearly any hair length will work for the oval face including an oval shape, although if your neck is short you are most flattered by hair above the shoulders. A double chin? Wear your hair well above your shoulders.

The Round Face

To balance the round face, hair usually looks best when shaped to add width and height at the top of the head. Think about upswept styles, less volume at the sides, variation in lines, asymmetrical cuts, side parts that run at a diagonal to the crown, and other arrangements that elongate the face versus adding more roundness or width. Part the hair on the side, not in the center. Avoid a blunt cut at the back of the neck. Full bangs are difficult to wear because they shorten the face. If you must, try them wispy.

The Oval Face

The Round Face

The Square Face

If your neck is short, your hair shouldn't be cut any longer than the ears, at most. An illusion of height and some softness are needed to offset the angular width of this face. The widest volume is best kept above eye level, with hair at or below the ear worn close to the jawline. Asymmetrical cuts and wispy bangs can work, especially if shaped with fullness or height at the crown, but avoid a straight-across-the-forehead bangs line and a blunt cut at the nape of the neck (which will widen the neck).

The Square Face

The Oblong Face

Your face was born to wear bangs! Look for cuts that add volume and softness to the crown and to the sides of your angular face. Avoid long, straight styles, center parts, and unnecessary height.

The Heart/Diamond Face

These faces look best framed by hair shapes with more width at the jawline to support the forehead. Soft bangs usually work well, as do soft sides, covered ears, fullness at the nape of the neck, and blunt cuts. Avoid hair that's too flat or too high.

The Oblong Face

The Heart/Diamond Face

The Triangular Face

The Triangular Face

The best hairstyles balance the width of this face at the jawline with height and fullness above the cheekbones. Upswept styles work well, as do some asymmetrical or fluffy bangs, an exposed forehead, or waves and curls that direct the eye up and out at the eyeline and above.

Other Features to Consider

- *Short neck:* Wear your hair close to the head and above the ears. (I suffer with this one. In photographs or on TV you can always tell how pudgy I am by how short I'm wearing my hair.)
- *Sloping shoulders:* A straight horizontal hairline helps balance the slope. Avoid any style that ends in a V in the back.

- *Prominent nose:* Balance by arranging hair with height and fullness high on the back of the head.
- *Double chin or jowls:* Arrange the hair up and back with upsweeps or asymmetrical cuts.
- *Small chin:* Balance with fullness low at the back of the neck.
- *Dowager's hump:* Don't expose it—keep hair fluffy or loose over your nape.
- *Full face:* Wear some hair close to the sides of the face (the balance can be pulled back if you want).
- Hair shouldn't extend wider than two-thirds of the distance from neck to the shoulder.

Color Magic

Having your hair professionally colored is one of the best things you can do to improve your looks and feel great about yourself. Even if you plan to color your hair yourself, it pays to go to a professional the first time or two to find out what he or she recommends in terms of color and product type.

Your objective should be to get hair color as natural and flattering "as if it grew there"—for an investment of time and money you can afford. Covering gray? Looking for a brighter look? Want to lighten up and flatter your changing complexion? Just want to know what life would be like as a blonde? Whether you spend five minutes to color at home with a temporary rinse, or spend two hours every four weeks getting a touch-up at the salon, you still want great hair. But before you take the leap, know your options. Covering gray is an inevitable step for many women, but enslaving yourself to monthly touchups just to have lighter hair is another.

I've tried growing out my hair to escape touch-up hell, but even my mother begged me to highlight it again—and I was in college at the time, with great skin! Having been a light blonde baby, my skin and eyes just look better with the hair color I had as a child. Not every woman looks good with lighter hair—in fact some would look better with darker or just more intense color, but they mistakenly pursue that American Girl look with bigger, bolder, blonder. Every time I walk through a mall I'm struck by the number of misguided hair choices. Blonde is not better, it's just more yellow. Remember, if you lighten your hair more than just a single shade lighter than your own, you will have roots at the rate of at least a half inch per month. Madonna notwithstanding, roots are simply not chic.

There are so many coloring products on the market it's hard to tell them apart, so here's a guide by type. (Note: It's important to do a patch test on your skin to see how you react to hair-color products. Your scalp is tender and will react more strongly to harsh chemicals than other skin areas.)

Temporary Color

These products sit on the surface of the hair shaft and wash out with the next shampoo. They rub off, though, so be careful. (A word of warning: If you have already lightened your hair, all temporary or less than permanent colors can have the nasty effect of being a little more permanent than you'd like. The color-stripped hair shaft will absorb and hold color, unlike virgin or previously colored hair.)

Semipermanent Color

This color penetrates the outer layer of the hair but isn't absorbed because it contains no peroxide or ammonia. While it can't lighten, it does provide enough color to cover your gray (if you're less than half gray), and will intensify your natural color. Semipermanent colors wash out after about six shampoos, but are easy and economical to use. They usually come out more red than you expect, so plan accordingly. After a few months you may need to see a professional colorist to even out the color front to back and ends vs. roots, since the older hair will absorb more color. For best results, choose a color a shade or so lighter than your color, use the plastic cap that comes in the box, and apply a little heat with your hair dryer after applying the color. Lighter/blonder semipermanent color over gray can turn drab to highlights.

Tip: *Even if you color your own hair go to a professional every five or six colorings to get a professional touch and be certain it's even and acurate.*

Permanent Color

This is the best way to cover gray and the only way to radically change the color of your hair. (It permanently stains everything else too, so use plastic gloves and be careful.) Pick a shade that works with your skin tones (cool vs. warm, intense vs. subtle, etc.). Be sure you choose a shade that doesn't contrast too much or it will age you. Generally, you should go just a little bit lighter than your own hair color. Pay strict attention to the directions on the box. You'll need touch-ups every three to six weeks.

Highlighting

This process lightens or colors selected sections of your hair—strand by strand, section by section, etc. It's the most natural looking, is a good way to start to disguise gray, and doesn't leave a sharp root line the way single-process color does—and doesn't need maintenance as often, either. In the salon this process is most often done by the use of foil wraps, where tiny sections of hair are delicately sorted out and bleached or colored independently. They often use multiple colors and vary the degree of lightness for a natural look—lighter around the face, darker in the back. You can do this at home with a commercial kit by pulling your hair through a little cap with dozens of holes, but it isn't easy! Be sure to arrange your hair the way you usually wear it, with the part in the right place, and get a friend to help. You'll need touch-ups every six weeks to six months depending on how light you go. Fortunately, your colorist can do full head, three-quarters, half head, or face framing. The less you do, the lower the price.

Avoiding Color Disasters

It only takes one time to mess up your hair, and months or years to correct it. The more hands you have involved in your hair color, the more chances there are for big mistakes. So take a little care in how you choose and use hair color products and professional services. Call the toll-free customer information on the side of the box to speak to a professional about your hair type and expectations before you select a product or use it at home. If you intend to use a salon, get a free consultation with the colorist before making an appointment, and ask lots of questions about how often you will need touch-ups, and whether the color will negatively affect your hair's manageability, etc.

The Care and Feeding of Hair

Short hair needs a good cut and regular trims every four weeks or so. Medium-length hair (ears to shoulders) needs cutting every six weeks to maintain shape and proportion. Trim long hair every eight weeks.

Hair products today work so much better than their predecessors of even ten years ago that you're bound to be having a lot fewer bad hair days than your mom ever had. For instance, did you know you do not have to shampoo, lather, rinse, and *repeat*? Unless you wear a lot—I mean a lot!—of hair-styling products, or wash your hair less than twice a week, the average shampoo will lather enough the first time to get your hair clean. Follow with a light conditioner. If you blow-dry your hair every day, color your hair, or use a lot of rollers or a curling iron, you may need to deep-condition your hair weekly or so.

Remember—hair is also subject to sun damage, so protect it with some conditioner or one of the new sunscreen products for your hair. I have very light, very sensitive skin and I lighten my mousy blonde hair, so you won't catch me at the beach without a hat. Besides, there's no better way to balance a plus-size, nearly naked body than with a lovely, large-brimmed hat!

The Best Tip for Knowing and Keeping Your Style:
Photograph your new 'do. There's nothing like a few Polaroids of the front, back, and sides to remind me how to get and keep the look I fell in love with originally.

Salon Tipping Etiquette

No matter what price you pay for a cut or color, as long as you are satisfied with the service you should plan to tip about 10 to 20 percent of the bill. This is just standard for the business—the same as for a waiter. Be sure to tip the person who washes your hair, as well. Most salons have little envelopes that allow you to be discreet, so ask at the desk if you don't see them. Remember to put your name on the envelope, or the stylist/colorist/assistant won't know who paid them. The only exception: Don't tip the owner. This handy rule could actually get you the best service at the same price!

As with all service businesses, if you are not satisfied for any reason, let your displeasure be known. If the operator can't or won't help you, tell the manager. Their main concern is making you happy, since bad word of mouth could seriously hurt their business.

> **A Great Tip for Those Afflicted with Hard Water and Dull Hair:**
> *Once or twice a week, rinse your hair with a solution of lemon juice or vinegar and water. Use about one tablespoon of lemon or vinegar to each cup of water.*

The Changing Faces of Fashionable

Some women fall into a common trap of not adapting their hair and makeup to keep up with their age and the changing tastes in fashion. Retro is one thing, but frozen in time is something else! Unfortunately, these women usually maintain a hairstyle (a bouffant, for instance) or makeup (blue or green eye shadow) in the mistaken belief that it's what *becomes* them most. At one time, the woman probably did look her best in that style, but people and the styles of the times change. While she may have been at her physical zenith when

Blow-Dryer Tips

The keys to using your hair dryer effectively are:

- Use more air than heat.

- Use a round brush.

- Keep it moving so you don't fry any particular section (the leading contributor to split ends and frizzies).

- Dry the roots first.

- To add a little volume, hang your head upside down and scrunch with your fingers while you dry.

- To protect the hair cuticle and keep it shiny, direct the air from the root out, the way the hair grows.

- If your hair is short, start at the nape and dry sections around your head, ending at the crown.

- If your hair is long, dry section by section. Put your brush in at the root and follow with the dryer out to the ends (rather than keep the dryer focused on a single place too long, repeat the root-to-end sweep a few times).

- For lift at the front, use a round brush. The bigger the brush, the higher the lift.

- For volume all over, use a vented brush: Put it down in the hair at the root, brush back an inch or so. Then, keeping the brush flat on the head, pull it back forward again, which lifts the hair up at the root so you can direct the air through the brush to the root.

- Use a styling product to hold your 'do, and protect it from humidity droop.

she wore that particular hair or makeup style, it wasn't the style that made her look her best—it was probably her youth.

As a woman ages, she needs to adapt hair and makeup to her evolving face and body—as well as the changing social fashions. While it's understandable that some women hate to keep up with hair and makeup, or feel they have no talent applying makeup in a new way, or styling their hair into a particular style, with the right teacher (makeup artist or salesperson, and hairstylist) to help her choose the best styles and show her how to execute them, any woman can learn to emphasize her most attractive features.

CHAPTER Twelve

Wardrobe Planning for Every Body, Every Lifestyle, Every Budget

Wardrobe Strategy: The Coordinated Wardrobe

Okay, so you know what your body type is and which clothing styles are right for you. Congratulations—you're ambitious, organized, and dedicated. Now you need to develop the skill to look at your current clothing and new purchases from a perspective that makes sense for you.

The goals of successful wardrobe planning for most people include:

1. Getting more looks from fewer pieces
2. Updating easily
3. Spending less time in the stores and the closet deciding what to wear

"One and one are sometimes eleven."

KASHMIRI PROVERB

247

Do you have other goals in mind when you think about simplifying your wardrobe? You might want to write them down and take a look at them in six months or a year and decide if you are still heading in the same direction you set out in. Maybe you want to shift your personal style away from one category and move toward another that communicates the real you. Maybe you want to leave a particular color or color category behind and include others that feel more comfortable. You decide, but do so *deliberately*. As a client of mine once said, "I want a happenin' wardrobe, not one that just happened."

Three simple rules for acquiring a dynamic wardrobe right for you:

Rule #1: Coordinate everything with everything else.

Rule #2: Buy the best quality you can afford.

Rule #3: Think in terms of Cost Per Wearing.

Clothing Teamwork

The most efficient way to look at your clothes is to regard them as coordinated sets, or capsules of clothing that work together toward a common goal. In her book *Working Wardrobe*, Janet Wallach introduced the capsule concept as the perfect way to manage a working woman's wardrobe. Most designers now offer their lines of seasonal clothing in similar groupings of garments all with the same fabrics, designs, and functions. Both ideas are the same: a coordinated set of clothing that harmonizes in color, fabric, and shape to be worn interchangeably.

Think of the capsule as your own personal team of communication advi-

sors complete with specialty subunits that each have their own mission. Most women have many teams, or capsules, working for them to cover a multitude of personal and professional situations and seasons. For instance, when you've got a big meeting coming up that demands you look sharp with a touch of razzle-dazzle, you might call on the power-playing red team.

The garments in a capsule have similar fabric weights and textures, and share scale and proportions. They also travel really well together because they're all multipurpose and give you flexibility. In this scenario the red team is designed to give you confidence and power because of the color and intensity, and makes you feel good because it makes you look good. The red team might have a couple of jackets, coordinating skirts and pants, a dress, a few blouses, etc., all in black, white, and a couple of prints, and its own accessories and finishing touches. Everything on that team works together mix and match, each building upon the other to fit your body, style, personal coloring, and specific aspects of your lifestyle.

Some teams are for power, some are for strict functionality, some say what a nice person you are, and others say Ooooooowwwweeeeeeeeee— Lookin' good, girrrllfrieeennnnddd!!! They all extend the possibilities of your wardrobe without adding expense. If you have a closet of mismatched "finds" that sometimes work together and sometimes don't, read on. If you can't get packed because you don't have the right things to wear, or can't go two weeks without wearing the exact same outfit twice, this chapter's for you!

The Ground Rules for Building Coordinated Capsule Wardrobes:

- Use four or five colors, maximum—preferably two neutral and two brighter accent colors.
- The neutral colors complement each other, the accent colors complement each other, and all the colors work together perfectly.
- The patterns coordinate.
- The styles and scale are compatible. (The blouses look good under several jackets, for instance.)
- Each piece is appropriate for the same lifestyle function (professional or informal business, evening and entertaining, sports, casual, etc.).

Color and Pattern

By limiting the number of colors on each "team," or in each capsule, you can make more combinations that work together. Of course, you need to choose colors that complement your skin, hair, and eyes, and be sure that they all work together. Putting individual outfits together within the capsule is safer if you choose only one, or at the most two, bright colors. Every other color should be a lighter color or a neutral.

Any pattern or print in that capsule must use a color from at least two of the solid pieces in that same capsule. Remember that bold patterns work best on bold styles, and smaller, more subtle patterns work on small or medium-scale garments. Other details to know about combining patterns:

- Combine two or more patterns only with those that share the same colors.
- Combine geometrics with other geometrics, florals with florals.
- Combine similar designs.
- Smaller patterns mix easier.
- When mixing patterns, one pattern should dominate.

When selecting colors and combinations, remember that *contrasting colors make you appear bolder and more authoritative. Minimal contrast makes you appear more casual, friendly, and approachable.* Monochromatic looks are most elegant. What do you want the clothes in each capsule to say about you?

Looking at your clothes now, how many capsules do you think you have? Looking at how you spend your time, what types of capsules do you need—what percentage of work versus formal versus casual? If you live in a climate with distinct change of seasons you may need several different types of capsules. What key pieces do you need in order to make each capsule work? Make a list of these items and carry it with you!

The typical core of a capsule wardrobe includes a few key pieces that you build around. The pieces vary by the purpose of a wardrobe, but all contain workhorse tops and bottoms, shoes or boots, and accessories. A dozen or so items in the typical capsule will yield thirty or more outfits using combinations offered by the close proximity of color, texture, style, and purpose. Here's an example from a professional working woman's closet that adds up to more than forty outfits (if the dress was two pieces it would add several more looks):

- A matching suit with skirt, pants, and jacket (in a neutral, solid color and simple style)
- A second unmatched suit (in a complementary color and style) or a jacket, another skirt and a second pair of pants to be worn as separates
- Six tops of different styles and colors:

  One blouse the same color as the suit (or a shade of that color)

  One blouse in contrasting accent color

  One blouse in a complementary, coordinating print

  One blouse in white or cream

  One sweater or knit top in the same color as the suit

  One matching knit cardigan in the same color as the suit
- One dress

In addition, each capsule should include accessories, such as neutral pumps, flat shoes, boots, scarves, earrings, necklaces, handbags, etc.

Division of Labor—How to Build a Wardrobe That Supports Your Lifestyle

How do you spend your time? Working in an environment that requires a traditional look? In a casual atmosphere? Are you an active mom? Do you have

A Capsule Wardrobe

civic or charitable duties? Are you a student? Do you spend a lot of time in the garden, on the court, or in the gym? What percentage of your time is spent relaxing in clothes that no one will see you in? How important is how you look while doing these activities? (I'll admit to you that sitting alone in front of my computer writing this right now, I am not wearing anything I would want any other person to see me in—and my entire writing wardrobe is the same. For this activity I allocate about six dollars per year.)

In a perfect world you would spend money on clothes in the same percentages as you spend your time. For most women, however, your exercise gear, relaxing togs, general mom clothes, and gardening duds cost a whole lot less than anything you would wear to work or to a formal event. So you need to temper your allocation by the actual cost of goods. This may seem simple, but even the "experts" can be led astray by the allure of an outfit too cute to pass up. A couple of years ago I sat down confidently to do a simple exercise much like the previous one, and found to my horror that I was spending way, *way* too much on casual clothes. I had all I needed, and yet was tempted each season to add a few new T-shirts, some new cotton knit shorts, a sweatshirt here and there, a darling little denim skirt, new Keds.... Wow! The expense can creep up.

When allocating funds, consider how important clothes are to you. Do you like them, love them, or merely tolerate their existence? Do you like to spend some time in the morning getting dressed, and "communing with your mirror," or would you rather be out the door as quickly as possible? What's your style type? Naturals can mix and match with fewer pieces, while the Elegant and

Dramatic types will need to devote a little more time, energy, and expense to achieving their best looks.

What's a reasonable amount to spend on clothes per year? Only you can really answer that, but some women find that one month's net salary works as a good guide for them. What does it cost you to get dressed every morning? Not only is there an expense for what you do wear, there's a meter running on what you leave home in the closet, of course. If you pay a lot for a team member's time, you had better be using her, not letting her sit around in the back room playing cards! Treat your clothes as investments.

Wardrobe Strategy: Investment Dressing

Planning your purchases means you buy nothing haphazardly or emotionally. Since your wardrobe is an expensive necessity it deserves some thought and preparation, and it should provide you with a high return on investment in durability and appropriateness for your lifestyle. Think of your wardrobe as a portfolio. How much money do you have tied up in clothes versus stocks or other investments that could be paying dividends? If you devote even a fraction of the time to planning your wardrobe as you would to planning which mutual fund to buy, you would spend less and have more, I'm sure.

Some women give themselves a timeline for building their wardrobe. They work toward a good coat one season, a couple of dresses another, etc. No matter what your budget, you can eventually have a wardrobe that works for you if you prioritize your needs. Naturally, this is easiest to do if you invest in clothes that are timeless enough to look good for many years. It's easier still if you can define your personal style and limit the number of less than perfect garments and accessories you buy. *Bargains are only bargains if you would have bought them anyway at a much higher price.*

The Cost per Wearing Approach: Cost Plus

In all of my wardrobe and style classes, I show the same Cost per Wearing example, which never fails to bring a hush over the room and some shocked gasps of recognition. This simple formula is the single best way to compare the relative prices of clothing and accessories, and decide what are good long-term investments versus short-term indulgences. I never shop without a little calculator that helps me keep a total of the immediate "damage," calculate the tax if there is any, and decide what's a bargain. You should, too.

The Cost per Wearing calculates the cost for each wearing of a garment based on its total cost over its lifetime. If you want, you can add in the maintenance costs as well. This is helpful to judge the difference between a garment that must be dry-cleaned versus one that's washed. This analysis reveals that some things that seem expensive may actually be very efficient, while seemingly inexpensive items are unbelievably costly over time. If you have anything hanging in your closet right now that you've never worn or worn only a couple of times, you need to use this formula every time you shop! These are the questions to be answered:

1. What is the price of the item?
2. How long will you keep it?

3. How often can you wear it (weekly, monthly, yearly) in its lifetime?

4. What is the cost *per wearing* in total?

If the cost of a light wool-gabardine navy blazer, for example, is $200, and you expect to wear it approximately once per week 6 months of the year, you'll wear it 26 times per year. If you think the blazer will last three years before you damage it, grow out of it, it goes out of style, or you just get tired of looking at it, you'll wear it 78 times (3 years *times* 26 times per year). Looking at how much you paid, its cost per wearing is $2.56 ($200 *divided by* 78).

How does that compare to another garment—say a $75 lime-green linen jacket that you can wear about twice per month during the four months of summer? (We remember brighter colors more than neutral or dark colors, so if you wear it too often, people will notice!) If you keep it for two years, it will cost $4.69/wearing ($75 *divided by* 16).

If you take into account how much it will cost to own a garment, including cleaning costs, the blazer is an even better bargain. Linen wrinkles and absorbs more dirt and perspiration than wool, so if it requires dry-cleaning every other wearing, you'll pay an extra $25 to $50 in cleaning bills for the linen versus $10 to $20 for the wool, which only needs cleaning about once a year. So the blue blazer is $2.69 per wearing at best, and the green is $6.25! Furthermore, because the blazer is a classic that can be worn on the weekend with jeans, or even more months of the year if the weather isn't too hot and the wool is light enough, the cost per wearing could be much, much lower.

You can go all the way through the calculations or just get an idea of directional costs when you shop, but cost per wearing is the best measure of any garment's real cost. It certainly sheds new light on the $300 cocktail dress that makes you drool, or the perfect-but-pricey outfit you have your eye on. If you combine this method with your wardrobe plan, you'll be shopping smart without even trying!

White Cotton Blouse Example:

1. What is the price of the item? *$50*

2. How long will you keep the item? *3 years*

3. How often can you wear it in its lifetime?

   4 times per month, 9 months per year

   (36 times total) × 3 years = 108 total wearings

4. What is the cost per wearing?

   $50/108 wearings = $ .46 per wearing

High-End Suit Example:

1. Price: *$450.*

2. Life: *4 years*

3. # Wearings: *4 times per month, 10 months per year plus at least 6 other jacket wearings with other outfits = 46 × 4 = 184 total wearings*

4. Cost: *$2.45*

What you will find if you're honest with yourself and your wardrobe, is that some expensive garments are very good buys, and some seemingly cheap clothes are very expensive. Consider your spending patterns. Are you buying lots of moderately priced pieces and wearing them very little—and not looking as well in your clothes as you might if you bought fewer, higher-quality garments? *Most expensive of all are the clothes still hanging in your closet, unworn!*

How to Dress for a TV Interview or Photo Session

So many of us in our work now take advantage of video information delivery, teleconferencing, and so on, that it helps to know how to look your best in front of the camera. QVC host and plus-size fashion maven Renai Ellison and I recommend:

- Be sure you aren't overpowered by your clothing or accessories. Wear things that make you comfortable.
- Wear a simple, flattering neckline that falls at least two inches above your cleavage.
- Be certain your top fits perfectly through the bustline—especially when seated. Chances are very good you will be seated. I choose my television outfits differently depending on whether I'm standing or sitting.
- Do not try to cross your legs if you can't! It's actually more correct to sit at an angle with your legs together and your ankles crossed.
- Be sure your skirt is long enough to cover your thighs while seated.

- Wear a solid color that's not too dark, too light, or too bright. Avoid stark white and solid black. Your best neutral will work, as will most blues, greens, and purples, but avoid reds, which "bleed" on the screen. A monochromatic look is always good.

- Wear dress shields or a white T-shirt under your outfit. You will perspire under the lights no matter how you dress.

- Wear a jacket or sweater—it hides the little lumps, and it's much easier to wire your mike under a jacket than a dress alone.

- Don't do anything fancy or different with your hair that day, it will only add stress. Keep the lines simple—no Elly May ponytails or pageant hair. Keep the spray to a minimum. *Beware:* Dark roots will be emphasized on camera.

- Neutral nails are always best. If they're chipped, the camera will see it.

- Be sure your eyebrows are groomed. Even if you don't pluck or shape them, pencil is a must to get a good arch.

- Get rid of unwanted facial hair. There are no secrets on TV or in portrait photography!

- In a photo shoot the makeup will look very different, whether it's color or black and white. Don't try to do it yourself. It's well worth the investment to hire a makeup artist. If you trust the photographer, let him recommend someone.

- When in front of any camera remember: powder, powder, powder for a non-shiny, matte finish.

- Earrings: Smallish hoops or elegant solid shapes—no more than an inch in diameter—are always a winner. Movement is very distracting, so choose a style that remains still.

- Glasses can be distracting by reflecting light and separating you from the audience. Wear contacts or go without them if you can. Never, ever wear tinted glasses.

- *KISS*—Keep it simple, sister—is the best advice on TV, as it is with most things in life. Avoid busy prints, stripes, dots, etc. Sequins, beading, satin, and very dressy fabrics are only appropriate if you are accepting an Oscar or Emmy.*

* In which case, contact Suzan directly and she'll dress you personally!

CHAPTER Thirteen

Conquering Your Closet: Giving Up and Letting Go

Getting Started

Before you can revamp your wardrobe you need to deal with what's already in your closet. Face it, there may be demons in there: expensive fashion mistakes, bad advice, yesteryear's fashions that once were hot and now are not, other bodies big and small, cousin Evelyn's fantasy wedding number, etc. Not to worry, you're only a human, and hey, live and learn!

The key to getting out of bad habits and into new ones is to face the music and make a conscious decision to change. Of course, whether the new activity is exercising, singing, learning a new language or any new skill, all coaches would tell you to practice, practice, practice. Ditto for solving your wardrobe blues. You need to put your new knowledge into practice so it becomes routine and you learn to make the right decisions

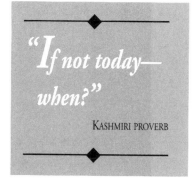

"If not today— when?"

KASHMIRI PROVERB

for you first time, every time. Since you have to build on what you already own unless you've experienced a natural disaster, or come into money, you might as well practice your judgment skills on the clothes in your current wardrobe. Besides, you'll have more closet space.

I find it's helpful if you focus on the positive changes you are making rather than what you are giving up. Take your time, breathe deeply, and forgive yourself your mistakes. You may find you want to organize by season—warm-weather clothes versus cool—especially if you keep those clothes in separate places. If the two wardrobes don't overlap you can evaluate them one at a time. If they interchange you should look at everything at once.

In my experience, closet revamp requires several preparatory steps:

1. *Privacy and Relaxation.* Select a quiet morning or afternoon when you won't be pressured by the phone, kids, husband, work, etc. You shouldn't have to hide from prying eyes and incriminating looks. This task is difficult when you're overtired and self-critical, so if you choose an evening when you've been working hard all day, a glass of wine may have medicinal value. (Some women find that it helps to throw everyone else out of the house, close the blinds, turn the stereo up, and turn off the phone.)

2. *The Trusted Assistant.* If anyone else is present, be sure she is a trusted friend with your best interests at heart. If while shopping with her in the past she has ever suggested you try on clothes you wouldn't be caught dead in or that look suspiciously like her own unique and very particular taste, she's the wrong friend to share this experience with now. I'm sure she's loving and supportive, but she won't give you unbiased advice.

3. *Take Notes.* Have a yellow legal pad (or its equivalent) and pen on hand. For the first time ever you will record your wardrobe balance sheet. This is an excellent job for your friend—very fulfilling and responsible; it will take her mind off criticism.

4. *Removal Made Easy.* Have several heavy-duty garbage bags on hand for removal.

5. *Proper Environment.* Be sure the lighting is good, and that you have access to a full-length mirror. Have enough room to make four large piles (each the equivalent of about two loads of laundry).

Painless Sorting: The Five Essential, Acid-Test Questions to Decide What Stays, What Goes

Now, take everything out of your closet and pile it neatly on the bed, sofa, or in the middle of the floor. (Be sure the floor is cleanly vacuumed, especially if any of the garments are knits, because they will pick up all the dust and pet hair. Or you might want to throw down a sheet.) You will be establishing four piles: (1) Discard Pile, (2) Fix and Alter Pile, (3) Wait and See Pile, (4) Keeper Pile. Every garment must find a home in one of these piles.

As you pick up each piece of clothing, try to evaluate it against the Acid-Test Questions. Assume you'll have to try each one on, and be sure to put on the proper undergarments to make each item look its absolute best. Have your trusty assistant record each garment on the chart, which includes space for skirts, tops, dresses, jackets, suits, slacks, activewear, swimwear, coats, robes, and possibly lingerie.

Take special note of those clothes that served you well, that you have worn frequently and been happy with but now need to give up. These are clothes that should be replaced first. Think about each one—was it the color, the fabric, the design, how it coordinated with other things, or the general panache of that garment that you liked so much? Once you figure it out, replacing it is a snap. The flip side of this exercise is looking at those things you bought and never or infrequently wore. Why? What can you learn from these mistakes?

What you will end up with is a catalog of all your clothes, which will be really helpful in developing a shopping list of items that you need to round out your wardrobe and make it work as hard as possible for you.

Acid-Test Questions

Now, let's begin. For each article of clothing, ask yourself the following questions:

1. *Is the style right for me?*

   Is it one of your recommended silhouettes? Does it flatter you, or merely cover you up? Do you get compliments when you wear it? How does it make you feel? Is it in style?

2. *Is the color and fabric right for me?*

   The wrong color can make you look tired, old, unfriendly, too timid, too aggressive, etc. The right color will bring out your best. Remember that you are more comfy in fabrics that aren't too stiff or confining—if

Your Clothing Catalog

Clothing Type/#	Garment	Season/ Fabric	Color	Also Works With	Best Accessories
Skirts					
1.	Long with center pleat	Winter/wool gabardine	Navy blue	All white and cream blouses, Jacket #4, Sweater #9	Hermes scarf w/ blue trim
2.	Short straight	Winter/ Wool crepe	Chocolate brown	All white and cream blouses, and #12, 15. Jacket #8, Sweater #7	Stacked-heel light brown pumps

you're very curvy the fabric has to curve too, or the clothes turn into refrigerator-box clothes. What's the pattern like? Plus women look better in moderate-scale prints, not teeny, tiny patterns and huge Tahiti designs. Match your personal patterns for optimal flattery—smooth and shiny vs. matte and textured. Also, is it still in good shape—is it free of stains or wear and tear?

3. *Can I accessorize it for variety?*

What jewelry, shoes, hose, scarves, etc., do you wear with it? Can you wear it with several things? Would you like it more if you had the right belt, necklace, scarf, or something else? If you need to buy an accessory to wear with it, what else can you wear that accessory with?

4. *Does it flatter me?*

   Be critical! Too big, too loose, too wide, uneven hems, too long, too short, anything missing? Does it fit perfectly or can it be easily and inexpensively tailored to fit? Tailoring is your very best clothing investment. If in doubt, take it to your tailor and ask. Take a step back and look at yourself in the garment. Does it *flatter* you or just cover your body? Just because it fits doesn't mean it flatters!

5. *Do I love it?*

   Life is way too short to compromise on how we see ourselves and how the world responds to us. Hold out for fabulous—you'll never be sorry.

Start with your jackets and tops and work your way through all your skirts and pants. What does each jacket go with? Is there a way to create new combinations that would extend your wardrobe? Look especially closely at all blouse and skirt or trouser combinations, and how scarves might tie colors together. Think about what you could buy that would really add to your wardrobe's flexibility.

As you evaluate each piece, these are the piles to set up around the room. Put them all within easy tossing distance:

Clothing Sort Piles

1. *Discard Pile*

   This is home base for clothing that clearly no longer works for you according to the Acid-Test Questions. Remember, you don't have to worry about what to throw out, only what to keep. Be ruthless—your closet will thank you.

2. *The I-Guess-It-Will-Be-Okay-If-I-Just… (Fix and Alter) Pile*

These clothes will be okay, as soon as you get them altered, cleaned, repaired, or otherwise attended to.

3. *The Gosh-I-Love-That—I-Can't-Give-That-Away! (Wait and See) Pile*

These are clothes that have meaning too deep to bear parting with, at least for now. That's okay. Everybody feels connected to some things, like the suit you wore to christen the baby, or the first dress you bought yourself after the big raise, or those really expensive trousers you bought after you lost all that weight on that crash diet and got to that hoped-for size for about 20 minutes…. In six months look again. If you're still ambivalent, put them away for another six months. Give yourself permission not to decide, and stash them in one of those flat cardboard boxes that fit under your bed. You'll derive comfort from sleeping over your favorites for a few months. Then see if you can give them up.

4. *Keeper Pile*

These are garments that pass all the tests. You'll re-sort them in the closet when you're done.

Last winter I went through this exercise again, and decided I needed a pair of brown pleated trousers, a new crisp white cotton blouse with some pizzazz, a jacket in the russet/crimson/red family, a very long black knit skirt, and a new black belt with a big gold buckle. None of the pieces proved hard to find (all were fairly classic pieces), and because they were carefully planned, they created a new synergy with the things I already owned. I got dozens of new looks.

I promise you that this method works terrifically well, and actually makes the whole process easier than trying to sort "freehand." Once you get going, you'll fly right through, empowered by the criteria. This kind of process takes decision-making out of the emotional zone and puts it into the rational zone where these things belong. Remember, they're just clothes!

Two notes of caution:

1. There are some things that you really should never throw away even if they don't fit. These include:

- The clothes that make you feel really good (that you enjoy wearing around the house) even if they look like hell.

- Sentimental connections like the sweater Grandma knit for you, which never did fit right, but represents her love.

- Very, very expensive formal clothes that are too small or large just now. These things are rarely worn, and the fewer you need to buy the more you'll have to spend on clothes you wear all the time. If you lose or gain weight in the future, you'll kick yourself for not having those special pieces around.

2. Some clothes can be saved or dramatically improved with the right buttons and bows. Consider replacing the buttons on that tired dress with some really nifty ones. I have salvaged thirty-five-year-old suits of my mother's this way. The designer Adrienne Vittadini made a nothing-much jean jacket into expensive but spectacular wearable art with dozens of brass buttons around the collar and cuffs. I love this jacket, wear it all the time, and get compliments on it wherever I go. Great buttons can be found in sewing shops, flea markets, resale bins, and by catalog.

The Details—Accessory Evaluation

Be sure to go through all your accessories, as well—hats, gloves, scarves, bags, belts, jewelry, hose, shoes, etc. Take them out and subject them to the Acid-Test Questions. Decide if they still work for you, and if they do, do they need to be cleaned, polished, or repaired? Remove those worn-out items that you liked and put them on the shopping list for replacement. What's left? What do you need? As you go through the clothing evaluation keep track of which outfits have, or might need, accessories, and try to get an idea of what you need to make your wardrobe perform.

The Afterlife of Clothes

Remember that there are lots of women in need who would love and treasure your clothes—especially the plus-size women. Think about their circumstances and give what you can. All charities will give you a receipt for the clothing, which you can use as a tax deduction. Itemize everything, and use fair pricing.

If you don't want to give them away, you can resell old clothes at one of the growing number of resale consignment shops around the country. The Yellow Pages should list several in most major cities under Clothing: Bought and Sold. Call them and ask if they accept plus sizes and what their requirements are for sales. Some are more restrictive than others—certain types, ages, and sizes of clothing. Others are more broad-based in what they accept, but all will want clothes freshly cleaned and pressed. Since you own the clothes until they sell, it's in your best interest to prep them perfectly. You can expect to keep 40–60 percent of the selling price, which you will negotiate when you drop them off. I find that some shops will give you a much better deal if you want exchange credits for other merchandise in the store, rather than cash. It might be a great way to round out your wardrobe—be sure to ask.

Lastly, remember that nothing cleans and dusts so well as old cotton! Recycle those old undies and T-shirts. Or if you hate to throw anything away, try redyeing natural fabrics to cover light stains. I've successfully resuscitated a couple of simple silk T-shirts this way. It's tricky though, and the stain may end up uneven and lighter or darker than you expect, so have patience, a very large pot to do your stove-top dyeing in, and a willingness to give up gracefully and throw the garment away if the process doesn't work. Tie-dyeing old T-shirts is a fun project for the kids, though.

Becoming the Ultra-organized Woman

Before you put anything back in that closet, vacuum it out well, paint it if you can, and line the bottom liberally with cedar blocks or packets of cedar chips to keep the moths at bay. These are cheap and easy to find at most hardware and discount home stores. They're a great investment because dust and moths will kill your clothes almost as fast as overcleaning will—maybe faster, and cedar smells much, much better than mothballs—and has got to be healthier to breathe.

The objective to rearranging things is to hang everything where you can get at it most easily, where there is enough room for every garment to preserve its shape so you don't have to steam or press it, and where you won't forget it. My home and office may be cluttered, but my closet is a well-organized and well-oiled machine! That's one of the secrets of plus style.

I suggest you separate clothes by season to cut down on confusion. While many fabrics cross seasonal boundaries, it's difficult to wear a heavy wool skirt in July, so take it out of contention during the summer. Next, group all your similar items together, graduated by color, with the patterns together—suits, jackets, trousers, dresses, jeans, etc. I prefer to group all the blouses together, separated by color and weight (one section has my much-loved white cotton shirts, another the patterns, another the colors, and the last the lighter and more formal silks).

Take note of the colors you see left in your closet. Surprised? If you love everything you see, great. If not, what doesn't pass inspection upon closer examination, or what do you need to add to complement your existing pieces?

A Place for Everything...

Hang woven trousers neatly on skirt hangers with clips, with center and back creases maintained. Hang knitted pants folded over a padded hanger. Nonknit garments can hang from the hem, waistband, or shoulders; knits should be hung from the waistband to avoid stretching. Skirts should also be hung from clip hangers.

You can minimize the space suits take in the closet by hanging the jacket, trouser and/or skirt together. I use little plastic adapters that slip over the jacket hanger hook and provide a loop to hold the skirt hanger. They work great, and the separates never separate.

Sweaters should lie flat on a shelf or in a drawer to keep from stretching out of shape. Fold them horizontally, tucking under only the arms, so that the creases fall out easily. Scarves should also be folded or hung over a trouser hanger. Hooks pull them out of shape and can easily damage the delicate material. Belts should be hung to minimize the leather cracking. Look for belt hangers at your local hardware, houseware, or bathware store.

I store my many pairs of hose in three different sizes of decorative floral hat boxes that stack in the corner. I roll them up, tuck in the ends, and toss them in by color. The rest of my collection of hat boxes really do store my hats, and find a happy home on top of my armoires.

I recommend hanging necklaces somewhere visible but not in the way. I hang most of my ropes and chains from four heavy-duty pins stuck discreetly into the molding on my armoire, but heavy beads are best wound and stored flat. My earrings are held in a big velvet-lined jewelry box, separated by type. It's not a good idea to store pearls with any other type of jewelry, since they are easily scratched. Pearls like to be worn, and actually are improved by coming into contact with your skin.

I leave shoes to you. Good luck, and may the force be with you.

Mistake-Proof Shopping Strategies

All of the best advice in the world won't help you get the perfect wardrobe unless you have a solid strategy for acquiring it. You may never have thought about shopping as a contact sport requiring a game plan and a technique— so listen up!

The Shopping Plan

Essentially, you need to think about getting your clothes-buying out of the emotional realm and into the objective world. A perfect wardrobe that fits, flatters, and feels good truly requires planning. What's in your plan?

If cold, calculating clothes-hunting sounds like a job, like no fun at all, you're partially correct. Acquiring the perfect wardrobe isn't easy. Of course, if you want to shop casually as recreation, have fun. But that's not

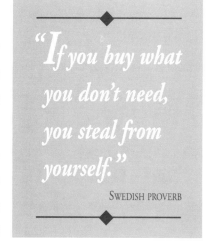

"If you buy what you don't need, you steal from yourself."

SWEDISH PROVERB

shopping to maximize your wardrobe, that's entertainment. If you're going to be buying a lot of clothing on these informal expeditions, you may want to consider putting aside a small amount of "mad money" to use for impulse items. Spending mad money means you won't be taking money out of your wardrobe budget in dribs and drabs, and you won't end up with an impulse-driven, uncoordinated closet. Of course, if you do come across the perfect what-have-you on one of these trips, you can consider it against the plan, and if it works, terrific! Otherwise, it's best to forget it and move on.

What can be fun is to know exactly what you need in theory, and shop around to find the very best items to fulfill your plan. You'll find that shopping is uncomfortable only when you are pressed for time, or are feeling out of control because you are overwhelmed with choices, or don't know how to separate good choices from bad. Those aren't your problems anymore since you know how to judge clothing silhouette, shape and proportion, color and intensity; you know what you own and you know what you need; and you have a price range to work within.

Shop alone. Keeping a positive attitude about ourselves while choosing clothes is hard enough without any outside interference. She may be your best friend, but she's a distraction. To have somebody else influencing you means that you have another whole set of "tapes" to listen to. She might choose things that she finds attractive in general, or are right for her—not necessarily for you. If you must go together, plan to separate at the store and agree to a luncheon catch-up session.

Shopping Strategies That Work

- Shop with a plan—know what type of item you want and your price range (but always buy the best quality you can afford). If you haven't got a plan, go back to Chapter 12.

- Shop only when rested and prepared—keep your cool under pressure. Drink lots of water. It keeps you awake and refreshed.

- Only buy things that you love and that are absolutely perfect for your needs.

- Shop alone and use the salespeople efficiently.

- Think outfit, not garment.

- No punishments! Agree to not criticize yourself for the day. Avoid making faces, real or imagined, at yourself in the mirror, or thinking about how much you dislike certain body parts, etc. Suspend self-negativity for just one day.

The Five Acid-Test Questions on the Road

The same Acid-Test Questions that worked in your closet analysis will guide you when shopping. If you know what type of garment you're looking for, aim for that rack first before you get distracted. One of the reasons some women hate to shop is that in today's department stores and shopping malls, everything is bigger, louder, and more visually intense in order to attract your eye and rein you in. It works! This visual stimulation strategy is confusing and creates the sense of being visually overwhelmed, out of control (you buy more when you lose your sense of self, of perspective, of reality). That sensory overload makes some of us feel like giving up and walking away from our shopping plan very quickly. So if that's your problem, stick to the project at hand—shop for what you need by evaluating against an objective criteria, and don't allow yourself to wander. Remember to consider everything in its own light, as well as for what it will bring to your wardrobe. "It will do" will never do well.

When trying on clothes, ask yourself:

1. **Is the style right for me?**

   Is it one of your recommended silhouettes? Does it flatter you, or merely cover you up? How does it make you feel? Is it in style?

2. **Is the color and fabric right for me?**

   Pay attention to fabrics that aren't too stiff or confining. The right color will bring out your best. What's the pattern like? Plus women look better in moderate-scale prints, not tiny, tiny patterns and huge Tahiti designs. Match your personal pattern for optimal flattery—are you smooth and shiny or more matte and textured?

3. **Can I accessorize it for variety?**

   What jewelry, shoes, hose, scarves, etc., can you wear with it? Would you like that garment or outfit more if you had the right belt, necklace, scarf, or something else to wear with it? If you need to buy an accessory to wear with it, what else can you wear that accessory with? Can I wear it with other things?

4. Does it flatter me?

Be critical! Too big, too loose, too wide, uneven hems, too long, too short, anything missing? Take a step back and look at yourself in the garment. Does it *flatter* you or just cover your body? Does it fit you perfectly or can it be easily tailored to fit? Just because it fits doesn't mean it flatters! If it doesn't fit you now, can it be made to fit?

5. Do I love it?

Really *love* it, not "like it"; not "it'll be fine"—is it a "10"?

Holding Out for Perfect 10s

Life is way too short to compromise on how we see ourselves and how the world responds to us. Hold out for fabulous—you'll never be sorry, you'll spend less, and you'll get exactly what you want. Hold out for a 10: the garment that suits you and your body in style, fit, color, and every way possible, and makes you feel terrific.

Holding out for a 10 may seem impossible, but if you can't find what you're looking for where you've been looking, cast a wider net and look at all the resource possibilities: specialty stores, department stores, major catalogs, small specialty catalogs, home shopping TV outlets, custom clothing, etc. If the Appendix at the end of the book doesn't help, try Royal Resources for a comprehensive listing of clothing, accessories, and every other kind of resource for plus-size people. Royal Resources, c/o Janice Herrick, P.O. Box 220, Camas Valley, OR 97416.

Can't afford what you want? Maybe you're looking at the price-value relationship all wrong. If the most inexpensive garment you can own is one that you wear over and over again, what's the cost per wearing likely to be on that perfect whatever? It could be a lot less than you might think—and much cheaper than an inexpensive outfit you rarely wear.

Based on your wardrobe plan, what type of garment are you seeking? How often will you wear it? What cost per wearing are you willing to pay—and therefore what's your price range?

Size Is a Four-Letter Word

If the actual size of a garment bugs you, plan to cut out the tags when you get home. Don't let the manufacturer's definition of size stand between you and a great piece of clothing. I do this all the time—especially on jackets that might sit behind me on a chair and say something about me I don't want the world hearing. My size is none of anybody's business—I just want the best fit I can get. How about you? If you pass over a great garment because it's one or two sizes larger than *you know you really are*, you aren't really buying clothes for you, you're buying them for somebody or something else.

Think Outfit

Experienced, stylish women of every age, style, budget, and background agree on this: Buy complete outfits. You will *always* be glad you did. For years I would see a terrific suit, and thinking I was saving myself money, I would buy just a single piece—usually the jacket. If I was really feeling flush, I bought both the jacket and the skirt. I figured I was a pretty savvy shopper, and I could easily find something in my closet, or at a lower price somewhere that would finish off the look. The problem was, I often ended up buying even more things and spending more money on individual pieces than I would have with the whole original outfit! When you buy a complete outfit, you look polished, put together, and complete—and you never have to spend time in your closet wondering what goes with what.

Cost Plus

When you're standing in front of your closet dreaming about the dress or blouse or suit or trousers or other piece of clothing you wish you had, what do you think about? Color? Style? Fit? Price? You probably think about clothes in terms of what they can do for you and your wardrobe, not about what they will cost you. So when you stand in front of the racks in the stores, consider color, style, fit, and how a new garment can make your wardrobe work harder for you. Think about expense in terms of what the *cost per wearing* will be. How many more outfits will you be able to construct out of that new outfit, and how many times a month will you wear that garment? If you combine this method with your wardrobe plan, you'll be shopping smart without even trying!

The Confessional

The mirror is a tool that you control. Try to avoid thinking of the fitting room as a confessional. Think of it as a gateway to great possibilities of self-expression and positive self-esteem. Claim this time as your own and take as much time as you need. That fitting room is your castle, so relax, take your time, and think positively.

Secret Strategies of Smart Shoppers

Try these tips for getting in and out of the fitting room with your ego and wallet intact:

1. *Before entering a fitting room, find a salesperson to take charge of you.* Let her get you the clothes you need and suggest alternate blouses, etc. If the store salespeople can't perform that function for you, consider shopping where they can. You deserve service and attention. Think about how much time you can save by not having to get dressed and undressed while you hunt for another size, another color, or anything else you need.

2. *Wear the proper underclothes and bring the right shoes with you.* There is nothing worse than trying to feel good about an expensive new business or formal dress while staring at yourself in short white socks, tennis shoes, and no hose or slip.

3. *Accept the fact that dressing rooms are badly lit,* that fluorescent lights add pounds and lines and destroy the look of your makeup and your hair color. If you look less than fabulous, you're not alone. Even size 6 women look lousy in there, really. It's not you, it's the lighting, and lighting is everything. Trust me on this.

4. *Take complete outfits into the fitting room, and don't look in the mirror until you are fully dressed in the outfit you are trying.* Smile! Do *not* make faces. Dress as you would wear the garment and try to get a sense of how it *feels* as well as looks.

5. *Back up as far as you can from the mirror to get a long view.* This is what most people will see. Try walking, turning, bending over, sitting, moving in general. Clothes are meant to move, so try them out, especially if they are sports clothes intended to support you while you walk, run, play a sport, etc. Stretch and swing your arms a little. How do the clothes *feel?* Remember that once you're out of the range of the mirror you will care more about how the clothes feel than how they look.

6. *Check the fit from the top down,* and remember that when people are close enough to carry on a conversation with you, their focus will be on your body from about the waist up. Double-check the neckline, collar, bust, and sleeves. How does the color look against your skin? Does it flatter? If you have to settle on something, settle on those details farthest from your face.

7. *Ask other women in the fitting room what they think of you in the outfit* (out of the range of the salesperson). Don't ask what they think of the outfit—it might not be their style. Instead, if they comment on the outfit, ask them how they think *you* look. It will force them to see the whole picture, not just the clothes. Then ask the salesperson what she thinks. Of course don't take her word for gospel, but listen for the evidence she supplies to support how great you look, as in "that front button placket really makes you look taller," or "that color is great for your complexion." Do you agree? Does she sound authoritative, enthusiastic? If you feel strongly about something, but can't decide if it's good or bad, listen to the comments of the other shoppers. If they give you raves, you've probably found a new (untried) terrific style or color. Listen to them. Listen loudest to any unsolicited compliments.

8. *If you have to choose between fit and looks, choose fit.* Great fit will make you look better and feel better than any other aspect of a garment—more than color, pattern, fabric, or price.

9. *Get in there!* Don't ever, ever buy anything without trying it on first. Never!

Dealing with Choices

Some women are a little overwhelmed by all the new choices. I understand. For years we plus-size women had our own short list of shopping resources, both department stores and small specialty retailers. Whatever they carried, we saw, a few times a year. Whatever fit the body, the budget, and hopefully our lifestyles, we bought. Now there are more department stores and specialty shops offering dozens of new labels, brighter colors, and more selection than we would have thought possible. Intimidating, overwhelming, exciting, exhilarating, a pain in the neck? Not for the savvy shopper. Opportunity knocks!

Your point of view on the pleasures and pains of clothes-hunting probably depends on whether you see clothes shopping as a potentially productive or painful experience. If you see shopping as a real-life reminder of your worst fears realized, and an encounter with a body you dislike and don't want, try instead to think of shopping as a source for good news and good feelings. Try to think objectively, not emotionally. These fabulous new clothes can make you look and feel marvelous.

The French Approach

The single most important thing you can do to deal with all the clothing choices on the racks is to ignore what isn't right for you in terms of style, color, size, and cost. Focus only on what is right. Sounds ridiculously simple, right? It is. A great sculptor was once asked how he created such deeply beautiful, evocative, female sculptural masterpieces out of cold marble. He said it wasn't difficult, he simply cut away everything that looked like it didn't belong. Who says there isn't greatness in shopping?

In legend and oftentimes in reality, French women are the very best-dressed, most glamorous, and self-assured women in the world. They also tend to own only a small percentage of the clothes that American women do, because they are remarkably picky about fit, style, and quality. They prefer to own just a few perfect things than a closet full of mediocrity. Unlike American women, they have learned to maximize the amount of style they exude while minimizing the long-range expense, and they worry more about quality than quantity. Their method of dressing is bound to be less expensive in the long run (even if they spend twice as much on their typical purchase than the average American woman would) because French women own fewer clothes. All of which, when you think about it, has far-reaching effects on your cleaning bills, closet space, shoe selection, accessory assortment, and overall ease of wardrobe maintenance. If you shop wisely, you can find those perfect 10s fairly easily, and be done with the whole process very quickly.

So the lesson is simple: You need only a few perfect things to look great; quality, not quantity, counts. A wise French woman once told me to always buy the very best quality I could afford because quality would never disappoint me, and I would never regret my choices. Never have. Neither will you.

Buying in Multiples

This is really, really important: When you find greatness, get as much of it as you can afford. You don't get many Brownie points for variety! If you find the perfect pair of shoes that don't hurt and that add just the right touch to your wardrobe, for example, buy a few pair. You can buy them in different colors or snap up the same favorite and put them aside for the future.

If you don't actually buy multiples and store them, write down the item description, the brand, the style name and number, where you bought it, and what you paid for it so you can save yourself some time shopping in the future. If shoes were Kellogg's cornflakes, I'd be able to find them over and over again everywhere, and I'd be a happy woman. Instead, I'm a smart pack rat. When my current pumps die, I'll have another pair, thank goodness. Try it!

The trick to buying smart in multiples is to buy early in the season, wear the items at least once right away to see how well they road test, and go back immediately to find the same item. This is also very important: If the store doesn't have the thing you want, ask the salesperson or manager to call the other store branches to see if one of them has it in stock. If that doesn't work, call the manufacturer's customer service number and ask what other stores bought that particular item or line, and call those stores. It's your money, your clothes, and your life—you're entitled.

Keep in mind that salespeople in retail clothing stores usually work on commissions, so they would rather have a challenging sale than no sale at all. Don't be afraid to enlist people to help you in your mission to look your best. You are never obligated to make a purchase, no matter how much someone helps you. You'll find that if you build a rapport with salespeople, they are worth their weight in gold in the time they will save you shopping.

Matching the Original

If you need to match colors and palettes, textures, patterns, styles, or any other design element, be sure to take the original with you. Even if you have to haul around a big bag of clothes, you will never make a perfect match without the original. The peculiar thing about humans is that they have no precise color memory. Your brain remembers that something is red or yellow or a general version of a color, but it cannot remember the exact shade and tone. So be cautious!

Likewise, when having shoes dyed to match, bring your dress along and show the shoe repair person (or whoever is in charge of dyeing) the whole thing, even though you'll only leave a swatch. The dyer should get a chance to see the overall perspective or whole pattern, should his color palette force him to make a decision about whether to go lighter, darker, more muted, or brighter.

The Occasional Nightmare

Once in a while you have to run out to buy something for a special occasion or as a quickie replacement. In these moments, use the phone before you go anywhere. Call the store that has the most comprehensive selection or is most likely to satisfy your needs. Get the manager on the phone and share your dilemma with her. Tell her your needs, your size, your budget, and your time frame. Ask her what she would recommend were she in your shoes. Only spend the time and energy to go to a store that has a potential solution waiting for you.

People are nearly always happy to help solve your problem if you can get them involved and get them to empathize rather than just sympathize. (This works for any service problem you might have.) Generally, people have a lot of barriers up to protect themselves from added stress and mental effort. But underneath that, everyone wants to feel connected and appreciated. If you get someone to *feel* as well as understand your problem, you get them totally involved, and they will take on your problem as their own. And when they help you solve that problem, they will feel deeply satisfied and fulfilled for having been needed, and for being able to deliver. I'm willing to guarantee this piece of info, too!

Once in a Lifetime/Once in a While

Once in a while you encounter something so amazing, so wonderful, you have to have it. Whether it's a designer suit at a rock-bottom price, or a piece of wearable art that calls to you, or a formal dress in the absolutely perfect shade of aubergine, be prepared to grab it. So many women walk around with stories about "the one that got away." You don't need permission from anyone to have what you need and what will make you happy. Besides, armed with the five Acid-Test Questions, you'll never make that mistake, will you?

Once in a lifetime you encounter "The Great One." Be prepared to recognize it. Part of great style is feeling confident to recognize something that the crowd has overlooked. My Great One came one day as I was spending five minutes on my lunch break browsing the sale rack at a local boutique. It was the season-end double-sale week, meaning that everything was 50 percent off the price as marked—even on the sale rack. Underneath two rather shopworn, shiny suits was a red mess tied around the hanger by what looked like a dozen inside dress loops (you know, those ribbon or cloth loops sewn into

the lining to make hanging a garment easier). Intrigued, I took it to the fitting room and spent ten minutes untying it. What I got was a red French-lace gown with an ivory-colored organza silhouette stole collar from their defunct couture collection. This dress was handmade from very, very expensive fabric, and was virtually made for my high-hipped, hourglass body. It needed to be tailored and tapered slightly, but it was nearly perfect. The tag revealed it had been in the store for quite a while. This is what it said: $2500/$1250 (50% off)/$750 (40% off)/$375 (50% off)/$187.50 (50% off)/$93.75 (50% off)/$46.88 (50% off). That day, all sale items were 50 percent off, so I paid $23.44, or less than *one percent* of the original retail price. My tailor charged me about $35 to make it perfect, and I already had the shoes, the bag, and the wrap. I wore it to Sally Jessy Raphael's tenth anniversary party with a friend, and had over fourteen (*very thin*) New York women stop me to tell me how much they loved the dress and how nifty they thought it was for me to wear something besides New York Basic Black. Shopping smart is the best revenge!

Guerrilla Tactics

Insider information on resources, catalogs, personal shoppers, sales and bargains, secondhand stores, buying by catalog and TV

Sales and Bargains. This tip is worth the price of the book: Shop early, buy late. That is, browse the stores as soon as the new merchandise comes in to get a picture of the latest offerings, the colors, the fabrics, the designs being used. Decide what will work into your plans and which pieces you absolutely need to have now; those that you want to own—but at 20 percent or so less; and those that are perfect at 35 percent or more off. Keep an eye on the sales.

There are usually sales of about 20 percent off just a few weeks after the merchandise is out. Plan for this one, and call your salesperson to let her know you'll be in. Have her set aside your size (since you shopped as soon as the merchandise arrived, you tried everything on and know what size to buy). Keep in touch with your salesperson and let her know which pieces you want at 35 percent off or more. Sometimes stores have short-term or unannounced sales, which could mean terrific savings. If you maintain your relationships with salespeople they can alert you to these discounts. If they know you want to buy a piece or complete outfit but are waiting for the right sale, they also know they're better off getting you into their store—even at a large discount— than losing you to a competitor.

Make a point of finding and browsing the local outlets. With list in hand, you never know what you'll come across to round out your wardrobe. Keep in mind that some items are inherently worth more than others. Suits, blazers, and business-type dresses of high quality are always worth more if they will last. Leggings, jeans, shorts, T-shirts, sneakers, most shoes, and other casual things are worth less and can usually be had on sale. Keep reminding yourself that it's only a bargain if you would have bought it anyway at a higher price. Some pieces start out so expensive that even at a significant discount they're overpriced.

Strongly consider anything that is priced at 40 percent or less of its original cost. This poor thing has been around a long time for some reason. It was probably sized wrong, or it was done in a funky out-of-season fabric, or something was odd or wrong with it, or—and this is the best one of all—it was priced way too high to begin with. Since you know that size tags are meaningless, you're part of that tiny percentage of women who are willing to try things on for size before passing judgment. And as a smart shopper who watches the sales, you might be the lucky one to finally pick up that once overpriced garment for its real worth. The store's own private-label merchandise is likely to go on sale more often and at a bigger discount because it has the biggest profit margin. Of course, sometimes things are left because they were badly designed, badly made, or badly shop-worn. Caveat emptor!

The very best bargain strategy may be to shop the end-of-season sales for wardrobe staples. I regularly buy the most expensive items in my wardrobe, like suits and formal wear, several months out of season. While most women are gleefully browsing through the new linens, cottons, and lightweight garments at the beginning of the spring/summer season, I'm grabbing up forgotten woolen and microfiber pieces in dark colors. I always buy things I know are on my plan for the opposite season, those that will be timeless additions to my wardrobe. Of course, since I do so much traveling, I especially like seasonless fabrics and the highest quality synthetics that pack well and translate to any climate. For these items, the only difference between fall and spring, for example, is that the new stuff is priced 40–60 percent higher. Won't you join me at the sale rack?

Catalogs. If you haven't shopped by catalog for plus-size clothes, start now! Direct mail is the easiest, most convenient, and most private way to get just what you want without ever getting vertical. Most companies have excellent customer service to assure your order arrives on time, the way you want it. Be sure to ask about return policies because while a few catalogs will pay for the return of any merchandise (regardless of the reason you reject it), most will charge you both ways. Be sure to calculate shipping costs into the total.

Bear in mind that no two catalogs use the same set of measurements for sizing, and some even have their own size designations. Break out your measuring tape and check your stats against those in their size guide. See the Resource section (pp. 303-22) for some plus-size catalogs to subscribe to.

TV Shopping. The home shopping channels can provide you with some terrific bargains. Silks and blends in casual designs abound. For a year I was the spokesperson on QVC for Elisabeth, Liz Claiborne's plus-size line. On the air, the hosts and I spent a lot of time explaining the measurements and fit of the garments. That's very important, because to shop effectively it helps to have accurate expectations—but now you know your body perfectly!

When looking at a garment on the air, focus on the actual shape first. Where is it full? Narrow? Straight up and down? How does that compare to your body? Look next at the details of the garment. Where do they focus the eye's attention? Is that a place you want attention focused on your body? Lastly, look at the color both on your screen and as it's described by the host. What is the color's light/dark value and how will that flatter you? Will that color work with the rest of your wardrobe?

Be sure to ask when you will receive the items, how much the shipping costs will be, and about return policies.

Consignment or Secondhand Stores. Secondhand stores are a terrific place to find scarves, jewelry, jeans, some formal things, purses, and the occasional suit or blazer. Fortunately, more are popping up that cater to plus-size women, and since we tend to fluctuate in weight more than the average woman, great bargains can sometimes be found (in the clothes other women have outgrown or gotten tired of). Avoid buying shoes, which can carry nasty funguses, and be sure to spot-check everything before buying. If you buy it stained, assume it will stay stained.

Image Consultants and Personal Shoppers. Lisa Cunningham, AICI, a New York image consultant of the highest professional reputation (and founder of the foremost image certification program in the country at Parsons School of Design), says, "The benefits of working with an image consultant or personal shopper are fivefold:

1. You feel more confident about making choices
2. You have a clearer picture and plan of what to buy/avoid
3. It simplifies dressing
4. Over the long term, you save money
5. You feel happier and more secure about your appearance

"An image consultant," Lisa continues, "will evaluate your body by shape, size, and proportion, evaluate your coloring and personal pattern, and work with you on determining the best style personality and clothing silhouettes for you. Some shop with or for you, others advise only."

Lisa counsels that "an independent, well-trained consultant is your best consumer advocate, protecting your interests and helping you to locate the best clothing for you based on a variety of objective and subjective criteria. First, she will listen to what's really important to you and focus on your concerns, taking an accurate assessment of your current wardrobe/accessories status and then identifying what's needed or missing. If you want, she can help you to develop a realistic budget plan. If you plan to shop together, she may do advance scouting (pre-shopping). Last, she can keep a record of your wardrobe and accessory purchases (if you request it), and then call you next season if she spots items perfect for you.

"Using the Parsons definition, `An *image consultant* is a professional who advises individuals, groups and/or corporations on appearance, presentation, or image. A *personal shopper* is a person offering the service of shopping for and purchasing the personal accessories and wardrobe needs of other people for a fee. A personal shopper may or may not also be an image consultant.' Unlike image consultants, personal shoppers usually have less training in color, line, design, and/or wardrobe planning. But they may have access to specialized resources."

The Association of Image Consultants International is the professional organization that establishes the highest professional standards and rankings for members and helps promote quality training and service for clients. Lisa and I both strongly suggest you hire only AICI members to ensure the best advice. Call the association for a professional member referral at (800) 383-8831.

The best consultants have in-depth training from a reputable institute or school (preferably through a program that lasted more than one or two weeks). Unfortunately there aren't any legal require- *(text continues on p.302)*

The Last, Best Shopping-Advice Tidbits

- Don't shop on Saturdays. The crowds will frustrate you, the salespeople are overworked and out of steam, and the parking is unthinkable. Shop during the week for better service and selection.
- Never shop when you're in a bad mood.
- If something is flawed, ask the manager for a discount. You'll probably get one.
- Save your receipt until you've worn the garment at least once and are satisfied with it. Stores are not obligated by law to refund cash for returns, and returns without a receipt are never a good idea.
- Be adventurous, not silly.
- If you plan to shop at an indoor mall, leave your coat in the car or check it.
- Wear something you love that goes with a lot of other things you own.
- Some department stores offer a one time or one-day discount of 10, 15, or 20 percent for opening a charge account. If you are planning a big purchase, find out the details, like if the deal excludes sale merchandise. If not, wait until the big sale and get yourself a hefty discount.
- Even if you think you can't afford their clothes, take a walk through the top-end department stores to get an idea of what they offer in terms of color and assortment. A quick browse will tell you volumes about the trends, which you can use to shop for comparable looks at lower prices. A savvy shopper knows the value of things. While you're there, be sure to check the sale rack—the best bargains are found at the priciest shops.

The Very Best Packing Tips

1. Pack only in dry weather, or else in an air-conditioned room because humidity promotes wrinkles, and will make everything a lot heavier to carry. Cover all garments with plastic cleaner bags. That way, clothes slide across each other instead of wrinkling.

2. Hang several coordinated pieces together on a single hanger in their own bag to reduce hanger weight and prevent wrinkling. (Use large safety pins to hang skirts from hangers.) Organize these bags by color or outfit to really save time and hassle. (Some women even hang a bag filled with that outfit's accessories from the same hanger—an easy way to get dressed in a dark room without waking your roommate!)

3. Roll or fold each piece along a major seam or down the middle (in a plastic garment bag). Clothes will actually take up less space in the bag and get fewer wrinkles when folded or rolled—but be careful to smooth them out as your roll/fold. Delicate things folded individually with tissue paper in the middle will prevent wrinkles, too.

4. Keep your like-colored hose together by color in plastic baggies. Pack your socks in your shoes.

 **5.** Separate accessories into small zip-lock baggies. I organize earrings, necklaces, and every other small accessory separately. That way you can see everything clearly, and you'll never have to spend time untangling jewelry.

6. Bring a few empty large-size zip-lock bags with you to stash worn socks, hose, and underwear or wet swimsuits, if needed.

7. Pack the heaviest things (like jeans and bulky sweaters) on the bottom. Stuff undies into the little corners and small spaces.

8. Slip your shoes into plastic bags or into socks to protect the rest of your things from loose dust and foot odors.

9. Pack your jewelry, valuables, and cosmetics and toiletries in your carry-on bag. Never pack them in your suitcase, which is more easily damaged or stolen. Include one change of clothing.

10. Take along only as much shampoo, etc. as you need—no more, no less. Look for reusable travel-sized bottles which are larger than sample size and smaller than full size. (The tiny samples for sale in drug and food stores are much, much more expensive per ounce than full size, and are tiny. If you have to buy beauty aids at a resort or hotel you'll pay a fortune!) Be sure to leave a little space at the top of the bottle when you fill it. Things expand and overflow under low cabin pressure.

11. Pack a few cotton balls, cotton swabs, cosmetic sponges, Band-Aids™, prepackaged moist hand towels, a few tissues, a couple of rubber bands, and a few safety pins of assorted sizes, and a tiny sewing kit like those given out at hotels in a zip-lock bag and throw it in your purse. You can solve dozens of crises with this kit! Another handy addition I recently discovered: Summer's Eve® Feminine Wash towelettes for the inevitable ladies' room stall without paper.

ments for licensing or certification anywhere in the United States, but AICI members are generally the best qualified. Choosing the right professional for you is a little like shopping for a doctor—beyond the basic qualifications, bedside manner and listening skills are key. AICI recommends that you ask:

- How long have you been practicing?
- What is your area of expertise?
- Where did you receive your training?
- What is your fee structure?
- What will the process be like?
- May I have two client recommendations?

By all means, use the in-store shoppers available in many department stores. Fees are never involved, and you'll get better personal service. They offer larger, more comfy fitting rooms (and sometimes great freebies like special sales, complimentary beverages, etc.). Call ahead to give them a general idea of what you would like to see, and they'll have it in the fitting room waiting for you. They will pull whatever sizes you need—or find them in other stores and send them over—and help you coordinate an outfit. It sounds extraordinary, but there's no obligation to buy. This elevated service is actually a re-creation of the way shopping used to be when we all patronized small, friendly neighborhood boutiques. If you've ever wished for better service from a store, the in-store personal shopper service is for you. Just remember that you are still dealing with salespeople whose ultimate mission is to sell you something. Be courteous to them (use their service when you are really shopping to buy versus just browsing), and they'll make your life easier.

Clothing Resources for the Plus-Size Woman

I apologize in advance to any whose name, address, phone number, or other description has been omitted or presented incorrectly. I've done my best to avoid these errors, but perfection is impossible. Please send me new or correct info. Thanks!

Department Stores and Retail Chains

The Answer
(retail chain)
Call for store locations:
(212) 279-7676

Ashley Stewart
(retail chain; NY, NJ, MD, VA, IL, MI)
Call for store locations:
(201) 319-9093

August Max Woman
(retail chain—various)
Call for store locations:
(800) STYLE-YU (789-5398)

The Avenue
(retail chain)
Call for store locations:
(201) 909-2060

Bloomingdale's
(retail—department stores)
Shop for Women departments
(212) 705-2000

Bon Marche
(retail—department stores)
Call for store locations:
(206) 344-2121

The Bon Ton
(retail—department stores)
(717) 757-7660

Burdine's
(retail—department stores)
Call for store locations:
(305) 835-5151

Catherine's Inc.
(retail chain)
1878 Brooks Road East
Memphis, TN 38116
Call for store locations:
(901) 398-9500

Charisma
(retail chain NE—various, special occasion)
Call for store locations:
(800) 827-CHAR (2427)

Dayton Hudson
(retail—department stores)
Call for store locations:
(612) 375-2200

Dillard's
(retail—department stores)
Call for store locations:
    (501) 376-5200

Dress Barn Woman
(retail chain—discounted various)
Call for store locations:
    (914) 369-4500

Elisabeth
(manufacturer/retail chain—
    various; qtrly. trend newsletter)
Liz Claiborne
1441 Broadway, 18th Floor
New York, NY 10018
Call for store locations:
    (201) 376-5490

Ellen Tracy
(mfr./retail outlets)
Call for store locations:
    (201) 935-3425

Evan Picone
(retail-outlet chain)
Call for store locations:
    (800) 258-5663

Famous-Barr
(retail—department stores)
Call for store locations:
    (314) 444-3111

Fashion Bug Plus
(retail chain—discounted various)
Call for store locations:
    (215) 245-9100

Filene's
(retail—department stores)
Call for store locations:
    (617) 357-2978

Fitting Image/Modern Woman
(retail chain)
Call for store locations:
    (717) 396-9000

The Forgotten Woman
(retail chain/mail-order—various
    better day and eve)
34-24 Hunters Point Avenue
Long Island City, NY 11101
Call for store locations:
    (800) TFW-1424

Hecht's
(retail—department stores)
Call for store locations:
    (703) 558-1200

Jacobson's
(retail—department stores)
Call for store locations:
    (517) 764-6400

Jones New York Woman
(retail/outlet chain)
Call for store locations:
    (800) 258-5663

Kaufman's
(retail—department stores)
Call for store locations:
    (412) 232-2000

King Size
(retail chain—mens' plus sizes)
P.O. Box 9115
Hingham, MA 02043-9115
Call for store locations:
    (800) 846-1600

La Chine
(mfr./retail outlets)
55 Hartz Way
Secaucus, NJ 07096
Call for store locations:
    (201) 392-0421

Lane Bryant
(retail chain)
Call for store locations:
    (614) 577-4000

Lord & Taylor
(retail—department stores)
American Woman departments
Call for stores locations:
    (800) 223-7440

Macy's
(retail—department stores)
Macy Woman departments
Call for store locations:
    (800) 343-0121

Marshall Fields
(department store chain)
Call for store locations:
    (800) (312) 741-1000

Nordstrom
(retail/mail-order—department
    stores)
Encore Departments
Call for store locations and
    mail-order: (800) 695-8000

Personal Touch America e-mail
    shopping service:
6870401@mcimail.com
For info: (800) 925-4254
Fax: (206) 628-1441

JC Penney
(retail/mail-order—department
    stores)
Call for store locations:
    (800) 222-6161

PS—Plus Sizes/Plus Savings
(retail chain—plus, super)
3742 Lamar Avenue
Memphis, TN 38118-3727
Call for store locations:
    (901) 363-3900

Robinsons-May
(retail—department stores)
Call for store locations:
    (818) 508-5226

Saks Fifth Avenue
(retail—department stores)
Salon Z departments
Call for store locations:
    (212) 753-4000

Sterns
(retail—department stores)
Call for store locations:
    (201) 845-5500

Village East
(retail chain)
Call for store locations:
    (209) 434-8000

Woman's World/Fitting Image
(retail chain)
1166 Fesler Street
El Cajon, CA 92020
Call for store locations:
    (717) 396-9000

Specialty Retailers

A & E Apparel
(mail-order—knits)
2636 Walnut Hill Lane #100
Dallas, TX 75229
(800) 541-7057

Abigail Starr
(retail/mail-order—better career, special occasion, casual, custom)
Logan Square
1 Village Row (Rte. 202)
New Hope, PA 18938
(215) 862-2066

and

301 13th Avenue South
Naples, FL 33940
(813) 649-4999

Adini En Plus
(mail-order—dresses and sportswear)
725 Branch Avenue
Providence, RI 02904
(800) 556-2443

Alberene Cashmere
(retail/mail-order—capes, sweaters, etc.)
435 Fifth Avenue
New York, NY 10016
(800) 884-5478
Fax: (212) 302-2748

Allure
(retail)
356 Millburn Avenue
Millburn, NJ 07041
(201) 467-8900

Amazon Designs
(mail-order—various)
(800) 315-8332

Ambassador Showcase
(mail-order—various)
P.O. Box 28807
Tucson, AZ 85726
(520) 747-5000

Ample Annie
(retail—consignment)
717 Pacific Avenue
Santa Cruz, CA
(408) 425-3838

Ample Boutique
(retail—various)
895 North Academy
Colorado Springs, CO
(719) 637-1716

1307 Juan Tabo NE
Albuquerque, NM
(505) 293-4389

The Ample Tree
(retail)
Bedford, IN

Anita's Sizes Plus
(retail)
20335 Biscayne Boulevard
Adventura, FL 33180
(305) 935-4255

Annette's
(retail)
2406 Magowan Drive
Montgomery Village
Santa Rosa, CA 95405
(707) 528-8281

Annette's Armoire
(retail)
27 East Delaware Place
Chicago, IL 60611
(312) 337-6706

Anthony Richards
(mail-order—various)
6864 Engle Road
P.O. Box 94549
Cleveland, OH 44130
(216) 826-3008

Appleseed's Just Right
(mail-order—various)
30 Tozer Road
P.O. Box 1020
Beverly, MA 01915-0720
(800) 767-6666
Fax: (800) 755-7557

Arthur Robert
(retail)
2055 Green Bay Road
Highland Park, IL 60035
(708) 433-5100

Ashanti
(retail)
321 Millburn Avenue
Millburn, NJ
(201) 376-4799

Ashanti Bazaar
(retail)
Lexington Avenue
New York, NY
(212) 535-0740

Astárte: Woman by Design
(retail/mail-order—various career and formal wear)
24520 Hawthorne Boulevard
Torrance, CA 90505
(310) 373-0638
(800) R U WOMAN (789-6626)

Attitude Plus
(retail)
Wilmington, DE

Audrey's Fashions
(retail—various, some bridal)
645 Olive Street
Fresno, CA 93728
(209) 264-9855

Avon by Mail
(mail-order—clothing, beauty)
(800) 500-AVON (2866)

Barbara Stone Designs
(mail-order—washable silks)
1800 Shasta Street
Redding, CA 96001
(916) 246-1927

The Better Half
(retail—better various)
177 Columbia Turnpike
Florham Park, NJ 07932
(201) 377-8171

The Better Half
(retail—better various)
517 Avenel Street
Avenel, NJ 07001
(908) 634-5533

The Better Half
Grand Forks, ND
(701) 775-6261

Big, Bad and Beautiful
(mail-order—various)
19225 Ventura Boulevard
Tarzana, CA 91356
(800) 347-3593

Big, Bold & Beautiful
(mail-order/retail—sportswear)
1263 Bay Street
Toronto, Ontario
Canada M5R 2 C1
(416) 923-4673
(800) 668-4673

Big N Beautiful
(retail)
17D Farmington Road
Rochester, NH 03867
(603) 332-1960

Big Time Fashion Resale
551 Eglinton Avenue West
Toronto, Ontario
Canada MSN 1B5
(416) 481-6464

Billings Large Sizes & Maternity
(retail—various)
46 Main Street
Southampton, NY 11968
(516) 287-1616

Botticelli
(retail)
1330 Niagara Falls Boulevard
Tonawanda, NY 14150
(716) 837-1122

Brownstone Woman
(mail-order—various)
P.O. Box 3356
Salisbury, MD 21802-3356
(800) 221-2991; 322-2991
Fax: (800) 450-5551

Cathy
(retail)
40 North Dean Street
Englewood, NJ 07631
(201) 871-3788

Charlene's Fashion Plus
(retail)
46 White Bridge Road
Nashville, TN 37205
(615) 352-8896

Chezelle
(retail)
1417 Clarkview Road
Baltimore, MD 21209
(410) 821-1363

Choices Plus
(retail—various)
1247D Kailua Road
Kailua, HI 96734
(808) 262-2252

Classics Boutique
(retail)
Manassas, VA

Cotton Threads Clothing
(mail-order—casual)
Rte. 2, Box 90
Hallettsville, TX 77964
(409) 562-2153

Cynthia Rae
(mail-order/retail—suits, dresses)
4617 Excelsior Boulevard
Minneapolis, MN 55416
(612) 929-7593

Daisy's Corner
(retail)
120 Middle Neck Road
Great Neck, NY 11021
(516) 466-6589

Dallas Fashion
(retail—plus and super suits, dresses)
34 West 37th Street
New York, NY 10018
(212) 967-9744

Daphne
(retail—African-American apparel and various)
467 Amsterdam Avenue
New York, NY 10024
(212) 877-5073

Davidé Fur
(retail—furs)
330 Seventh Avenue
New York, NY 10001
(212) 268-0050

Deborah Gorra
(retail)
255 North El Cielo Road
Palm Springs, CA 92262
(909) 796-1982

Desert Rain
(mail-order—apparel, jewelry)
4705 Sanders Road
Tucson, AZ 85743
(520) 682-7335

Desert Tortoise Creations
(mail-order—various, Southwestern apparel)
P.O. Box 2181
Ramona, CA 92065

Designer Unlimited
(mail-order—offers discounted designer labels)
P.O. Box 523
Canoga Park, CA 91305
(800) 990-3033

Designs by Phillippe
(mail-order—loungewear, evening wear)
(800) 99 KAFTAN (995-2382)

Dimensions Plus
(retail)
280 West 34th Street
Anchorage, AK 99050
(907) 562-2313

Dion-Jones
(mfr./mail-order—various)
3226 South Aberdeen
Chicago, IL 60608
(312) 927-1113

Distinctions
(retail/mail-order—various)
8650 Genesee Avenue, #200
San Diego, CA 92122
(619) 550-1775

DJ's
(retail)
Missoula, MT

DJ's Plus Sizes
(retail/mail-order—various,
  plus and super)
4931 South Orange Avenue
Orlando, FL 32806
(407) 438-2183

Draper's & Damon's
(mail-order)
17911 Mitchell Avenue South
Irvine, CA 92714
(800) 843-1174

Eleganté Woman Boutique
(retail—various, plus, super)
75 Anderson Street
Hackensack, NJ 07601
(201) 487-6468

Elegant Lady
Fair Oaks Boulevard
Sacramento, CA 95825
(916) 922-9861

Especially for You
(retail)
915 Red Bank Road
Greenville, NC 27858
(919) 756-1600

Essence by Mail
(mail-order—various African-
  American apparel)
P.O. Box 62
Hanover, PA 17333
(800) 882-8055

E Style
(Mail-order—African-American &
  various apparel)
P.O. Box 182564
Columbus, OH 43218
(800) 237-8953

Exquisite Elegance
(retail—various)
460 West Main Street
Abingdon, VA 24210
(540) 623-0058

Extra Special
(retail)
976 Houston Northcut Boulevard
Mount Pleasant, SC 29464
(803) 449-8563

Fairy Godmother at Large
(retail—consignment)
133 South Murphy Avenue
Sunnyvale, CA 94086
(408) 737-7684

Fashion Friendly
(retail)
Jacksonville, FL

Fashion Lady
(retail)
2098 El Camino Real
Santa Clara, CA 95050
(408) 246-8696

Fashions Plus
(retail)
Grove, OK

First Impressions
(retail)
Kent, WA

Forget Me Not
(retail)
710 Washington
Bay City, MI 48708
(517) 894-0223

For Women Only
(retail—better, various)
210 West Merrick Road
Valley Stream, NY 11580
(516) 825-7347

FSA Plus Woman
(retail/mail-order—sweaters,
  various)
60 Laurel Haven
Fairview, NC 28730
(800) 628-5525
Fax: (704) 628-2610

Gourd Chips
(African designs)
(718) 797-2739

Grace Full Fashions
(retail)
3303C State Street
Santa Barbara, CA 93105
(805) 687-6811

Great Changes
(retail—various and better)
12516 Riverside Drive
North Hollywood, CA 91607
(818) 769-4626
Fax: (818) 769-7779

Greater Salt Lake Clothing Co.
(retail/mail-order—skiwear)
1955 East 4800 South
Salt Lake City, UT 84117
(801) 273-8700

Gypsy Moon
(mail-order—gypsy styles)
1780 Massachusetts Avenue
Cambridge, MA 02140
(617) 876-7095

Hammrah's
(retail—designer, limited plus sizes)
2 Piermont Road
Cresskill, NJ 07626
(201) 871-4444

Harper Greer
(mfr./retail/mail-order—better,
  various apparel)
580 Fourth Street
San Francisco, CA 94107
(415) 543-4066
(800) 578-4066
Fax: (415) 543-8813

Heart's Delight
(mfr./mail-order—various)
(805) 647-7123

Hovis Jeans
(mail-order—denim, etc.)
P.O. Box 1717 3204
Reefy Road
Cody, WY 82414
(800) 383-4684

In Full Swing
(retail—various)
285 Sutter Street
San Francisco, CA 94108
(415) 433-1564

Invitation to the Dance
(mfr./mail-order)
P.O. Box 215
Newbury Park, CA 91319
(213) 852-0601

Jalon Enterprises
(mail-order—leather and suede)
P.O. Box 750355
Forest Hills Station
Forest Hills, NY 11375
(800) 316-2877

Jill Saunders
(retail—better, various discounted)
435 Fifth Avenue
New York, NY 10016
(212) 685-8545
(800) GO LARGE (465-2743)

J. Jill Ltd.
(mail-order—various)
P.O. Box 3006
Winterbrook Way
Meredith, NH 03253
(800) 642-9989

John Sun Silks
(mfr./mail-order—better silks)
5782 East 2nd Street
Suite 600
Long Beach, CA 90803

Judith Ann
(retail—various)
321 Millburn Avenue
Millburn, NJ
(201) 376-4799

Just My Size
(mail-order—various, lingerie, hose)
P.O. Box 748
Rural Hall, NC 27098
(800) 522-0889

Just Right!
(mail-order—various)
P.O. Box 1020
30 Tozer Road
Beverly, MA 01915
(800) 767-6666

JW Ramage
(mail-order—lingerie, various)
P.O. Box 442
Lafayette, CA 94549-0442
(800) 715-7587
Fax: (510) 284-5776

La Bella Figura
(mfr./retail—custom collection)
Lisa Aldisert
525 Seventh Avenue
New York, NY 10018
(212) 840-3350

Lane Bryant
(mail-order)
P.O. Box 8303
Indianapolis, IN 46209
(800) 477-7070

Large Beautiful Originals
(retail)
257 South Robertson Boulevard
Beverly Hills, CA 90211
(310) 659-6955

Large Lovely Lady
(mail-order—dresses, suits)
P.O. Box 4385
Chatsworth, CA 91313
(818) 709-0950

Lisa Todd Inc.
(retail—multiple stores)
8235 South Dixie Highway
Miami, FL 33143
(305) 661-2646

Lutes Design Inc.
Peggy Lutz
(retail/mail-order)
6784 Depot Street
Sebastopol, CA 95473
(707) 824-1634

Magical Creations Boutique
(retail—various, plus, super)
4232 Northeast Sandy Boulevard
Portland, OR 97213
(503) 288-5450

Making It Big
(retail/mail-order—various)

For mail order:
501 Aaron Street

Cotati, CA 94931
(707) 795-1995
Fax: (707) 795-4874

For Making It Big store:
9595 Main Street
Penngrove, CA 94951

Michelle's
(mail-order—various)
6802 Ingram
San Antonio, TX 78238
(210) 521-8337

Miller Stockman
(mail-order—Western wear)
P.O. Box 5127Denver, CO 80217
(800) 688-9888

More to Love
(retail—better, various)
2924 Highway 365
Nederland, TX 77627
(409) 724-0175

and

4374 Dowlen Road
Beaumont, TX 77706
(409) 899-3641

Muggins
(retail—better, various)
The Waterworks Mall
929 Freeport Road
Pittsburgh, PA 15238
(412) 781-0771

Myles Ahead
(retail/mail-order—various plus,
  super, tall)
6652 Northwest 57th Street
Tamarac, FL 33321
(305) 724-0500
Fax: (305) 724-7177

My Mother's Star
(retail)
Edwardsville, IL

Nicole Summers
(mail-order)
Winterbrook Way
Meredith, NH 03253-3003
(800) 642-6786

Nieman Marcus by Mail
(mail-order)
P.O. Box 2968
Dallas, TX 75221-2968
(800) 825-8000

Nothing in Moderation
(retail—various)
801 Lake Street
Oak Park, IL 60301-1301
(708) 386-9750
Fax: (708) 386-9767

Paradigm
(retail/mail-order)
P.O. Box 4021-B
Los Angeles, CA 90051

Parsinen Design
(mfr./mail-order—dresses and
    separates, plus, super)
1011 Boren Avenue, #178
Seattle, WA 98104
(206) 329-4761
(800) 422-5808
Fax: (206) 329-0944

Peaches
(mail-order—natural fiber
    sweaters)
P.O. Box 268
Cedarhurst, NY 11516
(800) PEACH 03 (732-2403)

Peacock Clothes
(retail—plus, super)
558-B South Murphy Avenue
Sunnyvale, CA 94086
(408) 730-0941

JC Penney
(catalog for 16W+)
(800) 222-6161

Pernell's Clothing
(retail)
Ridgecrest, CA

PF-147
(mail-order—various)
824 South Los Angeles Street, #409
Los Angeles, CA 90014
(213) 488-1046

PFI Fashions
(mail-order—separates)
W986 Highway B
Genoa City, WI 53128
(800) 251-2112

Phillipp
(mail-order—dresses, coats,
    various)
3056½ Ivy Street
San Diego, CA 92104
(800) 995-2382

Plus Repeats
(retail)
Lakewood, CO

Plus Woman Collection
(mail-order—various, to 8X)
60 Laurel Haven
Fairview, NC 28730
(800) 628-5525
Fax: (704) 628-2610
pluswoman2@aol.com

Queen of Hearts
(mail-order/retail—various)
19 Merrick Avenue
Merrick, NY 11566
(516) 377-1357

Rainy County Knit Wear
(made-to-measure sweaters)
P.O. Box 7852
Everett, WA 98201-0852
(206) 653-7189

Regalia
(mail-order—various)
P.O. Box 27800
Tucson, AZ 85726
(520) 747-5000

Rennar Boutique
(mfr./retail—various)
586 Broadway
Bayonne, NJ 07002
(201) 823-3043

Richman Cotton Co.
2631 Piner Road
Santa Rosa, CA 95401
(800) 992-8924

Rivi Fashions
(retail—apparel and lingerie)
3035 East Tropicana #F
Las Vegas, NV
(702) 433-8707

Roaman's
(mail-order—various)
P.O. Box 46283
Indianapolis, IN 46209
(800) 274-7130

**Rocky Mountain Clothing/Blue
    Clover**
(mail-order—jeans, etc.)
8500 Zuni Street
Denver, CO 80221
(800) 688-4449

Roselyn Dress Shop
(retail)
347 14th Street
Oakland, CA 94612
(510) 444-7472

Rose of Sharon
(retail)
The Forum Shops
Las Vegas, NV

Rubenesque
(retail)
1020 B Street
San Rafael, CA 94901
(415) 456-5580

Ruthie's Big Galz Boutique
(retail)
1307 First Street
Napa, CA 94559
(707) 255-7737
(800) 655-7738

Sankofa
(mail-order—African motifs,
    natural fibers)
1870 North Vermont Avenue #530
Los Angeles, CA 90027
(213) 661-1431

Says Who?
(retail/mail-order)
3903 Piedmont Avenue
Oakland, CA 94611
(510) 547-5818

and

539 Bryant Street
Palo Alto, CA 94301
(415) 324-3511

Scarlet Crane
(mail-order—natural fiber
   apparel)
P.O. Box 1931-BB
Sausalito, CA 94966
(415) 332-5266

Seams to Fit
(retail—consignment)
6527 Telegraph Avenue
Oakland, CA 94609
(510) 428-9463

Sears
Woman's View Catalog
(retail/mail-order)
P.O. Box 8361
Indianapolis, IN 46283
(800) 944-1973

Sharon J
(retail/mail-order—various)
1327 Sartori
Torrance, CA 90501
(800) 998-1985

Shepler's
(mail-order—Western wear)
P.O. Box 7702
Wichita, KS 67277
(800) 835-4004

Silhouettes
(mail-order—various and petites)
5 Avery Row
Roanoke, VA 24012-8567
(800) 704-3322

Soho Woman
(retail)
375 West Broadway
New York, NY 10012
(212) 431-7803

Special Effects
(retail)
1433 Broadway
Hewlett, NY 11557
(516) 295-1059

Special Size Shop
(retail)
6215 Brooklyn Boulevard
Minneapolis, MN 55429
(612) 537-3034

Spiegel for You
(mail-order—various, talls and
   petites)
P.O. Box 182555
Columbus, OH 43218-2555
(800) 345-4500
Fax: (800) 422-6697

Sweet Cheeks
(mail-order)
P.O. Box 7767
Redlands, CA 92375
(909) 792-0454

Sweeter Measures
(mail-order—various)
819 Front Street
Box 340
Gibbon, NE 68840
(308) 468-5156
Fax: (308) 468-5287

SW Full Figure Designs
(mail-order—suits, dresses)
490 South Stone Mountain–
   Lithonia Road #59
Stone Mountain, GA 30088
(404) 469-6139

Ulla Popken
(retail/mail-order—various, petites)

For retail:
Towson Town Center
825 Dulaney Valley Road
Towson, MD 21204

For mail order:
5 Hampston Garth
Lutherville, MD 21093
(410) 494-8108
(800) 245-ULLA (8552)
Fax: (410) 494-8109

The Very Thing!
(mail-order—various)
P.O. Box 3005
Winterbrook Way
Meredith, NH 03253
(800) 642-6786

Warm Stuff
(Polar fleece)
(800) 753-3346

A Woman's Place
(retail—various)
191 South Main Street
New City, NY 10956
(914) 634-1076

Yeta's
(retail—better, various)
29 West 8th Street
Holland, MI 49423
(616) 393-5950

Zenoblie F. Creations
(mail-order—lingerie, swimwear,
   dresses)
129 Van Horne West
Montreal, Quebec
Canada H2T 2J2
(514) 277-6621
Fax: (514) 277-4705

Supersize Resources

Amazon Designs
(mail-order)
1473 Old Airport Road
Paris, AR 72855
(501) 963-6548
(800)315-8332

Armand's
(panties)
219-D Elm
Reading, PA 19606

Big, Bad and Beautiful
(mail-order—various)
19225 Ventura Boulevard
Tarzana, CA 91356
(800) 347-3593

Big Dreams
(mail-order—shorts)
P.O. Box 2195
St. Petersburg, FL 33731
(813) 824-7720

Big Shots Fashions
(mail-order—various)
74 Alabama Avenue
Island Park, NY 11558

Cello
(mail-order—various)
10401 Wilshire Boulevard, Suite 401
Los Angeles, CA 90024
(310) 446-9729

Charisma
(retail/mail-order chain)
(800) 827-CHAR (2427)

Colorado Coyote
(catalog)
1366 South Elm Street
Denver, CO 80222
(303) 758-5390

Color Me Big
(catalog)
P.O. Box 9773
San Bernardino, CA 92427
(909) 887-8969

Dallas Fashion
(retail—plus and super)
34 West 37th Street
New York, NY 10018
(212) 967-9744

Daphne
(retail—African-American
    apparel, various)
473 Amsterdam Avenue
New York, NY 10024
(212) 877-5073

Dion Jones
(retail—various)
3226 South Aberdeen
Chicago, IL 60608
(312) 927-1113

DJ's Plus Sizes
(retail/mail-order)
4931 South Orange Avenue
Orlando, FL 32806
(407) 438-2183

Elegance At Large
(mail-order—various)
3200 Adams Avenue, Suite 105
San Diego, CA 99116
(800) 884-0915

Entrance
(catalog)
P.O. Box 11627
Marina Del Rey, CA 90295
(800) 800-2394

FSA Plus Woman
(mail-order—various)
60 Laurel Haven
Fairview, NC 28730
(800) 628-5525
Fax: (704) 628-2610

Full Bloom
185 South Pearl
Denver, CO 80209
(303) 733-6264

Full Figure Designs
(mail-order)
490 South Stone Mountain–
    Lithonia Road #59
Stone Mountain, GA 30088
(404) 469-6139

Greater Salt Lake Clothing Co.
(retail/mail-order—skiwear)
1955 East 4800 South
Salt Lake City, UT 84117
(801) 273-8700

Harper Greer
(retail/mail-order—better career,
    casual, evening)
580 Fourth Street
San Francisco, CA 94107
(800) 578-4066

Have It Your Way
(retail—various)
10942 Balboa Boulevard
Granada Hills, CA 91344
(818) 831-1855

Hovis Jeans
(mail-order—denim, etc.)
P.O. Box 1717-3204
Reefy Road
Cody, WY 82414
(800) 383-4684

In Full Swing
(retail—various)
285 Sutter Street
San Francisco, CA
(415) 433-1564

Jalon Enterprises
(mail-order—leather and suede)
350 Warren Street
Jersey City, NJ 07302
(800) 316-2877

Large Lovely Lady
(mail-order—dressy, bridal)
P.O. Box 4385
Chatsworth, CA 91313
(818) 709-0950

Making It Big
(retail/mail-order—various)

For mail order:
501 Aaron Street
Cotati, CA 94931
(707) 795-1995
Fax: (707) 795-4874

For store:
9595 Main Street
Penngrove, CA 94951

Myles Ahead
(retail/mail-order—various plus,
    super, tall)
6652 Northwest 57th Street
Tamarac, FL 33321
(305) 724-0500
Fax: (305) 724-7177

Paradigm
(retail/mail-order)
P.O. Box 4021-B
Los Angeles, CA 90051

Parsinen Design
(catalog)
1011 Boren Avenue, Suite 178
Seattle, WA 98104
(800) 422-5808

Peaches
(mail-order)
P.O. Box 268
Cederhurst, NY 11516
(800) PEACH 03 (732-2403)

Peacock Clothes
(retail—plus, super)
558-B South Murphy Avenue
Sunnyvale, CA 94086
(408) 730-0941

Peggy Lutz
Lutes Design Inc.
(retail/mail-order)
6784 Depot Street
Sebastopol, CA 95473
(707) 824-1634

PF 147
(mail-order)
824 South Los Angeles Street #409
Los Angeles, CA 90014
(213) 488-1046

Rennar Boutique
(mfr./retail—various)
586 Broadway
Bayonne, NJ 07002
(201) 823-3043

Roselyn
(retail/mail-order—various)
347 14th Street
Oakland, CA 94612
(510) 444-7472

Says Who?
(retail/mail-order)
3903 Piedmont Avenue
Oakland, CA 94611
(510) 547-5181
Fax: (510) 704-0288

Scarlet Crane
(catalog)
P.O. Box 1931
Sausalito, CA 94966

Seams to Fit
(retail-consignment)
6527 Telegraph Avenue
Oakland, CA 94609
(510) 428-9463

Size It Up
(mail-order—various)
5621 11th Street NE
Calgary 101, Alberta
Canada T2E 6Z7
(403) 730-8466

Sweet Cheeks
(catalog)
P.O. Box 7767
Redlands, CA 92375
(909) 792-0454

Sweeter Measures
(mail-order—various and uniforms)
P.O. Box 340
Gibbons, NE 68840
(308) 468-5156

SW's Full Figure Designs
(careerwear)
490 Stone Mountain
Lithonia 59
Stone Mountain, GA 30088
(770) 469-6139

Uniquity Plus
(catalog)
320 2nd Street, Suite 1-C
Durham, NC 27717-2394
(800) 772-0272

XL's Inc.
P.O. Box 52394
Durham, NC 27717-2394
(800) 772-0272

Yellow Creek Originals
(mail-order—custom lingerie)
2901 Yellow Creek Road
Dickson, TN 37055
(800) 714-1410 PIN #3959
(615) 763-6147

Activewear

1824 Catalog
(horseback gear)
(703) 818-1517

Body by Rubens
(retail)
17109 Locust Drive
Hazel Crest, IL 60429

Danskin Plus
(mfr./retail outlets/mail-order)
Call for retailers near you:
    (800) 288-6749

Enell Sports Bras
(mail-order)
(800) 828-7661

Fit to Be Tried
(mail-order)
4754 East Grant
Tucson, AZ 85712
(800) 669-6409
(520) 881-6449

Full Bloom
(mail-order)
185 South Pearl
Denver, CO 80209
(303) 733-6264

Full Fitness by Jazel
(mail-order)
P.O. Box 40531
Philadelphia, PA 19106
(215) 386-5085

The Greater Salt Lake Clothing Co.
(mail-order—skiwear)
1955 East 4800 South
Salt Lake City, UT 84117
(801) 273-8700

Hep Cats
(mail-order)
P.O. Box 40223
Nashville, TN 37204
(615) 298-2980

Hot off the Tour
(mail-order—golf wear)
(800) 991-1211

Junonia Active Wear
(mail-order)
46 East Fourth Street #216
Saint Paul, MN 55101
(800) 586-6642

Miller's
(retail—horseback gear)
235 Murry Hill Parkway
East Rutherford, NJ 07073

Phillipe
(mail-order—special occasion)
3056½ Ivy Street
San Diego, CA 92104
(800) 995-2382

Tilley Endurables
(retail/mail-order—travel and
    activewear, hats)
(800) 884-3093

Women at Large
(mail-order)
1020 South 48th Avenue
Yakima, WA 98908
(509) 965-0115

Swimwear

Alice's Undercover World
(retail)
23820 Crenshaw Boulevard
Torrance, CA 90500
(310) 326-6775

All Ashore
(mail-order)
(210) 829-7813

Anne Terrie Designs
(mail-order)
129-G Derby Boulevard
Harrison, OH 45030
(800) 774-6898

Appleseed's
(mail-order)
P.O. Box 1020
30 Tozer Road
Beverly, MA 01915
(800) 767-6665

Big, Bold & Beautiful
(retail/mail-order)
1263 Bay Street
Toronto, Ontario
Canada M5R 2C1
(416) 923-4673

Big Day at the Beach
(mail-order—custom)
P.O. Box 271
Bryn Mawr, CA 92318
(909) 798-5652
Fax: (909) 792-9147

Big Stitches by Jan
(mail-order—custom)
2423 Douglas Street
San Pablo, CA 94806
(510) 237-3978

By Ro! Designs
(mail-order)
567 West 5th Street #1
San Pedro, CA 90731
(310) 221-0509

Fit to Be Tried
(retail/mail-order)
4754 East Grant
Tucson, AZ 85712
(800) 669-6409
(520) 881-6449

Grand Allusion
(mail-order)
200-4170 Still Creek Drive
Burnaby, BC
Canada V5C 6C6
(604) 878-1185

Helen Hirsch
(retail—swimwear, lingerie)
457 Mount Pleasant Avenue
West Orange, NJ 07052
(201) 736-4484

JW Ramage
(mail-order)
1007 Oak Hill Road
Lafayette, CA 94549
(800) 621-7587

Queen of Hearts
(mail-order)
19 Merrick Avenue
Merrick, NY 11566
(516) 377-1357

Red Salamander
(mail-order—swimwear, sportswear)
P.O. Box 2435
Riviera, AZ 86442
(520) 768-2424

Silhouettes
(mail-order)
5 Avery Row
Roanoke, VA 24012-8567
(800) 704-3322

Simple Solutions
(mail-order)
18102 Brookhurst Street,
  Suite 190
Fountain Valley, CA 92708
(800) 822-9467
Fax: (310) 928-8420;
  (714) 631-4440

Sweet Dreams Intimates
(custom fit)
81 Route 111
Smithtown, NY 11787
(516) 366-0565

Sweeter Measures
(custom fit)
P.O. Box 340
Gibbon, NE 68840
(308) 468-5156

Ulla Popken
(retail/mail order)
Towson Town Center
(800) 245-ULLA (8552)

Uniforms

Ample Aprons
(mail-order)
21210 Northeast 23rd Court
North Miami, FL 33180
(305) 937-1144

Bencone Uniforms
(mail-order)
P.O. Box 251
Winston-Salem, NC 27101
(800) 631-4602

Mixables
(health-care uniforms)
(800) 541-7057

NAAFA Feminist
(hospital gowns)
Lynn Meletiche
2065 First Avenue
#190
New York, NY 10029
(212) 721-8259

JC Penney Co.
(uniforms and scrubs catalog)
(800) 222-6161

Plus-Size Lingerie and Intimate Apparel

Alice Rae Shop
(retail—multiple stores)
2914 North Campell
Tucson, AZ 85719
(602) 326-1921

Alice's Undercover World
(retail/mail-order/custom
  foundations)
23280 Crenshaw Boulevard
Torrance, CA 90505
(310) 326-6775

Armand's Lingerie
(mail-order—panties)
219 Elm Street
Reading, PA 19606
(610) 370-2799

Barely Nothings
(mail-order)
897 Oak Park Boulevard, Suite 163
Pismo Beach, CA 93449-3293
(800) 422-7359

Big Shots
(mail-order—lingerie, leather,
  activewear)
74 Alabama Avenue
Island Park, NY 11558
(800) 331-1333

The Bust Stop
(mail-order—bras)
8270 East 71st Street
Tulsa, OK 74133
(800) 858-3887

Cameo Conture
(mail-order—custom bras)
(214) 631-4860

Carol Doda's Champagne & Lace
(retail—various)
1850 Union Street #1
San Francisco, CA 94123
(415) 776-6900

Comfortably Yours
(mail-order)
61 West Hunter Avenue
Maywood, NJ 07607
(201) 368-0400

Daphne
(retail—lingerie)
473 Amsterdam Avenue
New York, NY 10024
(212) 579-0479

DD&E Designs
(mail-order)
P.O. Box 32877
Palm Beach Gardens, FL 33420

Decent Exposures
(mail-order—natural fabrics)
P.O. Box 27206
Seattle, WA 98125
(800) 524-4949
(206) 364-4540

Designs by Norvell
(mail-order)
P.O. Box 37
Alexandria, TN 37012
(615) 529-2831

DiPierre
(retail/mail-order—professional
  fitters)
826 Lexington Avenue
New York, NY 10021
(212) 421-4314

Elegance Plus Lingerie
(retail—fit specialists)
136 Santa Barbara Plaza
Los Angeles, CA 90008
(213) 292-6283
Fax: (213) 292-5359

Extra Emphasis
(mail-order—bras: maternity,
  sports, nursing, all types)
P.O. Box 1725
Tahoe City, CA 96145
(800) 539-0030

Fine & Fancy Lingerie
(mail-order)
2325 Third Street #346
San Francisco, CA 94107
(415) 861-4576

Frederick's of Hollywood
(mail-order)
P.O. Box 229
Hollywood, CA 90078
(800) 323-9525

Goddess Bra Company
(mfr.—up to 56 I-cup)
Call customer service for retail
  location: (617) 569-3000

Hanes/L'Eggs/Bali/Playtex
(mail-order/retail-discount)
P.O. Box 748
Rural Hall, NC 27098
(800) 300-2600

Helen Hirsch
(retail—swimwear, lingerie, special
  size bras)
457 Mount Pleasant Avenue
West Orange, NJ 07052
(201) 736-4484

High Places
(mail-order)
P.O. Box 620155
Littleton, CO 80162
(303) 973-3412

International Marketing
1680 Dunn Avenue, 46A
Jacksonville, FL 32218
(904) 696-9226

Intimate Appeal
(mail-order—div. of Arizona Mail
  Order)
Palo Verde at 34th
P.O. Box 27800
Tucson, AZ 85726-7800
(520) 747-5000

Intimate Encounters
(mail-order)
540 North Santa Cruz #187
Los Gatos, CA 95030
(800) 464-8300

JaneEtte, Inc.
(mail-order—bras)
P.O. Box 26458
Tucson, AZ 85726
(602) 746-9474

Just My Size
(mfr./outlets/mail-order)
P.O. Box 748
Rural Hall, NC 27098

For mail order: (800) 300-2600

For outlet store locations:
  (800) 831-7489

JW Ramage
(mail-order—lingerie and various)
P.O. Box 442
Lafayette, CA 94549-0442
(800) 715-7587
(510) 284-7528
Fax: (510) 284-5776

Lady Grace
(mail-order)
P.O. Box 128
Malden, MA 02148
(800) 922-0504

Lane Bryant Catalog
(mail-order—not retail)
P.O. Box 8301
Indianapolis, IN 46283-8301
(800) 477-7070

Laughing Sisters
(mail-order—nightgowns)
4514 Manitou Way
San Diego, CA 92117
(619) 272-1976

Lillian Lavergne Designs
(mail-order—fine fabrics)
7401 Lunar Drive
Austin, TX 78745
(800) 416-0063

Madame X Lingerie
(mail-order)
3023 North Clark Street, Suite 271B
Chicago, IL 60657

Magnolia Lingerie
(mail-order)
1498M Reistertown Road #357
Baltimore, MD 21208
(410) 358-0120

Marcus & Wiesen
(mail-order—foundations)
27-01 Queens Plaza North
Long Island City, NY 11101
(718) 361-9025

Michèle's Lingerie
(mail-order)
(800) 871-7872

Nadina Plus
(mail-order—various, natural fibers)
1124 Lonsdale Avenue, #1176
Vancouver, BC
Canada V7M 3J5
(604) 985-2356

Pambra's Inc.
(mail-order—bra liners)
P.O. Box 983
Fontana, CA 92334
(909) 820-1769

Queen of Hearts
(mail-order)
19 Merrick Avenue
Merrick, NY 11566
(516) 377-1357

Regalia
(mail-order)
Palo Verde at 34th
P.O. Box 2780
Tucson, AZ 85726
(800) 362-8420

Romantic Interludes
(mail-order)
Box 206 LSF
Jenks, OK 74037
(918) 299-7401

Romantic Notions
(mail-order—leather)
P.O. Box 6783-X
Bryan, TX 77805-6783
(409) 822-0306

Roselyn
(retail/mail-order)
347 14th Street
Oakland, CA 94612
(510) 444-7472

Sally's Place
(mail-order)
P.O. Box 1397, Dept. B
Sausalito, CA 94966
(415) 898-5683

Sweet Dreams Intimates
(retail/mail-order—custom fit)
81 Route 111
Smithtown, NY 11787
(516) 366-0565

Uptown Bra Smyth
(retail—custom fitting)
905 Madison Avenue
New York, NY 10021
(212) 772-9400
(800) BRA-9466 (272-9466)

and

Village Bra Smyth
179 West 4th Street
New York, NY 10014
(212) 929-1917

Wacoal
(mfr./bras up to 44DDD)
Call for store nearest you:
    (800) 526-6286
In New Jersey, customer service:
    (201) 933-8400

Yellow Creek Originals
(mail-order—custom lingerie)
2901 Yellow Creek Road
Dickson, TN 37055
(800) 714-1410 PIN #3959
(615) 763-6147

Zenoblie F. Creations
(mail-order—lingerie, swimwear,
    etc.)
129 Van Horne West
Montreal, Quebec
Canada H2T 2J2
(514) 277-6621
Fax: (514) 277-4705

Plus-Size Maternity

Baby Becoming
(mail-order)
P.O. Box 7238
Cumberland, RI 02864
(401) 729-4702

Betsy & Co.
(mail-order)
P.O. Box 1911
Philadelphia, PA 19105-1911
(800) 77 BETSY (772-3879)

Bosom Buddies
(mail-order—nursing, maternity)
P.O. Box 6138
Kingston, NY 12401
(914) 338-2038

Maternity Matters
(retail/mail-order)
1410 Colonial Life Boulevard
Columbia, SC 29210
(800) 613-2982

JC Penney Baby & You
(mail-order)
(800) 222-6161

Custom Clothing

Abigail Starr
(retail—some custom)
Logan Square
1 Village Row
New Hope, PA 18938
(215) 862-2066

Alberene Cashmere
(retail/mail-order—free shipping)
435 Fifth Avenue
New York, NY 10016
(800) 843-9078

Amazon Originals
(mail-order)
1473 Old Airport Road
Paris, AR 72855
(501) 963-6548

Ample Image
Peggy Moore
(415) 344-2264

Antie Em's
Emily O'Neill
(415) 969-3156

B.A.S.I.C.S.
(retail/mail order—various, custom
  fit)
5540 North 103rd Street
Milwaukee, WI 53225
(414) 464-1918

By Ro! Designs
(mail-order—swimwear, special
  occasion)
567 West 5th Street, #1
San Pedro, CA 90731
(310) 221-0509

Color Me Big
(mail-order—various)
P.O. Box 9773
San Bernardino, CA 92427
(909) 887-8969

Cotton Threads Clothing
(mail-order—casual)
Rte. 2, Box 90
Hallettsville, TX 77964
(409) 562-2153

Cynthia Rae
(mail-order—suits and dresses)
4617 Excelsior Boulevard
Minneapolis, MN 55416
(612) 929-7593

Davidé Fur
(retail—furs)
330 Seventh Avenue
New York, NY 10001
(212) 268-0050

Great Salt Lake Clothing Company
(skiwear)
1955 East 1800 South
Salt Lake City, UT 84117
(801) 273-8700

John Sun Silks
(mail-order)
5782 East 2nd Street, Suite 600
Long Beach, CA 90803

Phillipe Originals
(special occasion)
(800) 99 KAFTAN (995-2382)

Positive Stuff by Sandy Mooney
(mail-order—unique, natural
  fabrics)
(810) 732-5303

Queentex
(mail-order—caftans)
111 Chabanal Street West
Montreal, Quebec
Canada H2N 1C8
(800) FOR-1X2X (367-1929)

**Rainy County Knitwear by
  Priscilla Bird**
(mail-order—cotton knits)
(206) 653-7189

Red Salamander
(mail-order—various, lingerie)
P.O. Box 2435
Riviera, AZ 86442
(520) 768-2424

RJ's Apparel
(mail-order—African wear, other)
(704) 527-9767

Sweet Dreams Intimates
(mail-order)
81 Route 111
Smithtown, NY 11787
(516) 366-0565

**Sweeter Measures by Marianne
  Schomburg**
(mail-order—basics plus requests)
P.O. Box 340
Gibbon, NE 68840
(308) 468-5156

Women Size Shop
(retail/mail-order—various,
  maternity)
319 North 2nd Street
Clarskville, TN 37040
(800) 729-0869

Yellow Creek Originals
2901 Yellow Creek Road
Dickson, TN 37055
(615) 763-6147

Hosiery

Andrew Barry Associates
(mail-order—hose)
565 Potter Road
Framingham, MA 01701
(508) 877-3131

Hanes/L'Eggs/Bali/Playtex
(mail-order—discount)
P.O. Box 748
Rural Hall, NC 27098
(800) 300-2600

Just My Size
(mail-order)
P.O. Box 748
Rural Hall, NC 27098
(800) 522-0889

Marietta Hosiery
(mail-order)
484 Lake Park Avenue, Suite #408
Oakland, CA 94610

No Nonsense Direct
(mail-order)
2515 East 43rd Street
Chattanooga, TN 37422
(910) 272-5671
(800) 677-5995

Scantihose
(mail-order—hoisery)
Limited Editions
P.O. Box 20
Farmington, CT 06034
(203) 677-9225

Plus-Size Talls

Amazon Designs
(mail-order)
Old Airport Road
Paris, AZ 72855
(501) 963-6548

Color Me Special
(mail-order)
(213) 852-0601

Dion Jones
(retail)
3226 South Aberdeen
Chicago, IL 60608
(312) 927-1113

Long Elegant Legs
(mail-order)
2-1 Homestead Road
Belle Mead, NJ 08502
(800) 344-2235

Myles Ahead
(retail/mail-order—various plus,
  super, tall)
6652 Northwest 57th Street
Tamarac, FL 33321
(305) 724-0500
Fax: (305) 724-7177

Tall Expressions
(retail/mail-order)
218 Sunrise Highway
Rockville Centre, NY 11570
(516) 766-6720

Plus-Size Bridal

Big, Beautiful Brides
(retail/mail-order)
Toronto, Ontario
(416) 923-4673

Bridal Exchange
4931 South Orange Avenue
Orlando, FL 32806
(407) 438-2183

Bridal Gown Outlet
2739 North Lombard
Portland, OR 97217
(503) 286-1992

**Chantal Wedding Center of
  San Francisco**
(415) 742-0160

Davide's Bridal Wearhouse
(retail chain)
Call for store locations:
  (610) 896-4360

DJ's Plus Sizes
(retail/mail-order)
4931 South Orange Avenue
Orlando, FL
(407) 438-2183
(800) 522-9099

Exclusively for You
1020 N. First, Suite B
Renton, WA 98055
(206) 277-8880

Femme Fancy
(retail/mail-order)
217 South Ellsworth
San Mateo, CA 94401
(415) 340-8392

Immediate Resources
1305 Wycliff #102
Dallas, TX 75207
(214) 634-8444

The J—Western Division
(customized gowns)
507 East 10th
Spokane, WA 99202
(509) 624-4795

Kathleen's Full-Size
(retail)
5447 Ballard Avenue, N.W.
Seattle, WA 98107
(206) 784-5996

Lynnbrook Bridal Center
(retail/mail-order/video)
414 Sunrise Highway
Lynnbrook, NY 11563
(516) 599-1151

Large Lovely Lady
(mail-order)
Box 4385
Chatsworth, CA 91313-4385

The Madhatter
(mfr.—hats, bridal accessories,
  videos)
(800) 728-7970

Nina's Bridal
23400 Woodword Avenue
Ferndale, MI 48220
(810) 399-0330

JC Penney Bridal Collection
(800) 527-8345

S.A. Simatos
(mail-order)
P.O. Box 653
Pottsville, PA 17901
(717) 628-9701

Plus-Size Kids

Big Kids
JC Penney Catalog
(800) 222-6161

Richman Cotton Co.
(retail/mail-order)
2631 Piner Road
Santa Rosa, CA 95401
(800) 992-8924

Larger Boots and Shoes

Active Soles
(mail-order)
29 Wapping Road
Kingston, MA 02364
(800) 881-4322

Alder's
Barnum Shoe
(mail-order)
1434-1436 Barnum Avenue
Stratford, CT 06497
(800) 582-7995

Comfort Corner
(mail-order)
P.O. Box 649
Nashua, NH 03061
(800) 735-4994

Coward
(mail-order)
P.O. Box 27800
Tucson, AZ 85726-7800
(800) 362-8410
Fax: (602) 750-6755

The Custom Foot
(affordable custom shoes)
136 Main Street
Westport, CT 06880
(800) 440-8814

Go Lightly Footwear
(retail)
222 North Main
Pueblo, CO
(719) 545-5539

Johansen Bros. Shoes
(mail-order)
1915 West Main
Corning, AZ 72422
(800) 624-9079

Lori Alexandre
(mail-order—boots)
7999 Boulevard les Galeries
   d'Anjou #N012
Anjou, Quebec,
   Canada HIM IW6
(800) 648-4735
(514) 355-8500
Fax: (514) 355-5407

Lorrini Shoes/Lori Alexandre
(mail-order)
1420 Stanley Street
Montreal, Quebec
Canada H3A 1P8
(514) 842-5925
Fax: (514) 842-0769

Maryland Square
(mail-order)
1350 Williams Street
Chippewa Falls, WI 54729-1500
(800) 727-3895

Massey's
(mail-order)
601 Twelfth Street
Lynchburg, VA 24504
(800) 462-7739

McB's
(retail/mail-order)
715 Market Street
San Francisco, CA 94103
(415) 546-9444

Mitzi Baker Footwear
(mail-order)
8306 Wilshire Boulevard #943
Beverly Hills, CA 90211
(213) 655-2743

Plus Nine
(retail—sizes over 9)
11 East 57th Street
New York, NY 10022

Reyer's
(mail-order)
(800) 245-1550

Selby Fifth Avenue
(mail-order/retail chain)
(800) 346-3348

Silhouettes
(800) 704-3322

Spiegel "For You"
(800) 345-4500

StatShoeEsque
(retail/mail-order)
Promenade West
2225 South University Drive
Davie, FL 33324
(800) 367-7167

Wide World of Mar-Lou
(mail-order)
157 V Arcade
Cleveland, OH 44114
(216) 861-0730

Yorke Fashion Comfort Centre
(retail/mail-order—all sizes,
   orthotics)
140 East 55th Street
New York, NY 10022
(212) 753-5151

Video Clothing Catalogs

Astárte: Woman by Design
24582 Hawthorne Boulevard,
   Suite 100
Torrance, CA 90505
(800) R U WOMAN (789-6626)

Distinctions
8650 Genesee Avenue, Suite 200
San Diego, CA 92122
(800) 467-6363

Greater Woman
10360 Ellison Circle
Omaha, NE 68134
(800) 689-6626

Accessories

Accessorize
(catalog)
P.O. Box 1198
Colfax, CA 95713
(916) 346-6834

Arizona Mail Order Jewelry Values
Brochure
(520) 748-8600

Astárte: Woman by Design
(catalog/retail)
24520 Hawthorne Boulevard,
   Suite 100
Torrance, CA 90505
(800) R U WOMAN (789-6626)

Barb's Abundent Jewels
(mail-order)
2000 North Racine
Chicago, IL 60614

Bigger Bangles
(mail-order)
P.O. Box 506
Morris, IL 60450
(815) 941-4678

Booby Bibs
Liz McGee
P.O. Box 1997
Dallas, TX 75221

C. Flaherty
(mail-order—crystal pieces)
634 North Glenoaks, Suite 4
Burbank, CA 91502

Coy
(bangle bracelets)
24843 Del Prado, Suite 249
Dana Point, CA 92629
(714) 496-7042

E Style
(mail-order Spiegel division—
   African-American apparel)
P.O. Box 182564
Columbus, OH 43218
(800) 237-8953

H.L.S.
(mail-order—belts)
4757 West Park, #106–410
Plano, TX 75093
(214) 985-0074

J. Lumarel Corp.
(mail-order—longer lengths)
801 South University Drive, #C-110
Plantation, FL 33324

JUS-LIN Belts
4757 West Park, Suite 106-410
Plano, TX 75093

Pendragon's
(mail-order)
P.O. Box 411
Whitehouse, NJ 08888
(800) 473-3011

The Right Touch
(mail-order)
95-60 Queens Boulevard,
   Suite B205
Rego Park, NY 11374
(718) 899-5743

Robin Barr Enterprises
(mail-order—jewelry extenders)
8306 Wilshire Boulevard, #614B
Beverly Hills, CA 90211
(310) 358-7351

Ross Simons Company
(catalog)
(800) 556-7376

Worldesigns, Inc.
(mail-order—fanny packs)
P.O. Box 355
New York, NY 10024

Other Videos

**Great Changes Low Impact
   Workout with Carnie Wilson
   & Idrea**
Great Changes Boutique
12516 Riverside Drive
North Hollywood, CA 91607
(818) 769-4626
Fax: (818) 769-7779

Work It Out, Inc.
(personal workout videos)
Kelly Bliss, M.Ed., CPFT
1594 Springhill Drive
Aston, PA 19014
(610) 459-5011

Yoga for Round Bodies
Kripalu Yoga Center
Lenox, MA
(800) 967-7279

Associations and Organizations

**Abundia Programs for Size
   Acceptance and Self-Esteem**
P.O. Box 252
Downer's Grove, IL 60515
(708) 897-9796

Ample Awakenings
(dance parties)
New Jersey/Philadelphia
(215) 602-2064
(609) 877-9116

Ample Opportunity
P.O. Box 40621
Portland, OR 97240-0621
(503) 245-1524

**Association for Full-Figured
   Women of Atlanta**
(404) 243-6862

**Association of Image Consultants
   International (AICI)**
(information, referrals)
1000 Connecticut Avenue, NW,
   Suite 9
Washington, DC 20036
(800) 383-8831

The Big Difference
(dance parties)
3131 Barrington, Suite E
Los Angeles, CA 90066
(310) 398-0168

Big Sensations
(dance parties)
New England
(617) 893-1985

Goddesses
(dance parties, newsletter)
P.O. Box 1008
JAF Station
New York, NY 10116
(718) 456-9119

International No Diet Coalition
Council on Size and Weight
   Discrimination
P.O. Box 305
Mt. Marion, NY 12456

Largely Positive
P.O. Box 17223
Glendale, WI 53217
(414) 454-6500

Largesse, the Network for Self-Esteem
(info clearinghouse)
P.O. Box 9404
New Haven, CT 06534-0404
(203) 787-1624

Majestic Travel Club
(trips for plus people)
(916) 889-8001

More 2 Luv
(dance parties)
Southern California
(310) 693-1844

NAAFA (National Association to Advance Fat Acceptance)
P.O. Box 188620
Sacramento, CA 95818
(800) 442-1214

Professional Association of Custom Clothiers
(free brochure on how to find and work with a dressmaker)
P.O. Box 729
Bodega Bay, CA 94923-0729

Publications and Directories

AHELP Forum
Association for the Health Enrichment of Large People
P.O. Drawer C
Radford, VA 24143
(703) 731-1778

Ample Information
P.O. Box 40621
Portland, OR 97240-0621
(503) 452-2542

Ample Shopper
P.O. Box 116
Bearsville, NY 12409
(914) 679-3316

B.A.S.I.C.S.
Newsletter
5540 North 103rd Street
Milwaukee, WI 53225
(414) 464-1918

BBW Express
(800) 453-7277

BBW Magazine
8484 Wilshire Boulevard, Suite 900
Beverly Hills, CA 90211
(213) 651-5400

Belle
475 Park Avenue South
New York, NY 10016
(800) 877-5549

Dimensions
P.O. Box 640
Folsom, CA 95763-0640
Personals: (900) 420-5575
(916) 984-9947

Elisabeth Newsletter
Liz Claiborne Company
1441 Broadway, 18th Floor
Attn: Marketing Department
New York, NY 10018

EXTRA Woman
P.O. Box 57194
Sherman Oaks, CA 91413
(818) 997-8404

Fashion News
210 Post Street, Suite 510
San Francisco, CA 94108
(800) 803-6613

Fat!So?
P.O. Box 423464
San Francisco, CA 94142

Healthy Weigh
7455 Broadway #219
Lemon Grove, CA 91945
(619) 464-4376

The International No Diet Coalition
Directory of Resources
A project of the Council on Size and Weight Discrimination, Inc.
Willendorf Press
P.O. Box 407
Shady, NY 12409

Jan Larkey's Flatter Your Figure System
(book and video)
P.O. Box 8258
Pittsburgh, PA 15218

Ken Mayer's Loving You Large Support Network
Newsletter c/o LYLSN
9974 Scripps Ranch Boulevard, Suite 172
San Diego, CA 92131
To place ads: (800) 289-5196
To browse ads: (900) 726-9004

Large as Life Newsletter
P.O. Box 573
Great Barrington, MA 01230

Living Large
P.O. Box 1006
Elgin, IL 60121

Love Handles
Vendredi Enterprises
P.O. Box 220
Dept. EVE
Camas, Valley, OR 97416
(800) 418-8379

Mastering Your Professional Image
(book)
Diane Parente and Stephanie Petersen
P.O. Box 262
Ross, CA 94957
(415) 258-0285

On a Positive Note Newsletter
Largely Positive
P.O. Box 17233
Glendale, WI 53217

Overcoming Overeating Newsletter
Jade Publishing
935 West Chestnut, Suite 420
Chicago, IL 60622
(800) 299-0577

Pretty Big
(quarterly publication)
One the Dale, Wirksworth
Matlock, Derbyshire DE4 4EJ
England
Phone: (0629) 824949
Fax: (0629) 824773

**Radiance: The Magazine for
Large Women**
P.O. Box 30246
Oakland, CA 94604
(510) 482-0680

Royal Resources
(product directory)
Vendredi Enterprises
1030 East El Camino Real, #314
Sunnyvale, CA 94087
(408) 739-4192

Rump Parliament
(activist)
P.O. Box 181716
Dallas, TX 75218

Sage Woman
P.O. Box 641
Point Arena, CA 95468
(707) 882-2052

**The Ultimate Plus-Size
Modeling Guide**
E.V.E.
P.O. Box 5516
New York, NY 10185-5516

Yes! Magazine
SM Subscription Service
6 Leigham Court Road
London, England SW16 2PG

Miscellaneous and Freebie Info

**AICI Fashion Update Information
Line**
(info on what's hot, what's not,
what works and what to wear;
updated monthly)
(900) 484-6243

**American Academy of
Orthopedic Surgeons**
*If The Shoe Fits, Wear It;
Steps to Proper Shoe Fit* (free
booklet)
(800) 824-BONE (2663)

Amplestuff
(mail-order—"Everything but
clothes")
P.O. Box 116
Bearsville, NY 12409

Attitudes
Beach chair for big folk
(800) 525-2468

Buttons & Things
(retail/mail-order)
24 Main Street
Freeport, ME 04032
(207) 865-4480

Color Education Resources
Jean Patton, AICI
*Color to Color: The Black
Woman's Guide to a Rainbow
of Fashion and Beauty*
P.O. Box 7704
New York, NY 10116
(212) 564-3082

Dress Shop 2.0
Liningsoft Inc.
(custom clothing design software)
P.O. Box 970
Janesville, CA 96114-0970
(800) 626-1262
Fax: (916) 253-2703

Eyes Ltd. Phase II
Dolly M. Wilson, ABOC, FNAO
(retail/mail-order—will
recommend eye frames based
on photos)
7930 North May
Oklahoma City, OK 73120
(405) 848-3937
Fax: (405) 840-5256

Goddess Greetings
(greeting cards, some clothes,
cartoons of plus-size women)
20583 Painters #D
Bend, OR 97701
(800) 344-7338

Great Fit Patterns
2229 Northeast Burnside, Suite 305
Gresham, OR 97030

**Oozing out of the Box: "An
Interaction with Mary Stanleigh"**
(publication)
(707) 441-1887
Fax: (707) 443-3601

S&S Industries, Inc.
Shape Your Bust in 30 Seconds
(free booklet on bra fit)
(800) 543-9154

Specialty Photography by Laurice
(boudoir and traditional)
65 Manchester Street
San Francisco, CA 94110
(415) 648-2675

Wheelchairs
Wheelchair Institute of Kansas
(big size chairs)
(800) 525-3332

> *For more information on
> seminars, workshops, and
> training, contact us directly at:*
> Plus Style
> P.O. Box 20765
> New York, NY 10021-0075

Index

About the Author

Suzan Nanfeldt, president of Suzan Nanfeldt Associates and founding partner of Emerging Visions Enterprises, is a leading advisor on plus-size style. In addition to her private coaching practice, she conducts workshops, seminars, and fashion shows around the country and is a marketing consultant to manufacturers and retailers. Her corporate clients include Liz Claiborne, Saks Fifth Avenue, Bloomingdale's, Nordstrom, QVC, and other major retailers and designers. A former advertising media director, she has been trained at the Fashion Institute of Technology and Parsons School of Design, where she now teaches. She is a member of The Association of Image Consultants International and The Fashion Group International.

If you would like to receive a free Easy Focus Shopping Card, or know more about products and services for plus-size women, send a self-addressed, stamped, business-size envelope to:

Suzan Nanfeldt
Plus Style EFSC
P.O. Box 20765
New York, NY 10021-0075